Passionately Striving in 'Why'

An Anthology of Women Who Persevere Mightily to Live Their Purpose

Nikki,

Here's to living with passion and working on purpose!

Alton

Published By: Something or Other Publishing

Madison, Wisconsin 53719
www.soopllc.com
retailers@soopllc.com

Contributing Authors

Sandy Beky – France

Neelam Chhiber – India

Dr. Alise Cortez -- United States

Cristal de Oliveira – Brazil

D. Renee Hamilton -- United States

Lauren Hollows – Australia

Stacy Jewel -- United States

Poonam Kasturi – India

Benda Kithaka – Kenya

Rikke Kjelgaard -- Sweden/Denmark

Nadalette La Fonta – France

Rachael Masaku – Kenya

Sabine Menon -- China (via France)

Salomé Meyer -- South Africa

Sharda Nirmal – India

Dr. Valerie Nkamgang Bemo -- United States (via Cameroon)

Julie Quinne -- United States

Tabitha Rose -- Canada / United States

Sheetal Shah – Kenya

Thear Suzuki -- United States (via Cambodia)

Tyneisha Ternent – Canada

Dr. Mavis Tsai -- United States (via Hong Kong)

Udie Soko – Zambia

Flavia Wahnfried – Portugal

Mirian Zacareli – Brazil

Table of Contents

Introduction

Passionately Striving in 'Why'
An Anthology of Women Who Persevere Mightily to Live Their Purpose

By Alise Cortez, PhD, Anthology Curator

Purpose. A word frequently used in today's vernacular but seldom truly understood or fully lived. It's both alluring and elusive. A fortunate few find purpose early in life, and its expression flows, fluid and effective. Yet, for so many others, purpose is that exasperating aspiration that is tantalizingly just out of reach, haunting its would-be captor with visions of a tranquil, fulfilling, and productive life.

Purpose is not to be confused with goals, passion, or meaning. That which we find meaningful can help us discern our purpose, as can our passions. The goals we set for ourselves can, in their reach and attainment, help us express our purpose. But purpose is better described as the forward-pointing arrow that motivates our behavior and serves as the organizing principle for our lives. Purpose lived is always about serving others, so we can think of purpose as the reason for our unique existence that makes the world a better place.

The world needs more people living their purpose, acting as examples to inspire us to find our purpose and act from it. That is why this anthology is in your hands now. But what if we created a worldwide culture that encouraged young people to see within themselves something special only they could offer the world? What if we taught them to see and celebrate the gifts in others as well?

Instead, what we're more likely to find is a significant number of purpose seekers hitting their stride and discovering their purpose well into their 40s and 50s, and only after years in unfulfilling careers. Paths they took largely on expectations to make a hefty income and create "the good life" they were promised in return. All at the expense of their self-respect and expression of their soul. We might call this segment of the population "the walking dead" while dreading to admit that we, too, could be part of it. The lights are on, but no one is home – a wrenching waste of one precious life after another.

Make no mistake—working toward finding and manifesting your purpose is arduous and painful; the meek need not apply. Hence, not everyone pursues purpose. It can also be daunting to honor purpose, once it's discovered. As you'll read in these stories written by women across the globe – from diverse cultures, socio-economic classes, and life circumstances – the business of discovering purpose and living it is intense. It requires unquestionable obedience to one's inner wisdom. These stories are raw and tell the truth about the path to discovery and then the sheer grit and determination it took to honor it and make a living from its execution. Some of the more traditional paths, such as attending college to acquire a particular skill in hopes of landing a decent, well-paying job, are enticing. That's one path to life, and perhaps over time, you find your way to purpose after financial and professional success. And yet, you might discover to your dismay that a persistent "emptiness" that registers as meaninglessness, or perhaps the proverbial "mid-life crisis," rears its head.

Still, the hunt for purpose is well worth the arduous struggle to attain it. Not only is discovering one's purpose a magnificent achievement, but it also expands our ability to experience a broader spectrum of emotion. So, we have greater access to feeling and sensing, making every moment more profound and giving us a more extraordinary ability to take in information about the world. In addition to feeling "high" on life, purpose has at least three other helpful functions. It gives us crazy confidence to go after what we want in life. It energizes us in the face of the unknown. It allows us to redefine our relationship with stress and thrive while postponing fleeting rewards in favor of leaving a sustainable, lasting impression and legacy. But the best gift of all? Purpose acts as a unique filter through which each of us sees the world. Looking through this lens allows each of us to see possibilities or do something that no one else could see or achieve quite as we do. That distinguishing difference is the source of creativity and effect to which we all aspire.

But where do you *look* for purpose? You will be introduced to the women in these stories through the paths they took to find their own. This segmentation is showcased as a way to illustrate how purpose can be accessed, and we hope that by sharing these paths, you may gain greater access to your own purpose through our examples. By reading our stories, we hope you gain a greater perception and understanding of your path. Doing so will enable you to access more meaning in the moments of your life and perhaps help you see the thread of purpose that has always been there for you to see and finally declare and activate.

Our stories are categorized among four paths to purpose.

The first group of stories showcases the path to purpose through a long-standing passion or life-orienting value among the authors. In these stories, you will meet six women who have found a way to orient their lives and work around a core value or central passion. That passion fuels their ongoing inquiry and dedication to its expression through who they are in the world and the work they do. As you read these stories, consider your own core passions or values and how they may be tied to or illuminate your purpose.

The next group of six stories showcases the path to purpose through the lens of a focus on overcoming a long-time ailment in life, a fixation or life concern that often emerges in youth or early adulthood and persists for years or decades. These stories illuminate the value of sharing with others that which we have passed through the journey of darkness to heal in ourselves. These stories showcase that pain has a *raison d'être* – that we did not endure it for naught – that, in fact, dealing with that pain gives us a way to live more fully and teach others what we've learned along the way. What ails you? You might be surprised to know countless other people struggle with something similar and could greatly benefit from your instruction on how you navigated through it.

The third group of stories features five accounts of women who passed through significant adversity or isolated crucible moment that, in doing so, elicited a higher version of themselves, a greater expression of consciousness and competence. It is the way these women took on the adversity that catalyzed them into a higher state of being and gave them a new or different way of being in the world and how serving from that distinguishes their path. That awful divorce, disease, or hardship you thought leveled you could very well be your ticket to purpose. It depends on how you address it.

The last group of eight stories share a proclivity toward devotion to a particular cause or boldly challenging a problem in the world. While the first three groups showcase a path to purpose primarily driven from within, this group is compelled mainly by a cause from without, more significant than their person. The women featured in these stories all saw something wrong, and they felt compelled to do something about it. Their unique life experiences made them keenly aware of things that they simply could not *not* do something about. What big, hairy problem in the world do *you* see that commands your abiding attention? That problem that just won't let you be could be your purpose.

We are a collective of women authors who share our intimate stories of how we discovered our purpose, live through it, and make a difference to ourselves and those we serve. We do this in the hopes it lights a fire in you to find and pursue your own. As the curator, I served as a "story catcher" for a few years before this book's compilation. Invariably, as I was out speaking to groups about nurturing passion, inspiration, and purpose, people would approach me after my talks and relay some hugely significant aspects of their lives they'd dealt with or overcome. Or, upon return home, an email or Linkedin message awaited me with a similar refrain. I came to understand I was "supposed to do something" with these stories and began hosting women's storytelling evenings first in Dallas, then in any city my travels for work took me to. And then, the opportunity to curate this anthology presented itself.

There's power in stories. Those contained in this book showcase that purpose is accessible anywhere, by anyone. And when we live and work from purpose, we can have an incredible positive influence and make the difference worthy of our one precious life. Our contributors hail from Australia, Brazil, Cambodia, Cameroon, Canada, China, France, India, Kenya, Portugal, South Africa, Sweden, the United States, and Zambia. We invite you to come along with us – be inspired by our courage, quest for your own, and follow your path to purpose. The world desperately needs your gifts, and you will find a kind of fulfillment you might not have thought possible. Together, we will join arms and help lift the world to higher consciousness, being, and contribution. Join us. The time is *now.*

Propelled
by Passion

The Lens of a Refugee Camp

By Cristal de Oliveira
Brazil

What are we supposed to do with our lives? This is the story about how in the middle of one of the messiest periods of my life, I found myself and how I'm now pursuing a journey with fewer restrictions on who I truly want to be. I'm a traveler who uses experiences to expand consciousness. I'm a listener who uses my ears to learn from others, and I'm a changemaker who aims to create a positive impact in our world.

For twenty-eight years, I tried to understand myself and my purpose. Still, I failed to reach any satisfying point because, somehow, things were disconnected and happening in a sequence of events without any evident cohesion. I had my family, a job, friends, and an excellent place to live. Everything was following its natural course, but I was unsatisfied with the legacy I was creating. To me, there was almost nothing to be proud of in my life. Life felt monochromatic as excitement became rarer. My body answered with weight and tiredness, and my mind was filled with stress. I saw no prospect of change.

A few weeks before I quit my job last year, I experienced something that helped me notice a few behavior patterns. I was part of a group in which I was asked to visualize a specific objective. I saw that there were obstacles to overcome on my way to reach it. These obstacles were represented by people in the room. I found it fascinating how my body was attracted to the barriers, making me disoriented. When I had the opportunity to let it go, I almost completely ignored it. I realized the weights in my life were unbalanced, and the connection with my values was far away from how I would have liked my life to be.

When You No Longer Recognize Yourself

It is possible and effortless to reach a point where you don't recognize yourself anymore. Everything turns into a blur. This was precisely what had happened to me, and I knew I needed a change, starting with my job. Since the future was unknown, that was a terrifying idea. I think part of the challenge was the fear of being judged by society. But, honestly, it was almost like I didn't believe that I could do better, overcome challenges, and achieve objectives that I set for myself. All these factors—combined with a lot of insecurity and passivity—left me feeling stuck.

It takes an extra dose of courage to confront everything and everyone, especially yourself, to assume genuinely who you want to be.

Now looking back, what I share with you is that it is worth pursuing the best version of Self, always. Things started to change when I took the time to recognize my ambition and determine what was holding me back. When I realized all of this, I knew I needed to put anxiety aside and let the process unfold.

The Call from the World Stage

In February 2019, I participated in a United Nations Conference focused on social development. I was sitting in one of the enormous meeting rooms filled with hundreds of people staring at representatives from different parts of the world, leading what looked to be an endless discussion about social inclusiveness, inequality, and women's representation in leadership. It reminded me of why I decided to study international relations in the first place: to understand how the world was connected and how it could be better integrated.

I realized that the high number of different interests made the discussion—an eloquent exchange of courtesies—more of a porous hands-on list of recommendations. At that moment, it occurred to me: I didn't want to stop at recommendations. I actually wanted to be part of tangible actions that could, in fact, contribute to social development.

In the same period, I started a postgraduate course in social innovation management. One of the core modules was about our "inner journey." That journey would allow us to get in touch with our deeper level, a deconstructed version of ourselves. Once I looked inside, I saw I was a fragmented, rambling scope of priorities that put others first in all aspects of my life. It was reasonable to imagine that I needed to do something about it, right? But it was not just about saying, "Yes, let's do it!" but about the "What?" What do I want to do with my life? What am I good at? What is my purpose?

The good part of working actively on my inner journey was that I had tools to facilitate my process and learned how to use them to discover myself. I understood I was good with people, and I loved to work with them and to help them. I loved to work to solve complex problems and create solutions for issues that are affecting our society. But most of all, I was in love with the idea of creating an accessible and equal world. Once I understood my likes and dislikes with clarity, it was easier to see beyond the barriers I had created for myself.

A few months after starting the self-discovery process, I was much more self-aware, and I created room for new perspectives. I was excited. Can you imagine what happened after that? Basically nothing. I wanted to start building social impact to connect with the cause and begin creating a legacy that I would be proud of. Still, the opportunities I was coming across weren't profoundly inspiring to me.

One late night, I had just finished a warm shower after work, and I was lying in bed, scrolling on my cell phone, almost falling asleep. Then, suddenly, I saw a post that made me stop everything I was doing. It took me a fraction of a second to understand that I had found my "how"! It was a post about a position to work with refugees on a social innovation project in Kenya.

There was no doubt that I needed to be part of it. The idea of working in Kenya was magnetic. My body was trilling, and my mind was running faster than ever. I found myself crying out of sheer happiness because I knew it was my way into a new period in my life that would have a purpose. I put all my energy into making it possible. Still, even without knowing what would happen, I wrote a message of comfort to myself during the process: "Everyone is equal and deserves to have opportunities, and I want to be part of a group or organization that is making it possible. I'll get there. It's international and multicultural. It's made of people for people. Believe in new beginnings. Life is incredible; don't let it pass by without enjoying it. Go with love and come back better, always."

The following day, I woke up and checked my emails as usual. I had received a message from the Xavier Project: "Dear Cristal, Thank you for your interest in the 3D Printing volunteer position in Kakuma, Kenya. I am delighted to inform you that you have been selected for the position." Everything changed after that message.

At that point, I realized that living with purpose is visceral. You feel it in your heart. You can't deny it, and you can't keep it away.

So, there I went: Kakuma, Kenya. The project's main objective was to use technology to generate income for a community-based organization called Solidarity Initiative for Refugees. They are one of the community organizations that the Xavier Project supports in Kakuma Camp, one of the biggest refugee camps in the world. They were in the process of creating a business ecosystem based on selling 3D printed products to generate income for locally based organizations to promote the project and new initiatives that could flourish with that technology.

Rolling Up My Sleeves with the Refugee Community

Aside from the business, the 3D printers had another purpose: to stimulate refugees to pursue solutions and create alternatives for their challenges by promoting and motivating them to use the technology for personal and collective benefits. The 3D printing project is part of a bigger initiative, which aid agencies are conducting as part of a new international work strategy—lowering the dependency on external financial support by creating and promoting a sustainable way to develop and evolve the local communities.

The idea is to provide the resources, knowledge, and initial capital to help communities start and grow initiatives and as a means to help them reach a sustainable economy. Our project was among these initiatives to encourage refugees to build their own futures. The business validation was already made before I came on board, and my job entailed "how" to make it possible.

We brought two 3D printers to the refugee camp and started working with the local organization. I don't know if you've ever had the chance to do fieldwork, but if you haven't and don't know this yet, I must say unpredictable routes will happen.

The project had different phases of development. We started with the basics: practical printing lessons, the 3D printing process, and its implications. We also worked closely with the local community to better understand the challenges in creating a new business, the different tools we could use to help people through the process, how to explore possibilities and transform data into insights. In the meantime, we created a pocket course about 3D printing to extend the knowledge to the community. At the end of four months, our hope was that we would start generating income from the business by selling the products in the local markets. This was an ambitious goal.

We started without electricity in the center where the printers were, so there wasn't any way to work with them from the beginning. We got a power generator which worked for two days before it broke. We tried to use solar panels, but they were not enough to power the printers as the Information Technology (IT) classes were also hosted in the center at the same time.

When it rained, the roads were flooded with mud, so we couldn't reach most areas in the camp. However, the most common complications were dust storms and intense heat. Dust was terrible for the printers, and the heat did not do any good either.

I discovered that I shouldn't invite people for a group discussion without offering refreshments. I didn't have a budget to buy them. How did I find that out? Imagine how many of the thirty people I'd invited showed up? Zero. It was challenging.

But despite all these challenges, we were able to build a prototype model for sales. This one, after validation, could integrate a portfolio of 3D printed products that the organization would offer to the local community through local markets, and word about the project spread throughout the camp.

We also managed to launch the 3D printer course to benefit the locals. For some in the first cohort of students, it was the first time they had ever had experience with any kind of printer. I remember when one of the students printed her first model, an airplane for her son. She was happy about how she went from knowing absolutely nothing about printers to being able to give her son a Christmas present in just three days.

It was complicated to put together a class that was equally made up of women and men. It was hard to find women with computer skills, availability, and encouragement to attend these classes.

The Power of Intolerance ... and Listening

Imagine the kind of creative things a person can build with the support and resources. The mother from my example represents how brave, strong, and powerful women are and yet how underappreciated they are nonetheless. Refugees taught me how to search for meaning behind the words, bodies, gestures. They made me more conscious of being aware of others beyond my bubble. They taught me that a smile is an international language for kindness. They showed me that I need to respect differences, especially when they conflict with my own beliefs.

I saw that intolerance is a deadly disease. How frustrated would you be if you were a refugee and feared death in a refugee camp? I heard stories that would make you stop and take a step back. For a long time, my ignorance covered my eyes to truly and deeply understand how much my skin color has given me countless privileges, how the income of my family determined my access to a chain of privileges, and how difficult it is to break this pattern. Kenya helped me to see all those things with a different lens, with *its* lens.

My role in managing the project was to simplify the process, create the appropriate environment so people could be comfortable enough to share their thoughts, encourage everyone to participate in the conversation, and guarantee that women and men had the same level of participation in the dialogue. Without intending to, my skin color put me in a superior position in front of the students. At the same time, I was supposed to be on the same level, supporting them. I tried several tools and types of approaches to make everyone's involvement in leadership equally. I used everything I learned while working in a conventional environment. Still, I didn't think that I was using the same approach in a completely different context.

I realized nothing could ever happen without a certain level of trust between us. From the first classes about managing the printers and building up a business from scratch to the meetings about planning and schedules, the most effective skill that appeared to work the best was having a dialogue and an open heart to listen. I learned that the most critical part of my job was listening to their stories about how they came to the refugee camp. Once we found the common language, everything became more fluid.

Using Justice to Promote Dignity

When you work with refugees, you are working in an intense environment with a potent mix of cultures, beliefs, perspectives, and knowledge. You work with people who were forced to be where they are since life back in their countries is no longer an option. There are many memories, traumas, stories, faith, and hope in people all mixed together. Sometimes it is hard to concentrate if you know your family is still in danger. Sometimes you don't even know if your family is still alive. Refugees are people, and they deserve to have the same opportunities as non-refugees. I know that I want to work for that to happen.

Providing equal opportunities for people is a way to reestablish dignity. How much potential is wasted because resources are concentrated in the hands of a few? The world could be a better place with more ideas, actions, and innovation if more people could participate in creating solutions.

Another part of the project was to conduct market research to understand the local context where the business would take place. We held classes about the design thought process to reach a consensus about the customer target for the 3D printed products, primarily, mothers from Somalia. The nationality was chosen due to access to income in the camps. Culturally, women are responsible for taking care of the house and kids.

In a refugee camp with twenty-seven years of existence, as Kakuma is, families are structured so that the role of the woman is integral to making life thrive. Walking through the camp, you could see them embodying that role. They fight daily against prejudice, tiredness, and poverty. They succeed every day when they can make sure kids are safe for another day. After deciding on the target customer, we interviewed women in the camp, specifically looking for "mamas" as they are known there. We talked to several of them with all kinds of backgrounds and reasons to be there. They were very particular with their own vision of the world. Still, they all had one thing in common: they had a thirst for providing better conditions for their kids, not themselves, but for the future they saw being still in process, as if their own was already defined.

There was so much hope inside people who had been through so much hardship. There were dreams for opportunities and a different world. Kakuma's mothers taught me to keep the faith and fight for what we believe is possible. We are powerful, and it is our right to be wherever and whoever we want to be.

It was not easy. It was not simple, and the job is definitely not over. How far do you think you need to go to change your behavior? In my case, I had to go to another continent to reconnect with myself and be able to unleash what was already inside of me.

I love people. I'm thrilled to serve as a facilitator to make connections easier, resolve conflicts, and make ideas flourish. Kakuma changed the way I see the world and helped me realize how excruciatingly unfair it is. Kenya taught me how to approach a conversation that has been there for decades. I can't turn my back on what I learned and experienced, and not do anything to help build a different reality for those who haven't had the same opportunities as me.

My purpose is to use justice as a tool to promote dignity for people. Everyone deserves to have the chance to choose, a chance to be the best version of him or herself. Everyone should have the right to try and fail and try again; everyone deserves the right to freedom. That's the kind of justice I'm talking about.

I am still in the process of discovering who I am. I'm still evolving, and I believe it will never end. The lens that I got from the Kakuma camp definitely changed my perspective, but it doesn't mean that it is supposed to work in the same way. The immersion in a journey of vulnerability accelerated the process for me. I didn't know what would or could happen with this experience. Still, it turned out to be the best and perfect amount of energy that I needed to discover myself.

I'm grateful for having been where I was before because it led me to be where I am now. I'll keep pursuing my purpose because one thing I'm sure of now is that I am on the best path that I can follow.

My Advice for You

There are a lot of lessons learned that I took back home from my experience working with purpose, and I'd like to share three of them because they might be helpful for you, as well. First: You are more resilient than you imagine. Working in a hostile place can be very challenging. Still, everyone can change his/her behavior and adapt to a new environment.

Second: you are not alone, but your purpose is only yours. People have different perspectives of the same objective, but our approaches and means of achieving it are often very different. Embracing the different perceptions of progress during the project helped the whole group move faster towards the objective because the track wasn't mine alone anymore but ours.

Third: it's not about what you do. It's about who you can be while you are doing what you are doing. The most amazing thing that I value working with purpose is to be entirely myself. It's not a coincidence that my most significant value is freedom. When I was in Kakuma, I experienced many restrictions because I'm a woman, a white person, and culturally different. Despite changing a lot of habits—like the way I usually dress, the way I talk to people, or address issues—being there was one of the moments in my life when I felt the most completely free. Because the moment wasn't about all those things like clothes or vocabulary, but it was about how I was dealing with all of those things in a way where my body and mind were in agreement.

After returning from Kenya to Brazil, I can see what a great chance life gave to me when I look back. I feel different from who I used to be, determined to pursue my purpose with courage and focus. I'm changing in a way that I believe is natural and healthy, as many things don't make sense anymore, so it's easier to let them go. My approach to certain subjects is different, and the way I see and listen to things has evolved. The world has expanded, and it's impressive.

Once I checked one of the notebooks I used while I was there, I found a text that I recorded towards the end of my assignment. Here's a part of it: "This is the night before leaving Kakuma, and my heart is full of emotions. It feels weird how much I could identify myself here. What an amazing feeling it is to be free." The whole point is I learned a lot about how to be free, to be the best version of myself with as few restrictions as possible.

That's the story about how I found a version of myself that I want to keep pursuing. My journey was not linear; no one's is. One great feeling I'm carrying with me is the peace of consciousness that brought tranquility to my anxiety. There's a long journey still ahead, there's a lot still to be discovered and understood, but I'm very excited to keep going. Are you enjoying your journey?

After returning to Brazil, my friends and family often asked me, "What's next?" Next, I will live my life pursuing my purpose and looking for ways to make it simpler. Sometimes it might seem difficult or even impossible.

I would like to make sure we all carry and never forget some lessons: trust yourself to do good; always be kind to others; and love your family, friends, and animals because they are precious.

Things will get hard. At some point, they always do but remember to trust your values. Remember to never give up and laugh as much as possible. Take care of your body and mind; they are your tools, and they need to be respected and treated with love. Make friends who are different from you and be open to learning with them. Buy flowers. Be honest with others, but mostly be frank with yourself. Go with love and come back better, always.

My name is Cristal de Oliveira. I'm a twenty-eight-year-old Brazilian passionate about people and the creativeness we can achieve with the right resources. My role in this world is to provide ways that give people access to opportunities democratically and inclusively. I want to do this by helping people in vulnerable situations, facilitating a sustainable future. I like to deal with the types of challenges that are too complex to describe but that, when resolved, have a significant impact. My work resonates with this through the development and implementation of projects from a people-centered perspective. I have a postgraduate degree in Social Innovation Management from Amani Institute. I'm a Millennial Catalyst at International Connector. I'm also a Fellow of the Starting Bloc Fellowship, a global network of entrepreneurs, activists, educators, and innovators working to create social impact. I love sunsets, music, and hiking. You can find me on LinkedIn by searching for my name. I look forward to connecting with you.

Purposeful Engagement in Meaningful Work

By Julie Quinne
United States

Living your purpose is exactly like bungee jumping. It's a warm, sunny day, and you are standing on a solid steel bridge spanning a deep, lazy river. You are surrounded by friends boisterously urging you on and by professionals trained to equip and guide you through the experience of a lifetime. The blood is rushing through your veins. You feel your heart thudding rhythmically in your chest as you look down at your bare feet. Each buzzing with anticipation themselves, toes curl over the edge of the trestle. Beyond your hot-pink pedicure—the color was called "Leap" and chosen just for the occasion—you can see clear down through to the bottom of the crisply cool water below. You've seen the others leap before you. You know your fingertips will barely break the surface of the river when you reach the end of the rope before being pulled back up to the firm ground. You're ready. You take the leap. You feel the charge of electricity coursing through your body and brain—the exhilaration, the terror, the desperate trust in strangers who are to have made sure of your ultimate safety. Living your purpose is precisely like that.

Gravity and Purpose

And if it's not like that, it's certainly what many of us envision it to be or are made to feel like it should be. We expect that there may be some epiphany of purpose realization and a moment in time, after careful preparation, that we take the metaphorical (literal?) leap into our new and more meaningful life. We imagine that we will only have to casually bat away any distraction or deterrent along the way, as we are propelled and powered by the passion that is our clear and present purpose. Except it's not like that at all. In fact, it's exactly like bungee jumping except for one critical difference: you jump without the help of gravity. In fact, you jump against a gravitational pull more akin to the atmosphere of the moon. And the rope is shorter and thicker and attached to something that you can't see, and no one is in charge of. And, like the moon, it's lonely and vast. Unfamiliar and inhospitable. So maybe it's the opposite of bungee jumping, except for the exhilaration and the terror. Let me explain.

I Had a Dream

I can recall the exact moment I discovered what I wanted to do with my life. I was a senior in high school and was working as a grocery checkout clerk. We clerks were always paired with a bagger, and the baggers, being next to each other at the end of the belts, would typically chat together as they bagged. Occasionally, customers would come through my line and pay for their groceries with food stamps. During one particular shift, my bagger noticed this and began speaking loudly and derogatorily to his colleague about the customer. The store manager, overhearing the commotion, came over to my line, loudly reprimanded the bagger, and returned to his office. The baggers looked at each other and snickered, the customers looked down in embarrassment, and I looked around in a bit of a shock.

At this moment, I realized that I wanted to train managers to help employees be better performers so that the customers, and, therefore, the business and consequently the employees all thrived. What I did not know was what this job was called or how one prepared for it. My dad was a teacher, and my mom was an entrepreneur herself, so "Human Resources" or "Corporate Training" weren't in our vocabulary. Applying to college, I searched for a major that could put me on a path to this goal. Interestingly, the school of management did not seem like a fit as there was virtually no coursework dedicated to people management or to communicating, educating, training, or inspiring. Wanting something more suitable to change people's minds and perspectives, I considered psychology and sociology, and I finally settled on "Interpersonal Communication and Rhetoric." Here, I picture myself standing in a field, attached to a bungee cord. I am preparing to leap.

Invisible Handcuffs

Like many of us who were encouraged toward college, I did all the right things: got good grades to get an excellent job to get good benefits so that I could have a good life. It's how things worked. It is the "physics" of life. As such is the gravitational pull that, by definition, can act against the realization of purpose. I graduated from college, became a corporate training manager (so *that's* what it was called!), and moved into more and more responsible positions within Human Resources, which culminated in running several HR teams at the executive level.

Indeed, I have had great jobs with great salaries and awesome benefits with wonderful people doing important work. I've been valued and impactful with influence and authority. I have had work-life balance, flexibility, and the freedom to be creative. I have had the best jobs you could imagine. So why on earth would I leave such a (pick one: secure / lucrative / comfortable / responsible / high-status / ...) job? I didn't. How could I? It would be career suicide and irresponsible and selfish and dangerous and wrong. So I stayed on the path to prosperity. Although I had toyed with the idea of going out on my own, the security of a good job and benefits is the physics of life, and fighting it can seem futile—at least until the pull of purpose started to grow large enough to create a force of its own.

Accidental Entrepreneur

The first time I left corporate, it was not necessarily my idea. Several business unit presidents were up for the "big job," and mine didn't get the position. Thus, I had the surreal experience of letting myself go:

"Julie …" "Yes, Self?" "… I have some bad news… ". Being laid off was wrenching. I'd been at the company for more than fifteen years and felt I had grown up there, both professionally and personally. I couldn't imagine myself anywhere else, which perhaps helped me see the cross-roads of opportunity a little more clearly. I had been spun out of the corporate orbit. I now had a choice: go back in or try my hand at stay-ing out and following my (barely formed) dream of being on my own to offer training and facilitation as a solo practitioner.

This was early 2009. I was the sole breadwinner for a family of five. My husband had become a stay-at-home dad in 2000 when our first child was born, and since then, we had added another son in 2003 and a daughter in 2004. We had a mortgage, two car payments, and a fair amount of credit card debt. So naturally, after discussing it together, we decided that now was the perfect time to start my own consulting firm with no experience, little preparation, and about fifteen weeks of severance to hold us over before certain success was achieved. Here, I picture myself standing in a field, attached to a bungee cord, and jump-ing into the air.

Leaping

The thing is, it wasn't until I had decided to strike out on my own, hang the proverbial shingle out, and get to entrepreneurial work that I real-ized how stifling my "great" job had been. The trappings of corporate employment seem so sound: the perceived security, the routine, the relative comfort. But once on the other side, it was easier to see that those trappings were more like a trap. Once I saw the possibility of doing what I loved and started experiencing the freedom, variety, challenge, and fulfillment of this new work, the force of purpose began to gain a bit of momentum. I started marketing—sending word to every human I had ever met—to let them know I was here to help and ready to set the world on fire. I experienced early success, lots of encouragement, and felt the exhilaration of building and growing something that was mine. I had launched Uncommon Consulting to help people become more purposefully engaged in their work. And then the Great Recession happened.

Fighting the Fear

Never underestimate the gravitational pull of other people's fears—and that's under normal circumstances, never mind during a Great Recession. As I embarked on my journey toward my purpose—at first buoyed by encouraging words and early success—I began getting all kinds of well-meaning advice from friends, family, and colleagues: "Your market is too broad, you need a niche, that niche isn't big enough, do people want to be purposefully engaged? Your marketing may be too feminine, you don't want to alienate men do you? ... ". If I wasn't getting direction, I was getting emails about open jobs in the HR field for which I might be qualified. To which I would respond, "I have a job. I am running my own business," while staring them down until they broke eye contact. Of course, they would immediately return to racking their brains for other ways they could make me stop making them worry.

Finding Purpose

Late 2009 was when I began finding my true purpose and my genuine community. The people you surround yourself with are so important when striving to stay true to your reason for being. I am grateful to have made the acquaintance of other women on similar journeys who were generous enough to lift me up, challenge me, and ultimately teach me so much about myself as I wandered around the empty, flat field holding my bungee cord looking for a place to jump. I call them my "Purpose Peeps."

One such woman is Helle Bundgaard, Founder of Motivation Factor™. Helle has been a successful businesswoman, turned coach, turned motivation expert, turned inventor who has created a remarkable framework that guides individuals, teams, and organizations to discover what drives them. It was working with Helle that I could finely tune my purpose, which is to create experiences designed to inspire purposeful engagement in meaningful work and life. By understanding exactly what I needed (freedom, personal power, to be heard) in order to get and stay motivated, by leveraging the qualities that give me the most energy (communicating, creating, catalyzing, leading), and by reflecting on the difference I feel compelled to make in the world (purposeful engagement in meaningful work and life), I was able to get crystal clear about how I wanted to contribute in this life. Knowing this felt like coming home, being whole. It had its own weight and mass, and it began to generate its own gravitational pull.

Life Gets in the Way

They say a new business takes five years to take root. I figured I could do it in two, but it turns out that whoever "they" are, they are right. It took four years to get the business to a place where I had the reliable infrastructure and an operational cadence that seemed to be working and proved to be something I could build on. I was home more, spent more time with my family, was less stressed, and felt more fulfilled by my work. Tragically, at the same time, my marriage of twenty-three years was ending. Further, having been the sole breadwinner for a family of five and with a stay-at-home dad taking primary custody of three kids, I felt I needed a more stable financial situation. So I unhooked myself from the bungee cord and went back to corporate, where I persevered mightily to keep the embers of my purpose burning.

Know When to Fold 'Em

The thing about a purpose is that it offers you a great deal of flexibility in terms of how you serve it if you define it well. While my goal of running my own consulting business was somewhat limiting (I'm running a business or I'm not), my purpose of helping people engage in meaningful work could be accomplished in myriad ways. With a bit of creativity, resourcefulness, and luck, along with a genuine passion for my purpose helping to fuel the effort, I approached a former colleague who was president of a small research company and pitched an idea: what if we joined forces—her research company, my engagement expertise and Motivation Factor's data—and created a new business? By establishing my purpose as true north and considering the widest set of paths to get there, I was able to stay on course through a tumultuous year that included a separation, a divorce, and a move for the kids. I was doing work aligned with my purpose, creating experiences (surveys, speaking engagements, training, etc.) designed to inspire, but I was challenged by two things. My personal life and obligations as a mom were being tested, given my distance from the kids and the expenses involved with funding two households. At the end of the day, we have absolute obligations that need to be met, and sometimes it takes more than purpose to fuel them. I was presented with an opportunity to double my salary, be closer to the kids, and secure a pension. Here I picture myself in enormous steel boots, rooted to a vast corporate magnet with my bungee cord nowhere to be found.

Keeping the Fire Alive

After all that work on purpose, the grounded feeling of being home, feeling whole, and the exhilaration of freedom and fulfillment, how could I? "How could I?!" Honestly, "How could I not?" I rationalized. I'm a mother, the primary earner. I have college-bound kids, two households to support, and the women in my family live to an average of nearly one hundred years old. *I have no choice.* I have no choice but to return to a VP of Human Resources job. I have no choice but to take this job for the money and the security. I have no choice but to sell my home and move closer to this new work and my children. To do otherwise would be *selfish* and *irresponsible*. And so I made that choice.

As part of the deal to myself, I kept the purpose fire alive as best I could. I changed the job's title from Human Resources to Talent & Culture. I outfitted my office in "Uncommon" purple. I brought my unique and somewhat irreverent approach to HR and transformational change unabashedly into my new corporate home's relatively more conservative environment. I pitched a constant yet quiet tantrum in the form of plum-colored hair and a "UNCMN1" vanity license plate on my car. I had reclaimed my bungee cord and was using it as a lasso to capture the hearts and minds of the employees in this wonderful organization. A good purpose provides some flexibility, and I took as much advantage of that fact as I could. At the same time, I was telling myself I hadn't sold out and was trying to believe my friends and family when they would say, "You can always start Uncommon back up again when you retire," and "It's a smart move," and "You're doing the right thing."

They were right. It was a smart move, and I had done the right thing. But I was paying a price I hadn't anticipated. I am good at HR, very good, according to most everyone I've supported in that capacity. I get great satisfaction out of doing an excellent job in that field. But just because we're good at something doesn't mean it's what we should be doing. Our talents, energy, and passions do act as fuel. When we leverage and incorporate them into our work, they can keep us motivated and engaged for a time. The problem is that they can be expended entirely when the environment's need for them is greater than the environment's ability to return the favor. On several occasions as an HR professional, I have found myself giving way more energy than I had and getting way less energy back than I needed. In this new environment—this wonderful, supportive, transforming, challenging, fabulous setting, I began to suffer.

Sick and Tired

About two and a half years into my tenure there, I began to fray at the edges with higher stress, more illnesses, crying in meetings, and difficulty concentrating. At about this time, a dear friend (a Purpose Peep) gifted me a custom t-shirt with "3.17" screen printed on the front. It was code for how long I had to stay to vest in the pension the organization offered. The idea was galling. Not so much that I had to muscle my way through three more years or so, but that I was now one of those people "waiting for retirement." This was in such conflict with who I was and what I valued.

It gave me pause. Of course, I got over it. I was making a difference, and I could see that I was inspiring people through experiences designed to engage. I could do this. In the meantime, physical custody of my three kids had switched back to me, so I never did sell the house to move closer to work. My commute was at least an hour and a half each way. My daughter had also developed some alarming symptoms that required a great deal of time and attention, not to mention access to medical benefits. Had I been paying closer attention, I would have recognized the pinch of those invisible handcuffs as I became ever more tethered to things not in line with my purpose.

Another year later, I was in the middle of a presentation when I suddenly lost the ability to form words. I lost my train of thought and tried to recapture the point I was trying to make. I quickly wrapped it up and sat down when the CEO came over and said, "I'm worried about you. Are you ok?" I wasn't sure. As it happened, I wasn't ok, and I didn't return to work for three months. During that time, I was tested for Lyme disease four times, rheumatoid arthritis, fibromyalgia, neurological disorders, and more. I could barely walk upstairs. My speech was slow, memory non-existent. I couldn't drive or think. I asked my doctor if it could be stress. She answered that it was unlikely since I had experienced a good deal of stress in the past and had never responded in this way before. So the tests continued. I embarked on a course of radical self-care, including yoga, acupuncture, meditation, regular sleep, and exercise. I worried that I would never get better.

Persevering

Toward the end of the third month, I was able to return to work on a part-time basis, though I was still quite fatigued. I had spent nearly ninety days reflecting on what was most important to me, imagining how I would provide for my family if I couldn't return to full capacity and considering what I needed to continue to get better. Upon my return in January, I wrote a memo to my CEO outlining my concerns for my own health. By June, I officially asked to go part-time to spend more time with my daughter, who was still struggling, and to begin to transition to a more consultative role outside of the organization.

By August, I had put in place a transition team that would allow me to continue contributing to the organization while making plans for income should I ever become disabled again. I had expected to stay on indefinitely, but the physics of life and of purpose conspired and, in October, tossed me off the bridge as I frantically buckled on my bungee harness. I found myself having come full circle and, again, at a crossroads of opportunity. This time, there was no question. Exhilarated and terrified, I woke Uncommon from its hibernation and began the work of aligning myself with purpose once more. Armed with more tools, more experience, and more humility this time around, I can see now that there is no leap into purpose. It is in us, right where we stand, wherever we are. When we ignore it, something withers, and when we honor it, we grow exhilarated—which feels terrifyingly wonderful.

Purposeful Engagement

I create experiences designed to help people move from leading incidental, uninspired, and draining careers and lives and from feeling stuck, self-conscious, beleaguered, and overwhelmed to being inspired to purposefully engage in meaningful work and life and to feel self-confident, contributing, balanced, and whole. My hope is that the people I inspire will be moved to inspire others to also engage in meaningful work and life. If more of us were more aligned with what we have to give the world and felt more confident about contributing to it, imagine what we could create!

I am wholly dedicated to this endeavor. I've felt the joy of committing to my purpose—to myself, really—and I have paid the price of ignoring it. In terms of joy and fulfillment at work, you may not be able to have it all, but I believe you CAN get what you need. You can experience energizing, satisfying, contributing, purposeful work and life. It can be scary and takes courage, even making small changes. But it's so worth it. Consider beginning by answering these questions:

- How is your energy? Are you waking up with a hop in your step?
- Are your needs being met? If being heard or having freedom, or being needed or having a sense of control is vital to you, are you satisfied?
- To what extent are your talents in play? Do you have plenty of moments in your work and life where you experience ease, flow, and sustained engagement in your activities?
- Are you aligned with your purpose? Is your work meaningful and gratifying? Are you contributing to something larger than yourself?
- If you answered no to any of these questions, it might be time for a reset. If you could, how would you re-shape your work and life? Consider these questions:
- What gives you a hop in your step?
- What work qualities are most important to you? How might you get more of those things?
- What are you best at? What moments of your work and life do you experience ease, flow, and sustained engagement in your activities? How can you do more of that?
- What would be meaningful to you to be a part of?

Julie Quinne is a strategic leadership development expert, author, and coach who combines brain science and practical frameworks for purpose-driven performance you can measure—in both work and life. Her greatest passion is to create experiences that equip and inspire people to engage more purposefully in their work and life. Her style provides a fun, irreverent, energizing environment to challenge yourself and grow. She has excelled by taking bold strategic approaches to work by making bold moves to support her own well-being and life purpose and providing actionable paths and inspiration for others to do the same. With over twenty years leading at the executive level across diverse organizations and her unique ability to develop straightforward business processes to address the complexities of human motivation, her leadership philosophies and frameworks have consistently been recognized for being uncommonly practical and effective. The results are greater motivation, better management, increased productivity, improved relationships, and more meaningful work and life at every level. She invites you to Be Uncommon and to learn more at www.uncommonconsulting.com.

Every Day, Showing Up with an Open Heart

By Sheetal Shah
Kenya

Big Bang or Gentle Breeze

I used to think that the big "why" of my life would appear to me as a big bang. It would be a grand epiphany; a thunderstorm would roll through my life, shift it, and the external expression of that shift would be vast and legendary. I also had the belief that if it did not appear in this grand way, then I was not really living on purpose.

I don't feel that way anymore. I have come to believe that it is not only in the grand creations that life is lived on purpose. It is how I choose to show up daily in all areas of my life, with my work, with my family, with my interactions, that my inner purpose can show up. This feeling is very recent. Even as I was invited to contribute to this anthology, I wondered and doubted: "Was I a woman truly living on purpose? What have I created in the world that is evidence of this? Is it big enough?" As I reflected further, I saw how these beliefs and external measures that I had placed on what a life lived on purpose should look like prevented me from valuing my journey and my commitment to stay aligned with my purpose and heart.

The markers that show a life lived on purpose do not have to equate with greatness, fame, or legendary creations. A life lived on purpose can be measured by the joy of small actions, daily movements that align with the call of the heart and that leave indelible marks on the hearts of others. A life lived on purpose can be measured by how it changes you from the inside out and how you inspire others by your way of living and being. And that is enough!

Today, I can see how my path of discovering my purpose has been like a gentle breeze that pushed me forward, opened up parts of me that I didn't know existed, bringing forth more of me into the world, and continuing to surprise me! I am not at the end of the path, and I wonder if we are ever done. I feel that purpose is evolutionary and dynamic and that as I move forward on this path of living on purpose, more of it gets revealed to me.

The current version of how I am articulating my purpose is:

"I choose to show up in each moment with presence, to be completely present, to see and hear another fully; to have an open heart, to surrender to the Source energy and to be an instrument of and a force for love in the world."

I currently work as an international leadership coach, facilitator, and meditation teacher. These roles allow me the structure to live my purpose. I also choose to be an eternal student, constantly looking inwards to find new ways to bring my purpose to life not just through these work roles but in all my relationships as a daughter, sister, friend, and colleague. My name is Sheetal Shah. I am a Kenyan with ancestral roots in India, and this is my story of uncovering and living my purpose.

Clues in Childhood

My parents tell me stories of how when I was a baby, I would stare into space and spend hours observing the world. My extended family regales me with stories of how I loved to write and read. They would go out, leaving me at home in a corner reading, oblivious to the rest of the world, and on their return, I would be in the same spot immersed in this reading world. My dad worked at Kenya Breweries as a laboratory assistant. Money was tight, but that never stopped us from buying books. He encouraged it. Books gave me the gift of imagination. I have powerful memories of using childhood holidays to rally my siblings to put on creative theatrical experiences for my family—fruits of my imagination, based on the many stories I'd read.

My mother grew up in a traditional conservative Indian family. Although she was living in Kenya, the Indians in Kenya remained insular as a community. Indians in Kenya had their own community schools. My mum refused to send me to one of those schools because she wanted me to have a broader experience. I remember being bullied by some students who looked like me and wanted me to stick to their little clique, but I wanted to play with everyone! When my mother found out, she knelt and told me how proud she was of me for wanting to play with everyone and how I should not care about the ones who were bullying me. It was a powerful message that has stayed with me to this day! I still marvel at my parents, who had no logical reason to be open to all races and value diversity. The social constructs they grew up with did not encourage such openness. Yet, they had an innate sense of humanity and equality that they passed onto me—for which I am ever grateful!

My maternal grandfather passed away when I was eight. My mother was devastated and unable to envisage life without her father. A friendly neighbor suggested that meditation might help her with her grief. She joined meditation classes at a local center in Nairobi, and I tagged along. I had some compelling experiences even though I did not know what they meant. I remember experiencing profound love and light. The teachers at the meditation center did not pay much attention to me or teach me anything at that age. It was only as I grew older that I began to value this practice. I devoted a lot of my time to exploring, learning, and diving deep into the study of the mind, meditative and reflective practices, and mindfulness.

I share these snippets from my childhood as I believe that they hold vital clues to my unique purpose. When I was having these experiences, I had no clue that they were significant or were pointing me towards my life purpose. As I have reflected on what is important to me, as I have looked inwards to discover what I was meant to be doing in my life, reflecting on my childhood has been necessary. It has helped me see the powerful messages that have shaped me and continue to speak to me until today, and it has allowed me to see some innate talents and strengths and claim them as my own. I would invite anyone who wants to get closer to their inner purpose to look back at their childhood as there are important clues.

Looking back is not always rosy. You will discover difficult moments and hurtful experiences in the past that shaped you. The messages are not always positively influential or empowering. Part of the journey to living my purpose has been delving deep into these demons of the past that hold me back and unshackling myself from their grip.

The Universe Knows, Uses Force If You Don't Listen

The year was 1989. By that time, my dad had been promoted to manager in the brewery where he was working. The company provided school fees for the children of their managers. I had been moved to a private school that followed the British curriculum. I had just completed my secondary school O-Level Exams. I had drifted away from the meditation center and wasn't practicing so regularly. With my exams over, I had more free time, and I remember going to the meditation center, and when I sat down, I couldn't connect!

I could not find that inner peace and that wonderful experience of love and light that had come so easy to me as a child! That experience of disconnection led me on a journey of learning and exploration. I asked the teachers at the meditation center to formally teach me what they had taught my mum. I read voraciously. I became active in the meditation center as a volunteer and as a regular practitioner. Back at school, I was a good student and top of the class. All these years of practicing meditation had left me with a super-focused mind and good concentration. Learning came easily to me. My parents, especially my dad, who valued education so much, had been saving up to send me to University in the United Kingdom. My teachers were all expecting me to apply to the top universities in the United Kingdom.

Yet, in my heart, there was something different stirring. I was so enamored by the spiritual principles of the meditation center and the mission of peace for all humanity. The teachings of the meditation center were predominantly influenced by Eastern tradition and had many references to Hindu mythology. I never found that strange as I had grown up with some of these mythological stories, but I had always seen them as metaphors. The message of universal brotherhood emphasized was essential for me. I still remember the first lesson of the meditation classes. It was about the soul—how all of us are souls, indestructible, beautiful bursts of energy that live in these bodies of different colors. We may all look different, but we are, deep down, all just light energy, brothers and sisters.

It was a message I took into my heart, and it shaped the way I wanted to see others and interact with others. All I wanted to do was to share this message with the whole world. As these longings grew in me, the world of a university degree grew less and less appealing. The life of the teachers who lived in the meditation centers was more attractive. They were all primarily women, wore a pure white uniform, and had chosen to live in this convent-like setup, devoting their lives to teaching meditation and spreading this message of unity and peace to all. I found myself, again and again, dreaming of serving the world in this way. I spent more time with these teachers, volunteering more to participate in the meditation center's outreach activities. I was only sixteen, and my odd and unusual interests in spirituality started to worry my teachers at school. My headmistress even called me aside into her office to counsel me to focus more on my studies than on this mission of spreading peace.

It was not just the idea of becoming part of an organization that had an essential and compassionate mission that appealed to me. A portion of my meditation journey was discovering my relationship with the Divine. The meditation center described it as the soul's connection with God. For me, it was a love story about finding the presence of a Source of boundless energy and love. I now define this Source as the field of infinite possibilities, as the spirit that moves through and within us all, as the sacred energy that can be called Universe or Creator, and as a larger field of pure and infinite consciousnesses that I can tap into. I now also feel that all these definitions are too limited to describe this Divine Source accurately. This sweet relationship that I was exposed to that pulled me led me to believe that the best way I could serve the world was to spread this message of love and peace.

I was torn. On the one hand, there was this all-consuming love story, and on the other hand, there were these expectations of conventional success—go to university, get a degree, and build a career. I got accepted into the London School of Economics (LSE) to read Politics and Law. My heart was telling me all along that this wasn't the path for me, but I did not dare to say no. How could I not want the benefit of a solid education? How could I disappoint my parents, who had worked so hard to allow me to have these opportunities? My logical brain said I would follow my spiritual aspirations better if I were to have this degree. My creative heart was achingly asking me to follow my true desires.

I completed my advanced secondary education in Kenya and went off to LSE. I hated it. I could not concentrate. I had always found it easy to learn, and the pursuit of knowledge was something I enjoyed, but I could not muster the enthusiasm and the love for learning anymore. I hated being in the city. I found LSE and London devoid of the warmth of the African communities I was so used to. I found it hard to make friends. I was an eighteen-year-old interested in meditating and thinking about serving the world! I did not fit in!

In hindsight, if I had known myself even better, I would not have chosen LSE as the university for me. I would have preferred a smaller, more rural university with green spaces and more community feel. I would not have made choices based on the prestige of academic brilliance. I would also not have chosen to read Politics and Law. I would have chosen a subject that was more about exploring the human mind or learning about culture or social constructs such as sociology, anthropology, or psychology. At that time, though, I didn't even know such subjects existed as possible degrees! It is amusing to me now how compartmentalized my life was.

I and others still treated my inner heart's desires and interests as a side pastime, a hobby but not a way of life or a field to be explored as a possible career. The lesson here for me that I now always share with others is that the more you know yourself, the more you understand your optimizers. These are the things that fill you with joy and energy. The more you know what's most important for your happiness, the easier it is to make choices that enhance your life and that allows you to grow to your full potential. For me, a life lived on purpose cannot be separated from a life devoted to self-development and inner discovery.

The good news is that if we suppress that song in our hearts waiting to be sung, the universe finds ways to lead us back to our hearts. That is exactly what happened to me! I contracted typhoid, typically a tropical disease that you don't often get in London. My doctor there wanted to hospitalize me at the Hospital for Tropical Diseases, where I would be isolated. When I phoned my parents, they asked me to fly home as we knew how to treat typhoid in Kenya without such strict isolation.

As I recovered at home, I found the courage to tell my parents how unhappy I was at university and what was stirring in my heart and what I longed to do. I am not a parent, but I am grateful to all the parents who ultimately want their child's happiness. My parents were disappointed, but my happiness was more important than the dreams they might have had for my academic achievements. They were concerned that I was making a decision based on emotion, so we agreed that I would take the next three years to do something other than joining the spiritual convent straightaway! I am grateful for their openness and the freedom they gave me to explore myself. I might not have seen the wisdom in waiting at that time, but looking back, I appreciate their wisdom in wanting me to be a little older before I made such a huge decision.

I spent the next three years that I would have spent at university doing so many things, including starting a business teaching computer skills to children and young adults, traveling around Kenya and Africa with the meditation center facilitating workshops, exploring writing and journalism through courses, getting involved in the leadership development activities that the meditation center offered to business people, and discovering my love for creative facilitation and passion for leadership development. It was a time to hone my skills and explore. Meanwhile, the inner journey continued. My love and connection with Source just deepened!

At twenty-two, I finally joined the meditation center in Nairobi as a full-time teacher. I shed my jeans and t-shirts and donned a white sari, and stepped into the life of a spiritual nun and meditation teacher. It was meant to be where I would spend the rest of my life! I thought I had found my calling, my place, and my purpose!

Well, it lasted only four years. They were four glorious years! I had the opportunity to design large-scale projects and was responsible for implementing experiential personal development learning programs. I learned what it meant to welcome people into a center with no prejudice and with compassion.

There were two experiences during those four years that I feel are incredibly significant. I had the opportunity to lead regular sessions for young people at the meditation center. We started with a group of twelve—a mix of teenagers and young adults, and at the end of the four years, we had a group of almost fifty young people coming once a week, sometimes twice a week. I had the freedom in these classes to test my creativity and facilitation skills! If I were to interest young people in spiritual principles and inner discovery, I felt I needed to find fun, exciting yet simple, down-to-earth ways to teach. I found ways to engage all the five senses and used color, paint, music, and movement. I know some of the activities we did were frowned upon by the older meditation teachers as taking away from the traditional and serious meditation practice. I also know that the young people who came loved it. It made a difference for them, and they looked forward to this class every week. I am still friends with some of them today!

The second significant experience is when I spent running the personal development center in Addis Ababa, Ethiopia. I spent two years there. I was on my own mainly, in a country that predominantly follows orthodox Christianity. It was a time where I started to find my voice, to experiment with teaching meditation to people without all the references to Hindu mythology. How could the study of the mind be made more practical and applicable to people's daily experiences? How could this meditation center that sounded and looked very Eastern create a safe and welcoming space for people from all walks of life without making people feel that they were being converted or betraying their religion? These were the questions that I was trying to answer and implement. It was a time of cultivating a deep respect for others and for acknowledging and appreciating the differences. I remember feeling very proud when the Patriarch of the Orthodox Church in Ethiopia, Abba Paulos, invited me to run workshops on personal leadership for his team of development advisors. I felt that there was something that I was doing right that was allowing for people from even the most traditional backgrounds to find value in what I was sharing.

As I found my voice and experimented more and more, I began to chafe against some of the ways I felt the meditation centers I was living in were run. I found myself rebelling against the rules and the senior meditators. I strongly felt my inner voice saying that we needed to change how we operated to reach more people. We needed to be less concerned with membership numbers and more concerned with adapting the teachings to make them more accessible to all people. I was so judgmental and full of arrogance that I knew better. I rubbed the leadership in the wrong way. It made my last year in the meditation center challenging! I was at the receiving end of some narcissistic behaviors. I was deeply shocked, as I had not expected my spiritual teachers to be this way. I became fearful, began to hide and lie at times to avoid the adverse reactions.

Again, I was torn! My inner voice told me there was a different way of living and being a spiritual teacher, and yet another part of me was saying, how do you leave a convent that you had decided was your place for life? How do you stop being a spiritual nun? It felt like I was divorcing God! How could I end the love story that was so important to me?

Again, the universe came to my rescue! My body just gave way, and I was seriously ill. To recover, I chose to go back home. If I hadn't fallen sick, I would not have left the meditation center. In the two years it took me to recover and start remission, I figured out what was important to me. I realized that leaving the meditation center was very different from abandoning my relationship with the Divine. I built up enough courage to shape my life differently, still choosing to live like a nun. I still wanted to serve, but I needed to do it differently. I found the courage to resign from my position with the meditation center formally.

Whenever I am now faced with dilemmas and challenging situations, I always go back to my heart. I go back to my inner voice as I know that it holds a message for me. When I experience internal conflict, I know that there is a part of the song of my heart that is wanting to come forth. I have learned that purpose widens and deepens. As we grow, our purpose asks for a new way that it wants to be expressed. I have learned to be alert to my evolution and the evolution of my inner voice.

I know that when I am misaligned with my heart, then something gives way. My body reacts and stops being an effective vehicle for my soul. I no longer wait for the universe and my body to come to my rescue, and I am listening keenly to and following my heart. I am more aware of my body's intelligence and my soul's intuition, and I use both of these as my guides as I move forward with my life.

All these experiences left me with absolute faith that the universe has got my back! There is a deeper reason for each of us to be on this earth; there is an extraordinary contribution that only each of us can uniquely make. The universe presents the opportunities in front of us to prepare us for this contribution and push us towards it! Every experience and moment up till this very present moment has been perfect, even the hard stuff, as it is preparing me to be the person I am meant to be. Each experience is opening me up even more; I am learning to be more loving and more welcoming. Every occasion is honing my skills, getting me ready to live my purpose! No experience goes to waste!

I would urge anyone who wants to get more aligned with their purpose to reflect on all their experiences—the choices and decisions, the moment when you took a stand because they all point to essential values and ingredients of living your unique purpose. I would also ask you to pause and listen to any pain, discomfort, or tension—perhaps there is a message there for you that something needs to change. Perhaps you are being pointed in the right direction.

Being, Becoming, Trusting

Suddenly, I had no title of meditation teacher, and I had no large projects to handle. Once I left the meditation center, I thought that I could go back to volunteering at the center and live independently. I was wrong! Every attempt I made to volunteer there was thwarted, or if I did volunteer, it was rife with conflict. I became very bitter and resentful. I was in full victim mode!

At the same time, I was in a discovery process of deep introspection. I wrote pages and pages. I used the automatic writing process designed by Julia Cameron of *The Artist's Way*, read Nick Williams' *The Work We Were Born to Do*, and followed the process designed by The Franklin-Covey Institute to take a hard look at my values, my purpose, and how I wanted both my values and purpose to show up in all my roles.

As my purpose became more evident to me, I saw in myself all the shadows, fears, and ego that prevented me from fully stepping into my purpose. The more I worked on letting go of my old beliefs and fears; opportunities started to appear. I was invited to give talks at organizations, at clubs, on radio, and on TV. As I became more open, as I let go of my anger and resentment, the opportunities opened up even more. In the beginning, I primarily gave motivational talks and coached young adults who were just back from university and starting their careers. Over the years, this has evolved into working with senior leadership and C-suite leaders across the world.

I see a direct correlation between my inner work and the growth of my career as a coach and facilitator. I have never yet had to market myself or do any serious promoting. Work seems to flow to me through word of mouth, and the more I grow, the more opportunities present themselves.

I have found that just saying yes to expressing one part of my purpose, taking one step to living aligned to my purpose, opens up more ways to express my purpose. One example of this is an e-zine I started in 2001. I was still recovering from my illness. My body was still weak, but I had a clear sense of what I wanted to share. The e-zine was called Food for The Soul. It was similar to what we would call blogs now, but these were email lists you could subscribe to. Every morning, I wrote an inspirational paragraph—a reflection or a realization I had uncovered for myself, and subscribers would receive it in their email. As the e-zine got forwarded around, it landed on the desk of the Chief of the

Staff Training and Development Unit of the United Nations in Nairobi (UNON). She invited me to become a trainer for some of their staff training programs. One thing led to another, and I was asked to design and oversee the coaching program for the United Nations Environment Programme, headquartered in Nairobi but has offices worldwide. This was an incredible opportunity to coach people all over the world from diverse backgrounds. I ran this program from 2007 to 2016, and it all started from saying yes to writing a small paragraph every day!

Whatever your heart says, even If you cannot do all of it, start with something small. That small leap of faith will open so many doors. Trust that the path will become clear as you take the first step.

I continue to remove all the barriers inside me that prevent me from showing up fully. I continue to meet my fears and embrace all parts of me. I recently embraced a part of myself that I had distanced myself from. After I left the meditation center, I did not think that I had the right to teach meditation. I had this illogical belief that to truly teach meditation and mindfulness, I had to live in a meditation center. I used to bring aspects of the mind and creative visualization during my workshops, but I shied away from teaching any meditation or mindfulness practices.

It was only about two years ago that I realized that I am a meditation teacher at my core, and I always have been. It is an integral part of who I am, and it shines through in many forms. I do not need to be wearing white robes for that. Fully owning this part of myself and fully embracing this gift has unleashed new energy in me. I feel the freedom to play with these gifts and allow them to come more to the fore in my work as I coach and facilitate. I found it quite amusing that I had not yet told anyone about this shift once I wholly owned this part of me. A friend even drove me to someone's house, saying, "There's someone I would like you to meet." When I got there, my friend introduced me as someone who would lead a meditation practice for everyone present. It is like the world was waiting for me to step back into this role. I now teach meditation more openly, record mindfulness practices, and even cus-tomize these practices for clients.

I also realized that one of my gifts is presence and being able to hold space for others. I had somehow always disregarded this gift of pres-ence even though it came so easily to me. I had thought that my con-tribution to the world had to be something more; it could not be this natural quality. I was always looking for something more. Over the last two years, I have begun to own that presence is the gift with which I serve the world. I am making room for presence to be the driving force for all my work, and in the last two years, I have had more new oppor-tunities to coach than ever before.

I do not know what is around the corner for me! I just trust that as I continue to step into being love, as I step into being an open heart, as I become more internally aligned to my inner purpose, as I remove all the barriers within me that prevent me from fully seeing, hearing and accepting another—the path will continue to become clearer and new opportunities will continue to appear.

I leave you with just one last piece of advice. Surrender to your heart's inklings and yearnings, let your soul light up your path, say yes, and trust. It will feel frightening, and you will doubt yourself and your worthiness. Do it anyway, as the rewards are immeasurable. The joy and the bliss that comes from continuing to find ways to live aligned to inner purpose are more than I could have imagined. You might feel alone at times, but you won't be alone. The universe will have your back and will send you allies and supporters, mentors, and friends who will bless you, comfort you and carry you closer to your purpose. As I look back on my journey, I am grateful to my parents, my brother Ashish, and my sister Sheetal for being such strong allies on my quest to live a more intentional, purpose-ful life. Would I do it any differently if I had another chance? I would not change any of it! It has been perfect!

Sheetal Shah is a creative learning and development facilitator and executive leadership coach. With over twenty-five years of personal research and experience in personal change, self-mastery, leadership, and creative mindfulness, Sheetal's expertise is in creating a space in which people can realize their leadership potential. As an executive coach, Sheetal pays close attention to the needs of her clients and is imaginative and intuitive in the methods used to help clients move towards their goals. As a mindfulness teacher, she is interested in supporting her students to find that sacred still place within, from which all is possible.

Sheetal has significant experience working with a broad range of international and national clients, including various UN agencies, CEOS, and senior managers from the corporate sector, small and growing business enterprises, government bodies, and non-governmental organizations. She is based in Kenya but has worked internationally in Africa, Europe, North and South America, and Asia. Her passion is to work with leaders and support them in creating inspiring, impactful places that foster cultures of creativity and collaboration. Her work centers around helping leaders to be authentic, ethical and exemplary in all their interactions. She sees her role as that of a transformation catalyst. She loves trees and often walks in the forest to find inspiration. Reach her at: https:// ke.linkedin.com/in/sheetalafrica or https://www.facebook.com/sheetal. shah.africa/

How I Got Knocked Down into Purpose

By Tabitha Rose
Canada / United States

"You neeeed to li-st-en," Dad said.

His words boomed across the kitchen table. The last letter of each word sharply cut as my mother tapped her hand on the plastic tray table of my baby sister's highchair.

"Eeeeeat. Yum yum yum," my mother said as she mimicked the oblivious one-and-a-half-year-old, picking up the tiny shreds of chicken and putting them in her mouth.

My baby sister continued to scream out for Dad, but his eyes remained fixed down on his food with his face red and angry. I felt it was at me, and a burning feeling rose inside. I thought to myself, *But I am always listening. I grasp everything you say, and most of all, everything you don't say.* My eyes welled up with tears. I loathed the intensity. Mom didn't notice. As usual, she was distracted by everything besides me. Her eyes would be focused on every other tiny detail in a room. She would see every little shred of chicken that made its way off the highchair table. Every pillow and hand towel in the house would be adjusted perfectly before her restlessness seemed to somewhat settle. By then, it was always too late. Besides, I didn't want her to notice because if she did, she wouldn't be comforting anyway.

I didn't want anyone to notice how much words affected me. There may have been a disconnect between how people saw me and how I felt inside. To be told I need to listen was astonishing, considering how I clung to every word spoken to me, even when I tried so hard not to. I begged, bargained, and pleaded to something outside of myself to, if anything, stop listening to others so intently as such that their words would not burn into me with insane intensity. I often thought about being the only one in the world that felt this way. Everyone else seemed to have figured this thing out, like life—the direction they should go in and emotions that come along the way.

When I carefully studied how others, like the kids in my class and my teacher expressed their sadness and anger, it always looked more attractive. They said what they meant, and it was on time. They wore their angst and innermost heart cries on their chest, gilded yet with guts. Whereas I kept everything inside like a slimy, sloppy stew, stuffing in more and more leftover ingredients over time. It was hot and heavy and left me feeling lethargic. Often after, I retreated to my purple-patterned bedsheets next to a stack of books where I would stare out the window at the silver lining of the clouds and doze off into a numb slumber.

Mornings at school were full of the buzzing energy of those around me. I was unsure of myself and felt wobbly amidst others who appeared to stand as tall as trees in their confidence. Even though I towered above most of my peers, their wounding words made me feel like I should shrink myself, so I slouched in my chair and when I stood in a lineup.

As days passed into the school year, I sunk further and further. The weight of each day took its toll on me. Then, one day, for no particular reason, I decided that I would do things differently. Today, I would try harder. I made the mistake of falsely sourcing confidence, which I would one day learn to be a fatal flaw. I held my head high and walked with the same stride I saw one of the popular girls had as I made my way past the coat hooks and into my classroom that morning. Copycatting had to be the solution, I thought. My chair felt tinier than usual as I half-sat on it, perched, piercing right through my fear as I scanned the classroom.

"Marcellooo. Sweatpants, again?" I cackled at the single yet only slightly less-liked person in my class.

He ignored me after muttering a soft, "Shut up," and plopping himself at his desk.

"Christina!" I welcomed the most confident girl in my class as she entered. I said only her name because that was what a worthy person would say. That was what her equal would say. That was what I had too wanted to say, just like many others, during the last six months of the year.

She said nothing, only glared down at me as she passed and made her way to the side of the classroom where she sat along with her actual friends. Once she joined them, she began to speak quietly. Sting. *They must be talking about me*, I thought. I could now hear them laughing.

As the teacher came in and the class began, the energy became more static than usual. It was as if I could hear and feel every word being said. It wasn't long before the comments started. The first came after I raised my hand to answer a question.

Shut up, Tabitha. No one likes you.

Still, I tried. First, I laughed the comments off. Next, I hit back harder, with words I felt would pound them into a place of submission. Nothing worked. One after the other, they came at me like tennis-ball machines on rapid-fire, from all angles.

The class made its way to our French lesson. This was a particularly boisterous time of day, and even I felt bad for our teacher. Her tone would flip back and forth from panic to pleading. For me, however, this was when it became exceedingly awful. The insults came at me at such a vicious pace, it was impossible to return what I was being served up. The stew inside me was so hot and furious, it made its way up to my throat and then to my bottom lip, which began to quiver uncontrollably. When

I could not stand anymore, my burning head fell into my crossed arms atop my desk, and I sobbed quietly.

Still, it continued—accusations and attacks far beyond anything I had ever experienced. The teacher did nothing to stop it. No one disagreed with them. I remained in the blackness of my arms for the rest of the hour. I listened as each student's footsteps left the classroom. I heard the sounds of the teacher rustling around at her desk. I waited in the same position, my sleeves and arms now wholly soaked with tears, for her to come over to me and simply ask if I was okay. Then, I listened as her footsteps left the classroom too. I was alone. Fluorescent lights never sounded so loud. *If she left, she agrees with them*, I thought. *I really am that terrible.* For the most part, from that day forward, I ceased listening. I don't think it was intentional, but that's what I did.

A Kooky Angel Appeared to Tap Me on the Shoulder

My grade-8 teacher was what my mom would call kooky, but she playfully uses that to describe most of her friends. My teacher too became a friend of my mom's. My grade-8 teacher was so much more than an educator, although it took a couple of decades to realize this. She was more of a dreamcatcher. I felt like she designed her lessons with only me in mind. The projects she gave were inspiring. We had monthly book reports, and I decided that instead of simply handing in some paper sheets and a plain cover page, I would compose a bookwork of sorts, interior formatting, and cover design, too, no less! I would stay up late the night before one was due, furiously writing, coloring, cutting, and gluing into the early hours.

Time didn't seem to faze me. I quite liked fighting my heavy dry eyes as I pressed on to completion. The following day, I would proudly place my product on her desk when she was there to see it. I would catch her eyes open widely as the vibrancy of the cover page caught her appreciative gaze, *I know*. I would think. *It's great, isn't it?*

My teacher and I spoke the same language, especially when we did not say anything to one another. Although, when it came time to hand back our assignments, she would take time to give a special mention to those that stood out. Mine, of course, always did. I received an A+ on every single book report. She would rave to the class about the time I must have taken to put the piece together and the attention to detail. *"Outstanding* job, Tabitha! You are a writer!" *s*he would exclaim.

Near the end of the year, students were asked to take a standardized test to determine their path and, ultimately, their purpose. Next year we would be going to high school, and the course stream we entered would set us on our way. As my stare shifted back and forth at the multiple-choice questionnaire next to the scantron sheet, tapping my pencil anxiously, I figured the whole thing out. I saw my future, or rather, didn't. A writer? A creative? Me and all these feelings? Just me. Quickly, I decided, no. Just no.

It was as though a gameshow buzzer went off in my head, indicating the incorrect answer. I am incorrect. In turn, almost robotically, I manipulated the questionnaire so that I would find myself swiftly slotted into the mathematics and business category. That felt safe. It seemed as though it was a choice that someone strong, fearless, confident, and secure would choose. I knew those people. I watched those people. I could be just like those people. Being like other people was who I would be for the next *fifteen* years.

Fast Forward and Pause

It was the first week in about two years that I had actually been on time for work every day. Not to mention, I was dressed well, beige dress pants and a white stiff, starched shirt to boot. I shifted uncomfortably in my chair as I watched the clock on my desktop computer switch to 9:00 a.m. EST. As I observed the unchanged office environment, I thought, "What is the big deal with being on time anyway? It's as if no one really wakes up in here until lunch."

The de-facto boss, but actually the head counsel, breezed by me and into his office and quickly shut his door behind him. No *"Good morning, Tabitha?"* I thought. I was trying to stack up as many of these as I could to make up for all the times he must have walked by my empty desk and graciously decided not to take action against me.

Boy, was I ever lucky, I thought. Suddenly, I started to feel warm and fuzzy about my workplace. I loved it here. It was my job, and I was lucky to have such a great job. For me, it was more than a job; it was the identity I boasted of so proudly. It was what excused me and permitted me to do all the ceremonious celebrating that had become so cyclical. So what if it seeped into the work hours from time to time? I made up for it when I was present but outperforming. Right? I suddenly began to regret how much I had taken this company for granted. If only I had been better. But this week had been good, I reassured myself. I would stay home this weekend, no drinking, no nightclubs, or after-hours antics, and do good next week again.

My VP appeared like a bolt from the hallway and asked me to please follow him. I rose from my chair with a puzzled look on my face, and before I could even answer to agree, he was back off down the hallway again. As I passed the offices which lined the hallway leading to the office entrance, my eyes quickly darted into each one to see if he was there and, if not, study the faces of my colleagues. Those who were there had their heads down at paperwork or fixed on their computer screens. *They were all on time*, I thought. *They are good employees. Why couldn't I just be more like them?*

I arrived at the front desk where the temp secretary sat. Although I already knew the answer, to stall, comfort myself, and collect my thoughts, I asked her, "Is Chris in the conference room?" She confirmed he was, with a friendly smile, and I thanked her.

I sat down across the conference room from my actual boss, VP of Investor Relations—although for the past year I had been unwilling to accept he indeed was as such, until now—along with a woman I had never seen before. He began to speak while holding a document of some sort in his hands. He was brief and swift, as most of our conversations. I was fired. He looked at me as though I were some sort of annoyance that he had been itching to get rid of and found even more irritating that he had to have the conversation to do so. Then, he left.

I sat with the woman I had never met before in silence for a few seconds. Fluorescent lights had never been so loud.

"Are you okay?" she asked.

I now understood she was a contracted human resources representative.

"I-I-I—just don't understand," I stammered.

I feared trying to say anything more, or else I would full-on break into sobs, and clutched my thighs, the liner of the annoying thick beige slacks now stuck to my skin.

Fuck, I hate these pants, I thought to myself.

She continued to speak, explaining the package I was receiving and highlighted the transitional support. This meant assistance in finding my way to a new job. I half-listened as my mind raced, remembering how I had once slept fifty-three minutes upright through an entire video conference call in this same room. I was told to leave straight from the conference room. I could only go back to my desk to collect my personal belongings and would have to immediately exit. I would have an escort and be watched closely, as though I could not be trusted. *The jig was up*, I thought. All the wrongs I had made, rules broken, lines crossed, and impossible days when I hid in the bathroom and escaped early flashed through my mind like a painful reel of shame. They must have known all along. Or maybe I just didn't belong. Did this mean I was a bad actor after all?

No. It's far easier to lie to myself than face a painful truth. I refused to listen. I refused to accept that I was the problem. I blamed it on office politics. I used nepotism as a loose argument and why they could no longer offer me special treatment. They were making significant changes in the company. It was time for me and all of my extended vacations and unexcused absences without consequences due to my boyfriend's father being the largest shareholder to end. Or maybe, my boss was just jealous that I was invited to our chairman's five-day wedding in Cartagena, Colombia, and he was not. Truth is the enemy of ego. In my case, ego won this battle.

When Taps Turn to Slaps, Carry On

Ego took me quickly to another job. This one was a big "Fuck you," not only my past employer but everyone else in my life who had ever made me feel small. My first six-figure salary and a Yorkville office were enough to shut anyone up who asked about the sudden job change. But it didn't last long. Missing my first day of work because I was still celebrating getting the job was tragic. So I made the excuse of a real tragedy, a death in the family. It was more like the death of my soul, as I lied and manipulated myself into more trouble.

The following three months of the job before losing it were insane. One day I was on top of the world, finding it unbelievable that I had made it to this level that I could boast so proudly. As my bragging persisted, as did my substance use, fueling the lies to others and, most of all, myself. Finally, the swanky uptown firm had had enough of me too. It was all just again, weird—my behavior, to put it flatly.

Months of sulking and sinking. I knew something had to change. I made my way to my first 12-step meeting for myself. Although I had been to others before. The first-ever was years earlier to support my biological father. He was a "greeter," and I was pissed off. I wore a hat and sat in the back with my grandmother. By the time it ended, I felt good, though.

I remember leaving the church and walking down the street feeling warm and fuzzy, as though every person in the room had magically somehow just became my friend, and all embraced me with a hug at the same time.

My drinking was not even a problem at that time, as I understood, at least. I was in my second year of university, and I drank as those around me did and frankly held my composure better than most. This meeting, the one I went to for myself, though, I was tricked into going to. I found myself partying with a friend of mine—odd considering I had previously seen her as the crazy party girl. In recent times we had gravitated toward each other, and I had been "outdoing" even her in our escapades.

One night, she came over to my apartment and passed out while I kept going by myself. It was indeed a weeknight in which I did not make it to work the next day. She got me to go to this meeting with her by calling it a book study. *A book study is good. I can brag about going to a book study like that on a Sunday afternoon*, I thought. I realized quickly what it was and glared at her with an "I see what you did here" face.

By the end of the meeting, I knew I needed to be there. I also fell in love with the stories. I did not want to be like any of the people sitting around me, and in many ways, I wasn't, but I also was. But I was only allowing myself to see the very little I could relate to. I quickly found the best-dressed in the room and identified those I thought had good jobs and money. It was a good thing she did for me that day. It was the right thing to do, and I will never forget it. Although, I was not ready. Surrendering (to anything) is not something we choose; I believe it is divinely chosen for us.

Haven't you had enough? Sometimes people share with me that this question comes to them when they are like a jaywalker, repeating the same pattern, getting crushed each time. For me, it did not. I tried again, another job with the same persona. I knew everything, could handle nothing, and unbeknownst to me, no one could tell me anything. It started off well this time. I was sober and slightly humbled by my new position as executive assistant to the CEO. The tasks being asked of me were simple. I am above this, but I am doing this because they need me.

Knocked Down at 30,000 ft

Then after a month, I retreated into my self-medicating, getting away with it at first as my boss traveled so often. I could plan my binges around this extensive travel schedule. That sounded reasonable, but that implied that I had some sort of control over this thing. Wrong again. I disappointed him, and I knew it. That was what hurt the most. I cried this time. I don't know if it was because I actually loved the job or because I had no choice but to stare my powerlessness right in the face. I binged and then slept, following it with a total of twenty-four hours of rest before I would get on a plane to visit my boyfriend. He had been in Texas for the last few weeks, reassuring his father against his own unmanageability.

At the airport, early the following day was when I began to feel queasy. I boarded the plane and took off, then went to the lavatory to be sick, but nothing came up. I passed out and awoke to my head in the sink, head hot and finding it difficult to breathe. I could tell by the pressure in my ears that we were well on our way. I made my way back to my seat, dizzy and barely breathing. I sat in my chair, clenching the armrests, eyes closed, trying my best to inhale breaths, but it became more and more difficult. The woman across the aisle asked me if I was okay. I told her that I felt sick. She was kind and gave me two wristbands with pressure points which she said would help. They didn't. Things got worse until it all became a blur—next, a wheelchair. The pilot asked me questions and told me about his daughter, who looked to be about my age. Then, an ambulance. Paramedics asking me if I had used drugs. I lied. Well, not that day, at least. The rest, I don't remember.

I woke up in a hospital in Houston, Texas. That was not the city I was headed for. My boyfriend was on his way, but it would take him hours. I was feeling better, but I did not feel safe enough to leave. I wished I could just stay there in the safety of doctors, quiet corridors, and the thin sheet I had to cover myself. That was the safest I had felt in a very long time.

"Why don't you come and stay with me for a while?" my boyfriend's mother sweetly suggested over the phone. I stared out the paned glass door of the colonial-style southern Texas home into the backyard, thinking to myself, *I wonder if she knows*. She was an intuitive, caring woman. She cared more for me than I deserved. This was another one of those occasions when she would rush in to save, only this time it wasn't her son. It was me. I graciously accepted her invitation. It felt safe. In fact, she was. Her lifestyle was simple and soft, and she and her home had a grace that I greatly admired. I flew west to Vancouver days later, arriving to find two adorable puppies and her open arms.

The next day I danced around what was really wrong in my life. She offered to send me to a "special person," who she explained was *just to talk, Tab.* I agreed. It felt safe. He was available later that day, and so I went. This was when I encountered who I refer to today as my magical mentor. I had no idea what we would talk about. However, I had had some experience with a therapist, and my boyfriend's mother had also graciously sponsored my sessions once before to "manage to deal with her son." Little did she know I used that woman to vent about my mother and convince myself I did not have a problem with alcohol or cocaine. I had confessed to that woman that I loved to write and had begun writing my grandmother's life story. She told me to view that as a hobby and essentially keep my day job.

On the other hand, Michael, the magic mentor, somehow had me talking about my grandmother's life story project in what seemed like the first few minutes. I had not planned to. Regrettably, I had not even thought about it in some time. I figured this mentor would be digging right into my issues and effectively helping me get back on my feet and get an even *better* job.

I remember him saying to me, "Why should we spend time in the basement when we can talk about your gifts and how you can start delivering them to the world?!" He said it with such enthusiasm. His blue eyes sparkled, and I knew he really meant it.

But my gifts. "Umm, politics?" I replied. Politics was something I saw a friend doing at the age of fourteen and quickly followed suit. My friend was confident, popular, funny, and had already earned himself status at a young age. These were all the things I wanted and had no idea how to get, so I followed. For years, I was like his shadow. Monkey see, monkey do. I followed him from youth politics into university, then a sorority because he was in a fraternity, and finally into a federal politics job.

"No," Michael replied. "Your gifts."

We talked for what seemed like a few minutes more, but somehow my whole life story came out. He listened to me telling him about the book reports in eighth grade and even more about the recent memoir project with grandma. In those moments, I admitted all the chaos in the last few years. Even all that which didn't appear as such, the only time I truly felt any sense of contentment or like there was nowhere else to be but exactly where I was at that moment was when I was sitting with my grandmother and listening to her stories. This feeling had intensified when she took me on a trip to Hungary to walk down memory lane and dig into her memory's recesses. I remember vividly sitting on the terrace of a relative's bed and breakfast, watching the rain, writing, and feeling utterly present at the moment. Every droplet landed in its perfect place. I was in my proper place. I had no idea at the time that something greater than myself had led me there and was giving me the most loving tap on the shoulder as if to say, here it is your purpose.

What was I to do with this newfound information? Michael said I should just start. Take one step in that direction—say it aloud. It took me a few attempts, but finally, I announced, "I am a writer."

Okay, I'm Listening

Ha! There it was. I felt a little silly, but then again, it felt good to feel silly. Maybe this was me. Next, I was instructed to leave his office and go for a walk through the market. If I were to smell something delicious, eat it! If I were to see something that caught my eye for some particular reason, buy it! This all sounded baffling to me considering the last five years and more I spent eating the food and listening to the music as others around me did.

One step at a time, I made my way into a brighter way of living. I started listening to my own voice and the one of something greater than myself, which I realized had been there all along. *Life to Paper* came to be one day as I sat at the desk in my grandmother's guest bedroom, dreaming up names for my new life story writing business. When I checked GoDaddy, and the .com was available, I threw my hands up in the air and exclaimed, "It is meant to be!"

My first client happened right on time, at least as I chose to see it. Suddenly, I saw everything as a miracle and began to see my life full of sweet serendipity. My first client referred me to my second, and opportunities to put extraordinary individual's lives on paper continued from there. Eventually, I learned that many of my clients needed help with launching and publishing books, and Life to Paper Publishing emerged.

My path in recovery continued, although as many are this way, it was not linear. It was all meant to be. My pain only drove me deeper into purpose. For the first time in my life, I had this grounding anchor of purpose pulling me back into a place of peace and contentment. When continuous sobriety into the years was maintained, the abundance in the growth of Life to Paper Publishing reflected back. The expression, "If you can dream it, you can do it," became my life's motto.

My memories float into my consciousness here and there, and I begin to remember the little girl who stared out her window into a sky of clouds but always saw the silver lining. I looked outside my window then, as I do today, and saw limitless potential. The difference, now, is that I am an arrow firmly pointed in one direction. I believe that stories can change the world. I help people fall in love with their lives and gifts, put their stories to paper, and guide them to inspire hearts and minds worldwide. I have worked with people toward healing, transforming into living lives beyond their wildest expectations, and sharing their knowledge to help countless others.

Today, my conversations with my dad are one thing that I hold most dear. I had no idea that when I was younger, he told me to listen, what he was really talking about. When we talk, I share what I am working on and my dreams to one day share this process with the world—for free— so that everyone can chronicle their lives. I tell him that I hope to live to see a world where there are no more lost stories, people who never had the blessing of finally starting to fall in love with their own lives and live to share that journey.

Three pieces of advice I can offer to those who want to live their purpose and monetize it:

1. Show up. Every single day. Whether it is for an hour or fifteen when you are first getting started, the most important thing is consistency. Some days I tackle big tasks that take months, while other days are for smaller items on my list. Every day is not going to look the same. Remember to be kind to yourself but set a standard that you are going to show up to your purpose every single day whether it's one social media post or a schedule of meetings. Just SHOW UP.

2. When you are starting out, I recommend having as many conversations as you possibly can. Spend most of the time during these conversations doing one thing - listening. It is not the time to *tell* people the kind of help they need. Rather, the time to *ask* people the kind of help they need. Start to notice a pattern in

the conversations of the kind of help people are looking for and how your gifts can help. You will begin to build confidence as you start sharing your gifts and see the transformation it offers people.

3. Pay attention to what your gut instinct is telling you. You know what that feels like! As you are beginning to monetize your gifts and purpose, don't feel obligated to say yes to everyone. You won't be able to help everyone and not listening to your inner voice which is signaling you that there is not an alignment may drain you of the energy you can devote to those within your ability to provide transformational experiences to others.

Tabitha Rose composes and conducts a symphony of stories that inspire hearts and minds worldwide. She is the Founder and Editor-in-Chief of Life to Paper Publishing, Director of Life to Legacy Foundation, and the Owner of The Bookshop in Buena Vista, Miami, Florida. Reach her at www.lifetopaper.com

Creating Positive Legacy and Family Wealth

By Stacy Jewel
United States

Finding your purpose isn't as easy as everyone thinks it is. Your purpose is something that you do without effort, and everyone appreciates you for it. You can have more than one purpose. The problem is that sometimes people confuse purpose with passion. They like doing something, even if it is hard for them, and they feel that is what they want to do. The thing is, your purpose isn't always what you like to do. It is what you are put here on this planet to do. You may not even realize that it is your purpose because it comes so easily to you. Learning my purpose was a journey because I wanted to do things that made money, but I couldn't always grasp them or wasn't that successful at them. I felt like whatever someone else was doing to make money, I should try it. Then I woke up one day feeling my purpose was calling me, and if I didn't go after it, I would die.

My purpose is to leave a positive legacy and family wealth in our name. I have quit my job and dedicated my time to my own companies: Stacy J Events, Stacy Jewel Beauty, and SJ Media. I am serving the generations of black women before me who couldn't strive for more based on their skin color, which limited available opportunities because of racism. This is important to me because long after I am gone, I want our family to believe that anything is possible and never have to work for anyone again.

After my husband passed in 2013, I realized that nothing is promised, and it was up to me to provide for our three children. After getting a master's degree, I was still working for someone else, and I was earning an hourly wage of twenty-one dollars per hour. I could barely pay all my bills and was forced to file bankruptcy. I felt like I was hitting rock bottom when I realized I couldn't work for anyone else and support my dream. I was scared because I needed secure income to pay bills, but I had no time to focus on my own business ventures. I prayed, meditated, went to the cemetery, and spoke to myself as if I was conversing with my husband. I was about to have a nervous breakdown, so I took some time off work, stayed home for a few days, and wrote down what was most important to me. After meditating most of the day and going over what would genuinely make me happy and fulfill my purpose, I decided that I had to spend as much time as possible working on getting my businesses off the ground.

Doing What I Love

My vision of living my purpose is to get up every day doing something I love, spending time with loved ones, making a difference in someone's life, and building bonds. Stacy J Events allows me to get up daily and help people with their goals, and I love being a part of that. Stacy Jewel Beauty allows me to help young girls build their business, see their inner beauty, and focus on self-respect. SJ Media allows me to write books, tell my story, and leave a legacy for those I will never meet and allow them to hear my struggle and go after what they want.

I get to make a difference in the world because I feel valued, excited for my day and inspired by the people I meet who hear how I decided to just go for it. I feel like I am actually living and not getting up daily to fulfill someone else's purpose.

Looking Inside When Life Knocks You Down

When I was sixteen, I met my soulmate and had our first child. She passed away at birth, and I was depressed for years. I had my oldest living daughter at eighteen, and my husband went to prison. I raised her until she was four, all alone. When my husband came home, we had our second child, and I found out he got another girl pregnant. That news put me in a more profound depression where I didn't want to do anything. A few years later, I had my youngest daughter and was still fighting for our marriage. As soon as we got to a good point in our marriage, he was killed. I felt like I never had a chance to live. I have traveled a little bit, but because of him being in prison and working on our marriage, I never felt like I could enjoy life to the fullest. I was always waiting for something. Waiting to marry, waiting for him to get out of prison, waiting for our marriage to be better, waiting for something in my life to direct me toward greatness.

When I looked inside of myself instead of what other people were offering me, I changed. I had to soul-search what God's purpose for me on earth was. I felt empty and had to do something fast. It took me years to figure out if I wanted to work for someone and grow with their company, put 100 percent into my own ideas, or just keep being miserable doing daily things that didn't bring me joy. I had to take a chance on myself and be serious enough about it to make some changes. I worked at my full-time job for five years, and during the last two years, I would take my breaks and lunches working on my own businesses and then go home and work on them until I was comfortable enough to say, "The next step requires 100 percent effort, so I have to quit."

The Joys in Entrepreneurship

I have taught my children the benefits of being an entrepreneur. I am helping others open and start their own businesses, and I am living my dream. I get up every day and feel like I am actually living. I may work longer hours some days, but I am doing it to build my brand and leave a legacy, so it doesn't feel like work. I am empowering young black women to think outside the box and shoot for the stars. I've had so many messages on Facebook, my blog, or Instagram with people telling me that I have inspired them, and that is what my purpose is all about.

One year ago, I was always tired, miserable at her job, frustrated, disappointed, and eager to find her purpose. I couldn't sleep at night because something in her would wake me up. My nerves were always fidgety because it felt like I was missing something. My soul was not shining through. People only saw the dark, edgy, and irritable Stacy.

These days, I am gleaming with delight. I am fun, adventurous, happy, and inspiring. When you are fulfilling your purpose, people are drawn to you. People I hadn't seen since high school have contacted me, asking me what my secret to success is. Life is full of energy, and it honestly seems like a fairytale. I have met a man who is into my goals and dreams, and he treats me like a queen. He was drawn to my energy and successful attitude. We are now engaged, and he is opening his own business. My life's purpose was hidden by the distraction of people, jobs, and negativity. When I cleared my mind and focused on what I was sent here to do, my purpose came to light. It isn't just making money and traveling the world. It is inspiring, motivating, and having fun doing it. My children will tell their children about our family name with gratitude for all my hard work.

What I Recommend

Three pieces of advice I would give anyone trying to fulfill their purpose would be to:

1. Think of yourself as the person you want to be. This means don't downplay your talent. For example, I was only charging people $500 to plan clients' events because I didn't think I was good enough to charge more. When I saw how much other planners were charging and I did more work, I stopped telling myself I wasn't good enough. I raised my prices to a little under the market price and stuck to it when people would ask me what my services cost. If you don't think you're good enough, neither will

they. Now, I have more clients charging more than I did when I only charged $500, and I get referrals.

2. Network with the class of people you want to be. Stop hanging out with people complaining or not interested in doing anything different than what they are doing. When you put yourself around people who are growing, you will succeed. I stopped dealing with negative people who thought my ambitions were too high. Most thought leaving my job was unimaginable. If you don't have supportive, driven people around you, you will second guess everything you do. Find people who are hungry for success, and they will help you stay focused. These people will also hire you to do things or introduce you to others that may need your services.

3. Make a plan. Figure out what you need financially to quit your job or open that new business. I have a mobile boutique. My goal was to have a brick and mortar, but they were too expensive, and I wanted something now. So, instead of the monthly payments of $3,000 for a rental building, I paid $11,000 for my own already put-together mobile boutique. Now, I don't have to pay rent, so I can afford to buy supplies and go to farmer's markets to sell my products. Think outside the box, figure out what you need to do, and then do it. If you have to stop going out to dinner for a year to save money to open your business, then it's worth it.

When you go after what is already yours, it is easier than you think, and the universe lets you take the journey. Not everything will be a piece of cake, but it will feel like your world has just opened all new doors so you can choose which ones to walk through instead of being forced or thrown into a doorway. Many of us feel like our purpose is passing us by, but you don't have to live your entire life waiting. Do a meditation retreat, stay home in quiet, think about what you're good at, write down ideas, and see what you get most excited about or do with ease. We only have one life to live, so what are you waiting for?

Stacy Jewel Ayiers has three children and was married for fourteen14 years before her husband's passing. She is remarried to a wonderful, inspiring man. Her dream of writing personal and newsworthy stories started when she was in fifth grade. She is inspired to write books based on life experiences that have changed her. She resides in Arizona and loves to travel and enjoy life. Her hobbies are shopping, writing (of course), reading, and spending time with family. She enjoys a great scary movie, HGTV, or cold case show. She is a graduate of Arizona State University. Stacy's goal is to leave a legacy behind for her children and to create stories that empower, change, and inspire others.

RISE—One Woman's Story of Passion and Purpose

By Lauren Hollows
Australia

Growing up in the Era of Female Empowerment

Strong women and respectful men raised me. There's no doubt in my mind that I had a very privileged upbringing. My parents worked hard and told me consistently that I could achieve anything if I worked hard and studied hard. I had a clear understanding that the only thing stopping me in this world was me.

From the music of Dolly Parton, Destiny's Child, the Spice Girls, and of course Madonna, to TV shows like *Buffy*, *Charmed*, and *Sabrina*, the media fed me a consistent diet that it was entirely possible to be a mother, entrepreneur, fight for justice and change the world, all while looking slim and stunning. My mother was evidence of this. She worked hard, was a fantastic cook, kept the house clean, always had time for my brother and me, and of course, looked stunning while doing it all. My aunts and my mother's friends all seemed to be the same, so of course, I planned to follow in their footsteps.

The result of this "girl power" upbringing was a clear sense of right and wrong, and I never hesitated to voice my opinion when I perceived injustice. This generally resulted in a combination of pride and embarrassment for my parents when, for example, my father came to collect me from Sunday school, only to find me in a heated argument with a pastor about how it was totally inappropriate to tell Sunday school children that Native Americans were "taught wrong" about God. The pastor naturally yelled back at me that he knew better and that I should be more respectful. My unwavering sense of righteousness at the tender age of eleven resulted in me telling my father I refused to go back to church, and if he made me, I would run away from home. In retrospect, I am sure that the pastor was happy to get rid of me.

Whether it was calling out the injustice of the slaughter of sharks and whales by Japanese ships, or the principal trying to cancel United Nations programs in my high school, or collecting and distributing food and gifts for more impoverished families, I was headstrong and active in wanting to change the world. My chosen career paths varied from journalist outing evil corporations and injustice to forensic pathologists hunting down serial killers, none of which sat particularly well with my mother, but she supported me unequivocally.

An Insidious Descent to Solitude and Fear

Born in Australia, we left when I was seven, and I spent most of my youth in Vancouver, Canada, and then in Oregon and Florida in the US. In 2001, I left Miami, my mum, dad, and brother to return home to my roots and extended family in Perth, Western Australia—one of the most isolated cities in the world—to study psychology and education. During my studies, I met the man who would be the biological father of my first son, a man who would have one of the most significant impacts on my life, who for the purposes of this book I will call John Smith. We met when I was called to jury duty, where I would serve as the jury forewoman on an aggravated assault and battery trial. We met while waiting for selection, and for the first year or so, we were happy university students studying and dating.

Honestly, I can't tell you, looking back, when things started to change. I began to change; he began to change. I can remember moments when he became sullen or fearful and expressed concerns he was losing me or that I was interested in others, so I stopped putting myself out there. I can remember moments of his overwhelming anger when I felt fearful desperation. What was initially most appealing about me, a carefree, outgoing, and almost hippie-like, affectionate personality, became an increasing cause of jealousy. In my attempts to make him happy, to be what I thought he needed me to be, I slowly walked away from everything I had been and everyone I loved. For three years, I lost touch with my closest friends. I stopped going to family events. I gave up my job until my whole world was the four walls that I lived within. I lived in them with the fear that I wasn't good enough and that I couldn't do anything right.

So there I was, no job, trying to finish uni, financially reliant on my partner—who at this point had convinced me it wasn't right to have individual bank accounts. I no longer wanted to socialize, as drinking inevitably led to fights, yelling, and me sobbing on the floor while locked in the bathroom. I was sinking lower into depression and desperately battling to maintain a front of normalcy when the doctor told me that I was pregnant, only six months after telling me that it was unlikely I would ever be able to have children. I was twenty-five and had a year left of university.

I was terrified. I sat in my car and cried, and then I went to my aunt's to cry and talk through what to do. That night, when I went home to share the news, the response was as I expected: unpleasant, angry, with a bitter ultimatum. I had to choose him or the baby. I had made the decision. By this point, my parents had returned to Australia from the US, and I could go and stay with them. I want to tell you that after years of being worn down, the news of a baby on the way made me turn my life around, but life is often more complicated. It wasn't until my son was a few months old that I finally got the courage to leave. I doubled down at uni during my pregnancy and handed in my last assignment four days before Mikey was born via C-Section as a breech baby. John's first comment was that I hadn't really given birth.

Four weeks later, I was back in hospital for what they thought was an emergency appendicitis. After seven days in the hospital with no sleep, being woken every two hours to pump, they decided it was a false post-labor.

It was at this point that I started planning. I knew I had to get out. John and I had been doing counseling, and I saw a separate counselor at a women's trauma center. I told my parents of my plan to leave John, and the counselor agreed we should tell him in counseling while my parents packed up a few clothes for myself and Mikey. The counselor would keep him behind after I told him, so I had time to get away. I was terrified. The only thing that worried me more was the thought of raising my son as a useless, helpless housewife in an abusive household.

I want to be clear here: this was how I saw myself at the time. I felt I had one decision: be a good partner and a shit mother or be a good mother on my own. I had parents and family who backed me 100 percent. Without them, I probably wouldn't have had the strength to leave and to be honest. I don't know if I would be here today. I know I wouldn't like the person I would have become. I know that there are so many women out there that didn't have the option that I did, where the violence was so much worse than what I endured. My only advice is that if you do get out, it will be hard. There will be times when you will doubt yourself, there will be days when you will cry on end, but it will get better, and you can rebuild. You can rebuild your life, your finances, and most importantly, yourself. You can become a happy, healthy person again for you and your children.

The first few months were easily the most turbulent and emotional of my life. Some days, there would be screaming calls and threats against me; there were tears and talk of change on others. There were talks about who got what and, most importantly, custody battles for Mikey. Amidst all this, I was a single mum, back living with my parents and working and trying to rebuild some semblance of a life. My first break came when my father introduced me to a small Registered Training Organization (RTO) owner, who ran a school that taught childcare. I had my teaching degree and was hired to help around the office. In doing so, I stumbled into what would become my lifelong passion.

A New Start

Terri had been a single mum herself who was now happily remarried and running a small successful Registered Training Organization, a college that taught job seekers, usually, single mothers who were trying to get a leg up after being in situations like mine, to get qualified to work in childcare. I started in administration and then got my certification to teach in Vocational Education & Training (VET), and I started training and working closely with the mothers. I will forever be grateful to Terri and my dad for giving me this chance. It was my reentry back into the world, but it was also a pathway to remembering who I was and how helping others was core to who I was as a person.

During my time at Childcare Training Professionals, I had my first inkling of the epiphany that this was what I was meant to do. I had been working closely with a group of about forty of two hundred women that were studying. Donna had recently come out of an abusive relationship—one far more physical and scarring than mine. Her husband had been a violent alcoholic; she had two small children and lived with a relative, and studied with us through a government-funded program called the Productivity Places Program. The program allowed individuals to register with a Job Seeker Agency at the time and then access the training at no cost. I had managed to find her a placement at a local daycare across the road from our school where my son went and where a few of our students did their placement. Halfway through the placement, the daycare agreed to hire Donna as a casual and act as a reference for her with other local centers.

The day Donna completed her certificate, I printed it out, along with a letter of reference that I wrote myself. It was late in the afternoon, and I was in the office by myself when she came to pick it up. When I handed her the certificate, she cried and hugged me. "Thank you, a few months ago, when I started, I didn't think I was worth anything. I couldn't work to take care of my kids. I didn't know what I was going to do, and worst of all, I thought he was right, my ex. I thought that everything he had said about me was true. Now, I have a job and this, and I really will do the Diploma once I can go part-time." At this point, I was crying too. I hugged Donna again, told her how proud I was, and that I couldn't wait to see her and sign her up for that Diploma course. She left the office. I closed the door, and I cried some more tears of joy—a reminder that things really can get better.

I resolved from that moment that working in VET was where I wanted to be. Working with kids and helping to shape their future is fantastic, and I truly put my hands up for all the teachers who can do it. I choose VET because we often deal with those that education has missed, job seekers who have to start over and retrain when an industry collapses, long-term unemployed, kids who the school system has failed for one reason or another. Of course, some apprentices want a trade, business employees, and small business owners who wish to improve specific skill sets, but they are not why I love VET. I love this industry because it's about finding a second chance. Education is about helping and igniting a passion and purpose in others, and I can't imagine wanting to do anything else.

The Rocky Road to Why

Once I had discovered the broad area of my purpose, I embarked upon a learning journey to figure out exactly where my purpose would take me. The thing about learning is that you have to be willing to fail, and boy, oh boy, have I failed! For the last twelve years, I have continued to work in VET and loved most of it. I have days where I'm not too fond of the tasks I have to do, but I don't think I have ever had a day where I thought, that's it, I am done with this industry. I have worked in sales, operations, management, training, administration, and quality. I have worked with big and little colleges from 50 to 20,000 students, domestic students, and international including a college with students from more than forty countries worldwide under one roof. I have worked in colleges that teach everything from technical skills like telecommunications, IT, and electrical safety to human services like aged care, childcare, and nursing, trades like painting, carpentry, bricklaying, and mining to agriculture, aquaculture, fisheries, and horticulture.

At times, my career has allowed me to deliver speeches to several hundred CEOs and managers, travel every other week around the country attending and preparing for audits and teach thousands of students and staff in the VET sector. It has also required me to do some less glamorous tasks, like inspecting mines in outback Western Australia to ensure the training is safe and suitable or touring piggeries and abattoirs to align tasks on the job with skills and units when designing training programs. Let me tell you; you will never forget the smell and sound of a piggery. The one thing that has stayed consistent through it all? My why, at the heart of every job was one core purpose—I was helping to ensure that the training that we offered matched the skills needed by industry and the needs of our students, to optimize their second, third, or sometimes last chance, to make a fresh start, a new start, or get a leg up. In other words, I get up every morning, believing that the work I do makes a difference.

This road has come with a lot of failures. I have failed in businesses, in partnerships, and sometimes in parenting in an attempt to meet the high expectations I set for myself as that little girl. At times, I had had to give up a job I loved because it took me away too much from my kids when they needed me. At times I have had to give up seeing one of my sons at an assembly because I needed to be at a meeting for work. I have also learned the hard way how a shared history doesn't make someone a good business partner or that a good business idea automatically makes a good business. I have taken every failure as a lesson, and each lesson has allowed me to refine my purpose.

My current purpose is dually influenced, but at its core, it has remained the same. I wake up every day to promote the idea that everyone deserves a first, second, and third chance to find their why and that we find our why best through education and lifelong learning. I work with companies who share that idea and action it through offering education and employment. My role is to help them do that better, more efficiently, creatively, and with a clear and a communicated sense of purpose to their staff. I also do this in my own home, with my children, who are seven and thirteen. I hope I have raised them with the same values that I was raised with—that with enough hard work and study, they can do anything they put their minds to because the only barrier they have is themselves.

Dealing with the Reality of Purpose

Of course, understanding your purpose, refining it, and making it happen are three separate things. Through the period of discovery, research, and operation, you will contend with the requirements of reality. As a child, it was easy for me to believe that the only thing stopping me was me. I had two loving parents who served as great role models. We were middle class, and though we struggled at times, I never had to worry about whether I was safe, where my next meal was coming from, or deal with an education system that wasn't built for me.

It was only as an adult that I came to face these realities, and it was through my children's experiences that I came to face two of them.

John continues to be part of our life, albeit not much; however, through Mikeys' childhood, he's had to deal with a harsh reality that he was not always safe. This reality had a considerable impact on him growing up, physically, mentally, and emotionally. It's only this year, three years into a long and expensive custody battle, that he has come to a place where he only has to see his father when he wants. As a little girl, I never imagined having to take my child to a police station. Yet, I have had this heartbreaking experience three times since 2015 when John was charged with aggravated assault occasioning in bodily harm against Mikey.

I can honestly say I would gladly experience any physical pain I have endured ten times over rather than the heartbreak of not being able to protect my own child or having to send him somewhere knowing that he wasn't safe. I can happily report now that, for the moment, Mikey is happy, healthy, coming into his confidence, and still one of the most caring and compassionate children I know. Born out of sorrow but raised spending most of his time in a home filled with love, this has come about in no small part because I have a wonderful husband who adores Mikey as his own. I have been remarried for nearly nine years. Again, I have to recognize my parents, who took on Mikey as their own and provided additional strong role models for him.

Zachie, my youngest son, is seven and has dyslexia. He spent the first three years at a school that attempted to teach him in a traditional pathway, and we moved him late last year after realizing that the school was never going to support him as he needed. After research, study, and many courses, I found some great resources to show me how to teach him in a way that met his needs. In the months we were in COVID lockdown, with one-on-one contextualized training, he's gone from not being able to add double digits and unable to spell simple words like "frog" to working on multi-syllable sounds and alternate spellings and, most important to me, having a love of reading and working on concepts such as decomposition and multiplication. Moreover, when something is hard, he now understands how his brain works and how he needs to work smarter, not just harder. When a teacher corrects him on spelling, his response? "My brain is different; it can get confused with some letters, but my brain can also do things that yours can't."

I mention each of the above because we all have our challenges. Sometimes, as a parent or a partner, you are going to have to put your purpose on pause, or you are going to have to take a step back because living your purpose first starts at home. If I don't make the effort to ensure I give my kids a leg up or a second chance when life throws challenges at them, how authentic can I be in promoting it with others?

Your purpose starts at home. It begins with you and those around you. Make it work there first, then when you take it out to the world, you are not only a cheerleader for the cause but a living result of it too.

Some Final Words of Advice

1. Find a cause that balances your day today

My purpose requires me to spend a lot of time on the computer, and I work a lot from home. This is not great for me physically and makes it hard to deal with the stress of the job. To balance this, I joined the *firies* back in 2018 and have never looked back. Becoming a firefighter means that I get to do something physical. It's a great way to connect with others from different backgrounds, and I get to give back to the community. Also, I can honestly say that when you are confronted with a thirty-foot wall of fire, you are not stressing about a work deadline—it puts life in perspective.

While it's not for everyone, look at your job. If it's sedentary, find a hobby or a physical cause. If your job is isolating, find a cause that allows you to be part of a team. Find a way to balance so that the journey to your purpose isn't all-consuming. It's often in the strangest places that we stumble into who we truly are. Giving back also gives you a chance to put things in perspective. While we all face challenges, it can be easy to let that consume you in today's current culture. Seeing life from others' perspectives allows us to appreciate what we have.

2. Focus first on your big purpose, then surround yourself with allies who share it

Once you have an idea about your purpose, it will take you a while to refine it. While you are working through that process, surround yourself with people who share that same purpose. A word of caution, figuring out who is genuine in sharing your purpose and those just looking to profit from it can be hard! I've worked closely with many professionals in my industry and learned from every single one of them. However, I have learned that there is a difference between being passionate about an industry and living for a purpose. Ask yourself, is this person trying to raise awareness about the cause, raise their profile, or make money? Find people who are authentic about helping others.

3. Never be afraid of change

This year has been, as many have said, a year like no other. COVID continues to impact the lives of almost everyone around the planet. Still, if I have learned anything from my life, it's that every challenge, no matter how difficult, comes with an opportunity for change and a chance to learn.

Through lockdown, my family discovered a renewed connection to each other that we had lost in the general chaos of life, we were able to help my youngest son gain a fresh start in his education, and I found a new way to support my why and continue to live my purpose. While I will continue to work with education providers to increase the quality of education and create new chances for students to discover their why, COVID taught us the important role that technology plays and will continue to play in the future in keeping us connected and providing access to those opportunities.

As a result, I started Learning Lifelines. This charity connects students trying to study with the resources they need to actively engage in that study, like laptops, the internet, software, or phones. It's hard to connect when you don't have the internet, and 14 percent of households in Australia still don't have internet access. This means that millions of people and households don't have access to online education, and they don't have the technology to allow them a second chance in a time when the country and the world are trying to rebuild again.

Over the years, I have tried many paths and figured out how to operationalize and monetize my purpose. I keep trying, keep moving forward, but I understand that happiness is not going to come from hitting a figure. Your purpose can be found in running your own business just as easily as it can be found in volunteering or as an employee where your *why* and your companies' *why* align. It's also ok to want change, and I would suggest that you expect it over time. Our purpose may remain consistent, but what that looks like should grow over time because it's only through growth that we can become better people.

It's only through becoming better people that we change the world and make it a better place for our kids and each other.

Lauren Hollows is the Director of Learning Lifelines and an RTO expert, working with various companies to increase the quality of training and assessment. Lauren runs regular professional development, training, and coaching for trainers, educators, and institutions within the Vocational Education sector across Australia. She is also a frequent presenter, podcaster, and vlogger around Australia at conferences and online through her social media channels covering auditing, quality training, assessment practices, employee and student engagement, and building purpose-focused organizations in education. Reach her on Twitter: @laurenhollows, LinkedIn: https://www.linkedin.com/in/laurenhollows/ Website: www.learninglifelines.org

Healing
Your Ailments

Bearing Fruit

By Tyneisha Ternent
Canada

It took some time for me to define my purpose. There were many years of mental struggle and self-sabotage. There were decades where I drowned in feelings of self-worthlessness and yearning for my life to be nothing like it was. I placed my self-value in the hands of others who were unworthy of carrying such a pure heart, as most cannot even entirely rely on themselves. After years of disappointments, I found the courage to try something different. I knew that people were not worthy of my soul, so I turned to God. God offered me redemption and peace like none I had ever received before. When entering my church, I felt a sense of respite and happiness that I had not previously found during my pursuit of identity. It became apparent who deserved to hold my life in their hands, so I gave my life over to Jesus. I placed my hope in God and found my purpose by walking with the spirit.

I intend to be true to myself. I aim to walk in my light, despite the shade that others intentionally throw my way at times. My purpose is simple— to be true to myself and write what is on my heart. Not to write what others would prefer me to write, but to write what I want to. For me, I need God to do this. Holy hands and my husband's hands are essential to hold me up when I am depressed. I need my Creator's strength, for he created me and can help me continue my path when I am at a crossroads. Unlike others' purposes, my purpose is unique, which makes it so special. With God's help and the family I have created, I can walk towards my vocation. Of course, this is extremely important because I know what it feels like to wander. I am too familiar with depression and hopelessness as if we used to be best friends. What makes my purpose so important is that I now refuse to live my life without it at the center of everything I do. I have grown accustomed to the light my calling has provided. It is no longer at the end of the tunnel; it is all around me.

My Road to Discovering My Purpose

As I mentioned previously, my road to discovery of this purpose was not stress-free. Only when I was utterly broken was I able to let the light in. Only when I put my ego aside and humbled myself would the light even shine my way. What led to this was the questioning of my existence. I interrogated my thoughts, words, and actions as if I was the prosecutor, plaintiff, and defendant of my own life. I became conscious of my characteristics and tendencies and paid more attention to my emotions and values. I reintroduced myself to my interests, hopes, and dreams with an attentive ear this time, as I was eager to demonstrate my ability to listen to myself. Next, I had to look in a mirror and study my reflection. I looked beyond my kinky hair, caramel skin tone, and chubby cheeks, and I truly reflected on my soul. I shifted my intentions from the superficial to the supernatural. I fixated on what was in my heart rather than my body's appearance, and I realized that everything I desired was staring back at me in my reflection. All I had to do was get out of my way and let God lead me to achieve it.

What Worked for Me

My discovery process involved:

- therapist visits
- distancing myself from toxic friends and family members
- meditation sessions with incense and crystals
- writing out my feelings

- attending local church events
- volunteering
- spending quality time with my daughter

I had no idea what would work for me on my discovery expedition. I tried numerous new activities until I found what gave me joy and permitted my mind to stop racing for a moment. That was the best thing I ever could have done for myself.

What a Purposeful Life Can Bring

Living in my purpose looks exactly like how you see me today—a published author with a bestselling poetry book. At the top of the charts on Amazon in the Poetry for Women and Hot New Releases category, it's evident that I am living my purpose, but all the self-work I put in is not apparent. My childhood goals are now realities. I replaced my self-sabotaging thoughts with positive self-affirmations. I set goals with full intentions of completing them, and I made them happen. I am aware of my talents and align myself with opportunities that are good fits for me. I have created a beautiful poetry book dedicated to my daughter, titled *Bearing Fruit*. Mothers and daughters now have a book that will connect them. Expecting mothers now have a poetic, intimate look at what pregnancy is really like. I have created a work that is emotional and real yet uplifting and inspirational. I have created a black-owned brand and defied various odds against me.

Staying Humble While Living My Purpose

I remain modest and blessed, eager to help anyone tired of suffering. Living in my purpose has allowed me to become an excellent example for young women, foster children, and people living in group homes, individuals living with mental health issues, and anyone who does not feel good about themselves. Walking in my purpose has created a path for many, leading those who are currently struggling to a path of redemption.

If you want to change your life from surviving to thriving, it is necessary to put in the work. If you've been feeling unnourished but wish to flourish, don't expect your transformation to be swift and effortless because it won't be. My story began with abandonment and mental health issues, abuse, and trauma—leading to low self-esteem, alcohol abuse, severe anxiety, and depression. I didn't trust myself and was continuously in a battle with my mind. I would start new jobs and quit at the first sign of confrontation or pressure. I put so much on my plate and overwhelmed myself, always trying to do too much in the hopes of gaining worthiness. I dated men that didn't deserve my heart and forgave those that wronged me time and time again. I knew my childhood survival tactics weren't beneficial, yet I still used them because I was not ready to do the work I knew was needed. To live and serve my purpose, I had to rebuild myself. I had to rewire my thinking and understand that what happened to me in the past wouldn't continue to happen if I decided to change. Electing to change is not enough; I had to give up everything I was used to to make my desired life. I had to leave the city I grew up in. I had to leave my job, friends, and everything that used to be "me." Departing was petrifying, and at times, I didn't think I would make it through. But through prayer, hard work, and dedication, I was able to persevere. I found my greatness by leaving environments that left me broken, which allowed me to believe in myself again. The journey to self-love and self-discovery can be lonely, so you must fully commit to your healing to win.

Words of Advice

If you are dying to live your best life, desperate for your season of change, and wanting your transformation to begin now, then listen to my words of advice. First, analyze your circle. Who you hang out with, what you watch, the music you listen to—everything affects you! Cut the negative people out of your life, and connect with people who have more positive outlooks on life. Listen to music that spreads positivity, as this will help uplift your mood. Be specific and consistent with this.

Clean up your social media pages and delete the Instagram models and the accounts you follow simply because everyone else is. Unfollow people you grew up with that you no longer communicate with or anyone who has hurt you in the past. Replace those accounts with motivational speakers, fitness pages, or healthy eating accounts.

What's the point of following accounts that don't inspire you? Social media has a way of making us compare our lives to others, so it is vital to be aware of our feed and encourage materials that will positively feed our minds.

Professionals Do Know What They Are Doing

Next, seek help in the form of a therapist, counselor, life coach, or group therapy session. Sharing your struggles will not only provide you with a sense of relief, but it will give you a different, educated perspective. These individuals have studied and are experts in helping others. They will not judge you and keep your conversations confidential as per the client and patient confidentiality clause. I know how appealing it seems to hold everything in. You might do that in an attempt to protect yourself and hide any feelings of shame or guilt you may have. I speak from experience when I say that nothing is wrong with talking to a therapist, and I promise you it will bring you liberation.

Don't Be Afraid to Put Yourself First

Lastly, don't be afraid to put yourself first. Most often, people who struggle put others' wants or needs above their own, always trying to please everyone else besides themselves. This approach will only have you feeling walked on and more abused. Don't be afraid to say no; you don't owe anyone anything. However, you do deserve to be happy. When you are tired, rest. If you crave alone time, cancel your plans with friends or family. If anyone tries to make you feel bad for loving your-self, then you don't need them in your life anyway. Don't feel obligated to give explanations, and don't feel guilty for saying no. You deserve to feel whole, and you deserve to live your best life.

I urge you, if you ache to operationalize your life and follow your dreams, then help yourself by taking my words of advice and the advice given by the other successful women in this book. We have transformed our lives and achieved financial stability by following our heart's callings; we are proof that this is possible for you.

Tyneisha Ternent is also known as Ty, the Poetess. She was raised in Toronto and shares her gifts as a poet, spoken word artist, and writer. Tyneisha is proud to be a mother, wife, and Christian. Tyneisha can be reached at: Instagram: @tythepoetess – or Email: tythepoetess@ outlook.com

Give Me a Reason to Live

By Sabine Menon
China (via France)

Back in March, four years ago, I was lying in bed. My body felt like a stone. It was impossible to get up. I felt "pukey," and all I wanted to do was force myself back to sleep, ignore the world, ignore my reality. I knew too well what was going on clinically: a burnout mixed with an existential questioning on "What is this life about? Is it worth living?"

Seen from the outside, I had a wonderful, privileged life with two great children, a loving husband, and a successful business. But I wasn't happy. I felt somewhat dissatisfied and lacking a sense of purpose; something essential was missing—something I couldn't name without sounding demanding or being like a spoiled child. I was abandoned as a child and learned to live with a constant sense of being rejected.

One element remained from my childhood: my desire to not be alive. I can love aspects of life: the sea, time spent with loved ones, my dogs, walks in nature, a good book, music...and chocolate. But I am also acutely aware of the world's miseries, human suffering, our endangered planet. As a child and a teenager, I was in survival mode, and as an adult, I sometimes feel that the happier times I live today weren't worth the early challenging years of my life. That it would have been better if I had not been born.

But my thoughts on that day in March weren't thoughts of someone depressed or reminiscing about an unhappy childhood nor the difficulties of adulthood. On the contrary, there were thoughts related to the present moment: "I have traveled all over the world. I have seen if not experienced human suffering, beauty, and trauma. My children are old enough. Yes, I love the sea and so many other things in life, but how many more walks on a beach can I take? Is this life really worth living?" For a while, I nurtured the fantasy of ending my life. I even went to the extent of writing letters, closing accounts, convincing myself that there would be no tomorrow, and I must say I experienced a new and most probably the best feeling I had ever experienced...one of utter liberation of all constraints and attachments.

What is Life Still Expecting of Me?

But here I am, writing this story today, so clearly, I didn't act on my ideation of suicide. Instead, I just did what I do best: rationalize. I pulled myself together and decided to prioritize others over me. I said to myself: "My children still need me, my husband will not understand; I have a meeting with a client coming up; what purpose will it serve? Once I'm dead, that is... what purpose?" I remember clearly being overwhelmed by a sentence from Viktor Frankl I had read many years ago in his book *Man's Search for Meaning*: "the question is not what I expect from life but what life still expects of me."

He said it in different words, but that's how I remember it, playing itself in circles in my head.

So, while searching for the answer to "What is life still expecting of me?" I carried on as if none of that existential questioning had ever happened. I didn't mention to anyone what I was going through. I continued pretending all was well, working, teaching, being a mom and wife even as I was running on empty. While I had not died exactly, something in me had. The old me, the false self, had died. Something had changed. It happened slowly, organically, but it happened. My true self—to put it in Winnicott's psychological terms—started fighting to emerge. This force beyond me was taking me towards my true path.

I'm French, fifty years old, and I am married to an Indian gentleman. I have lived and/or worked in France, Argentina, the USA, the UK,

Germany, Dubai, China—not to mention the (many!) countries where I have traveled. I have been an expatriate for over twenty-five years, and I've spent the last ten years of my life in Shanghai, China. I have a successful Executive Coaching business, and I teach leadership and team skills to highly successful executives. Most of my clients are very senior executives in the C-Suite: CEOs, CFOs, heads of country, heads of region, based in APAC or all over the world; the majority are male. They are highly successful in their roles, under tremendous pressure, and have the well-being of thousands of employees relying on them. It's not just about performance or success per se. It's about ensuring that the company is thriving, not just surviving in a highly competitive environment.

I love what I do. Well, I used to think I loved it until that day in March... until something started being wrong. I would find it more difficult to honor appointments, dragging myself to the next meeting, finding that instead of elating me, it would suck all my energy out.

Self-sabotage and Hidden Limiting Beliefs

That's when the self-sabotage started: perverse, insidious, discreet— that silent traitor. I would accept a client contract but would be drained by the time I was done honoring it. I would be called for a project and send one of my associates, knowing perfectly well that this particular associate had no loyalty whatsoever, and would then contract directly with the client, cutting me out. I stopped doing any business development in any shape or form. As I do have certain credibility and reputation, work kept coming, luckily, but I lost the spark.

In parallel, I started attracting another type of client: still-high-flying executives who were successful and performing, and the only reason why they were getting coaching was that, at this stage in their life and career, there were not many leadership courses they could attend. After all, how many more "leading for success" could they enroll in? So, calling an Executive Coach like me was a way for the company to say we care about you and don't want to lose you. In this context, the individual client had *carte blanche*, i.e., the coaching process was done with no specific objectives or expected outcome. It was purely an investment in the process and the individual.

Given everything that had been going on for me, it was a sudden realization when I noticed how much I loved those sessions. They asked about the meaning and the purpose of life, and they became curious about the fact that I teach meditation. They wanted to talk about their wife's loss of identity since the move to China; the choice they would soon have to make, go back home or extend the expatriation; their aging parents, sick parents, far-away parents; their relationship to a brother or sister; a fight over the last holidays; their fears; their dreams yet to be fulfilled. Whether they were really impacting the organization in terms of their legacy in the organization and in this world. We were so far from KPIs and performance, and I loved every minute of it. I thrived in it. I knew I was at my best.

I started craving more sessions like this. Sessions where I helped individuals make more sense of their lives, challenging or giving a different light or interpretation to their assumptions, giving them another grid to read what happened or was happening to them. I was giving a more therapeutic flavor to the sessions.

I trained as a psychologist, so switching from being an executive coach to becoming a therapist was not difficult. It's a different set of skills, but the roles are very connected. Except, you see, I grew up in a challenging environment. I was so lucky to be born in France, where there is free access to education and medical care. Yet, forty years ago, even under French standards, I was considered poor, and I know what it is like to not have and crave something.

It taught me a lot: I rarely desire things I don't really need or, as a little girl, I wouldn't go near shops to prevent myself from being tempted by goods I couldn't afford.

It also gave me the drive to do well at school and succeed. It gave me what we call *la gnac* in French, which means to have "fire in the belly" to get what you want. What motivated me professionally was not having money but *feeling* financially secure that whatever happened, I could provide for myself and my family. I wanted to be able to provide without struggling to make ends meet.

My business was thriving. At one point, I had over twenty associates working for me. I signed major contracts with multinational corporations, mostly Fortune 100s, and I felt very comfortable financially. I was taking care of that need to feel secure. That need was taking care of me, too. I didn't see it as a limiting belief but instead as empowerment, without realizing the vicious circle I was trapped in.

Whenever the idea of going back to being a therapist would emerge, I would shut it down strongly. How could I embark on a new "business" which, in practice, if I simply brought it down to numbers and calculated my fees by the hour, would reduce my income significantly? Was I out of my mind?

As life sometimes helps you make decisions, I received a call from an accompanying spouse who wasn't sure if she needed coaching or therapy while not wanting to embark on a long-term process. I am rarely approached for work with individuals, as my clients are major multinational companies. This person did because she personally knew someone I had coached. So, when she shared her struggles of how she was a successful lawyer back home but now, accompanying her husband, she became "the wife of" and " the mom of," losing her professional identity and self-confidence—I could relate. I wanted to help.

Mindful Coaching Therapy

I had to put together a different methodology, which would help me help someone at a deep enough level without being a quick fix. I knew

I could help someone by asking questions that were way beyond the typical boundaries of coaching, help someone be more self-aware and mindful so that she would be attuned to herself, listen to her body, and act accordingly. I knew I could provide enough support and help within a short period that would guarantee some effects in the long run. As a result, I created a methodology anchored and grounded in the seriousness of science and academia, which combined psychology (studying thoughts, feelings, behaviors), coaching (asking challenging questions hoping to provide insights towards a specific objective), and mindfulness (awareness of something happening, as it is happening, without judgment). Some would simply call it therapy! I like to think of it as *mindful coaching therapy.*

In parallel, some of my senior executive clients started to become curious about my Vipassana meditation practice (a ten-day silent meditation). Most of these executives are high performers, some marathon runners or athletes, so there was always curiosity about this other type of mind training. In the past, they would ask me to bring coaching or training to their organization so that their directors and managers would benefit from the same experiences they did. They slowly started to ask me to teach them some meditation techniques. After experiencing it, they would ask if I could teach twenty, eighty, or three hundred people.

Maybe it's my professional ethics or lack of self-confidence, but I felt a fine line between practicing meditation and teaching it, especially to such an audience. So I learned MBS—Mindfulness-Based Stress Reduction with Jon Kabat-Zinn and got accredited as a Mindfulness Teacher (with Tara Brach and Jon Kornfield).

I believed that teaching mindfulness to senior executives in organizations would cascade and add to the well-being of people. We all need to work and make a living, and we all want to have an impact and feel that we are active members of our society. We don't have to go through pain and suffering while doing it, and mindfulness can help release some of that struggle. I believed in mindfulness, but I was reluctant to be the one teaching it. I was concerned that it would affect my reputation and that I would lose my credibility. As mindfulness becomes mainstream, it also gets a bit damaged on the way because it is often misunderstood. It was important that I wouldn't be seen as "away with the fairies," but instead, I wanted to bring some level of credibility and seriousness to teaching mindfulness in organizations.

This is where trust in being aligned with my purpose came in. Because demand for these services came, I dared to do it. I trusted not so much myself but my purpose, and it has been very fulfilling since. People experience mindfulness as they experience individual one-on-one sessions, and they feel better during and afterward.

Shanghai is a city with 25 million inhabitants with an additional 200 thousand expatriates. It's a village! Word of mouth gets around fast, and I found myself receiving more calls from individual clients requesting coaching sessions that would include elements of therapy and requests to teach mindfulness in businesses.

Of course, as a coach, I work with individuals. As an experienced coach, I have always prided myself for saying to the person who contacted me, "Well, I might have contracted with your firm, but my allegiance is with your employee."

Indeed, I respect privacy and confidentiality. But I realized that for all those years, I was fooling myself. Because my client *is* the multinational corporation that contracts me... and my obligation is toward helping the individual executive reaching the coaching objectives agreed with his/her boss, carrying on performing and making an impact so that there is ROI—return on investment. There is an expectation and an obligation of delivery to the organization!

Don't get me wrong. I am not saying coaching for an organization is terrible. Actually, I am a firm believer and advocate of coaching. When I first came to China and launched my business, there iwas no question. This was my purpose: to help leaders be more excellent and better at what they were doing. In fulfilling that mission, it helped me progress as well. I learned from them; I gave; I received.

I am saying that my purpose that fit my younger self fifteen years ago evolved as my authentic self started to emerge. This true self revealed itself powerfully after thinking about suicide due to deep reflections and existential questioning.

For any outside observer, my work hasn't changed much: I have one-on-one sessions (face to face or remotely) with individuals, men or women, primarily expatriates, from all over the world. I still "teach" for an audience made chiefly of expatriates and business people.

From One Purpose to Another: The Essence of Being

What has changed is *the essence* of what I do, the intention, the purpose: helping people feel better about themselves. I added therapy to my services, and instead of only teaching leadership to individuals and high performance to teams, I now teach skills that bring back the "being" in human beings and reduce the doing. I am helping people live their life now, not just a life but the life they were born to live. While there is also an ROI expectation in the context of therapy and mindfulness practice, the essence of this "ROI" is what enriches me today.

There is a nasty side to being a psychologist, a coach, a mindfulness teacher: I usually have a high sense of self-awareness. I spent most of my professional life helping highly skilled, intelligent, successful people worldwide find answers, find their purpose, see what makes them happy, or at least prevent them from being so. I help them be courageous in making the tough decisions (to leave their job, partner, the country in which they live, etc.). One could say I am helping people find answers within (i.e., I do not provide the solutions), and these realizations are crucial to their well-being and mental health.

It was the usual "the baker's children who have no bread" story for a while. I would go through the day in full awareness that something was not right. Something must change while not doing anything about it myself. There were many reasons and excuses: tiredness, lack of time, work, other priorities, children to attend, the career of my husband, not being my own first priority. I helped people but wasn't helping myself. As my adviser used to say, "a bit of denial would be welcome," so that, at least, I wouldn't suffer from knowing what I knew. I was ignoring my true calling.

Being True and Taking Care of Myself as Well...

Since I have learned that to fulfill your purpose, you have to be a bit selfish and put yourself first. It is not egotistical; it is taking care of myself *as well*. Learning to say "no" or "not now," learning to take time off, learning to give more strength to the inner voice, or listening to the sign that our body gives us. By doing that, I have been much better at taking care of others.

In neuroscience, attunement (the felt sense of another's experiences) also refers to the notion of healthy emotional self-regulation. This term is also used in mindfulness as being in touch with the inner experience of oneself (self-attunement) or another. In living my purpose, I now feel attuned. It's not magic. It didn't happen by chance, but somehow, I feel good. I know it impacts my entire system—my family, people I interact with, friends—because they tell me they notice it. Someone even asked me recently if I had had a facelift. I didn't! Still, it seems that this inner alignment shows on the outside. Most significantly, I feel a sense of trust (call it trust in God, in Source, in destiny, in the universe) that is very new to me and puts me at peace with my choices. As long as I remain true to myself, in living my purpose, which might still evolve with time, I trust that whatever might come my way will be fair, and I will be ok.

It is not *la vie en rose* every day, though. At first, I had to stoically accept that I was losing business. I remember feeling like I was a Cirque du Soleil trapezist, jumping from one trapeze to another. You know that moment when they let go of the trapeze they have a grip on to catch the other one. In between, there is space and time when the trapezist is flying through the air with nothing in their hands. I wondered if, after years of practice, they still feel the fear. Clearly, they have the confidence and the trust that they will catch the next trapeze and that no matter what, if they fall, the safety net will catch them. They believe in their purpose of swinging fifty meters above the ground.

Excuse My French but "Fuck" the Guilt.

Then the feeling of guilt came and went. Until I decided not to feed it anymore. Instead, now I say, "Thank you! I know what you are doing." It's the voice of limiting beliefs, the voice of the inner child scared of being poor talking, the socially politically correct, the imposter syndrome. So many people within my head! But I say, "Thank you. I know you are doing your job. Except, I know better now, and you can't fool me anymore."

In this way, I teach people to be a bit more selfish, take care of themselves, prioritize themselves, and cut the noise, either their (negative) inner voice or even the noise coming from people who care about and love them.

A few pieces of advice:

When there is doubt, there is no doubt. Suppose you start feeling somewhere somehow that something is wrong. In that case, your energy level isn't the same as it used to be, your desire to go to work and do whatever action when you wake up has changed, if you start asking yourself questions (Am I in the right job? Do I still enjoy what I do?) that question is an answer...

Be Wary of People Around You Who Mean Well but Make You Doubt Yourself.

- Why would you leave a perfectly functioning and successful business?
- If you want to have some patients, why don't you do it on the side?
- You are such a spoiled brat: there are many coaches out there who would dream of the type of corporate contracts you are landing.
- You still have two children to take to university. Can't you wait at least until they are done?
- I don't get it: you are good at what you do, you are helping people no matter what, whether it's a coaching client or patient; why would you reduce your fees to do it? Your time is your time. Who cares about purpose?

And so on and so forth. It's tough at times to remain grounded and ignore these rational-like remarks, but try to do it nonetheless.

Your Body Never Lies

You hear all those comments from people you respect, whose opinions matter, and you start doubting your decision and convincing yourself that yeah, they are right. So, you pretend for a while; sometimes, you pretend for a long time. You put a face on. You smile. You keep going, but you keep running on empty. You start catching a cold. You catch a stomach bug. Your knees start hurting. Your sleep pattern is not what it used to be; you feel depressed but not clinically. No—you still function, still wake up, go to work, and perform.

Feel the fear and do it anyway (inspired by the title of a book). When I first started to reduce the amount of major corporate clients I was taking on to make space for individual clients, I also launched an *"online therapy"* practice. But I am not a big fan of marketing, social media, and other such tools. I have been fortunate all my business life to get referrals and work within a robust and reliable network. How would people start to know that I offer new services without entering into the nightmare of marketing them? I was so scared that I would lose everything—my business, credibility, everything I had worked so hard to build, achieve, and consolidate.

Trust yourself, follow your purpose. The universe will help. Trust that if you don't, it will remind you of it. Without falling into new age woo, life and work have shown me that if you are attentive to messages, an email, a call, a conversation, and most importantly to what makes you truly happy (even if sometimes happiness is overrated); if you are mindful of what makes you smile, lifts you up, doesn't tire you, those are usually signs that you are on the right path.

Irvin Yalom said: *A good therapist fights darkness and seeks illumination. I'm a guide on this voyage of self-exploration.*

If I had to cite my purpose today, it is not just to serve but help people feel better about themselves. I love sunflowers! I just want to bring a bit of sunshine to people's lives, bring a bit of light to guide them on their voyage of self-exploration. I am fully aware of how much I receive in return.

Sabine Menon (PhD) is an Executive Coach, a Psychologist, and a Mindfulness Teacher. She is the founder of Happy Consults and helps global nomads find their purpose.

Sabine can be reached at both www.sabinemenon.com and www.happyconsults.com

Turning Pain into Purpose:
The Way You Get Up When Life Knocks You Down

By Rikke Kjelgaard
Sweden/Denmark

In my life, I've had my fair share of both sh*t and sunshine. Growing up in Denmark with a family who cared for me in every way, I have no firsthand knowledge of poverty, racial discrimination, neglect, addiction, or abuse. I am a white female from a middle-class family. I understand my vast privilege, and I am blessed to have been surrounded by both people and a system that allowed and encouraged me to go to school, travel the world, and later get a master's degree in psychology. I have always been fascinated by the human mind, and I always insisted on essential changes in this world. I wanted things to be fair. I wanted freedom. I wanted connection. I wanted love. I wanted authentic living. I engaged in and expressed myself through music and theater, and I fell in love with the souls I encountered both at home and during my many years of traveling. Today, some people would probably label that girl as "chatty," "dominant," and "too much." I believe that she was articulate, determined, and fiercely passionate.

As I was growing up, vulnerable conversations were not our family superpower. Neither was having or expressing strong emotions. Truth be told: no one taught my parents how to handle or talk about all the messy psychological stuff we humans encounter through life, so they did the best they could to control their inner and outer environment. They did so by not addressing what was difficult, never asking for help, and by not showing anything that might resemble weakness. They *sucked it up*.

At the age of eight, I was taught one of my first hard lessons in life. Within 24 hours, I lost both my grandparents in horrible circumstances, and life as I knew it was changed forever. My mother was in such unbearable grief but did her best to get out of bed and get things done. She was drowning in sadness, and I know now that she was operating from these inner stories of having to keep up with her job, her house, her children, her marriage, and everything else—as if nothing had happened. *Be a good girl, now*. The show must go on, right? And there I was as a child in the middle of this epic horror movie. I had suffered a significant loss too, and I remember how I just could not burden my mother with my own sadness because, indeed, she had had enough. There was no apparent room for my loss and the inner experiences that come with that loss. As a result, I, too, learned to *suck it up*.

I also learned to be aware of other people's feelings and to adjust to them accordingly. I even learned to take responsibility for their feelings. Today, my mom tells me these sad stories about her finding me in my bed at the age of eight, talking secretly to a tape recorder (apparently the only one I could talk to), wondering whether my mom would ever smile again, and wondering how I could make her happy. You see, I made it my job to fix her. I just could not stand what she was going through, and I wanted to make it go away. I wanted *her* to feel better because consequently, then *I* would feel better. Since then, I have made it my job and my responsibility to make complicated stuff go away for everybody, which is a heavy burden to carry.

Now, as I am all somewhat grown-up, I see things from a different perspective. My parents loved me from the depths of their souls. There's no doubt about it. Misguided as their teaching methods might have been, I know that they were all about helping me get along in this world the best way they know how. Still, they taught me stuff I wish I never learned. Stuff that I hope not to pass on to my children. I now know that metaphorically I was supposed to *climb* the mountain—not to *carry* the damn thing!

Running from Tigers and Bears

Becoming a psychologist helped me gain a better understanding of human suffering and some profound perspective. I realized that many of us go through life with the experience of being entirely alone in our inner universe while not recognizing that we're all basically in the same boat. Suffering and pain are such an inevitable part of life for every single one of us, and we're all hardwired to get rid of unwanted thoughts, feelings, and sensations. While it makes evolutionary sense to run from tigers and bears and hence not be eaten on the great savannah, running from our inner world of pain and hurt can become a full-time job that doesn't pay off in much more than time wasted on surviving in a world where emotional tigers and bears seem to be lurking everywhere. While I'm a massive fan of surviving, I am a much bigger fan of living fully and mightily and thriving fiercely and fabu-lously in a world that is both painful and meaningful and everything in between and beyond. That, my friend, is exactly what makes my heart sing. Helping people live vital, authentic, and meaningful lives with purpose while moving beyond fear and doubt and other psychological tigers and bears.

Years ago, I found myself in yet another painful yet pivotal life les-son. My life had become something I was living on autopilot. My work situation was deeply unfulfilling, and so was my marriage. I did what I was passionate about—helping people live with purpose—but I really wasn't walking the talk myself. It seemed as if my life was living me rather than me living my life. For years, I had adjusted myself to my environment in an attempt to "be a good girl" and "to do what's right," and if truth be told, I was enduring rather than thriving. Worst of all, I wasn't the version of me I wanted to be. I was chasing other people's approval, and I was busy blaming everyone else for my own misery. As I crash-landed into the worst heartbreak I have known, I also decided to break free from a secure, well-paid, leading work position that was no longer serving me at all. Why not do divorce, a significant heartbreak, move the kids from one city to another, *and* quit your financially stable leadership job at the same time, right? Right.

But oh, the *pain*. And the *fear*. And the *doubt*.

This was not happening *to* me, however. These were consciously made choices to let go of what was no longer nourishing my soul. I wanted to do bigger and better things with my life. I wanted to *be* the change I wished to see in this world. I wanted to build a life and work situation that supported my purpose rather than accommodate my life to fit my work situation.

Most importantly, I wanted to show my children that change is possible and that failures are not barriers to success. I wanted to show them my lived examples of bravery, love, connection, authenticity, and vulnerability. They had seen me asking for help. They witnessed me cry. They heard me talk about fear. They saw me allowing myself to be carried by my parents and closest friends in times of great despair. They saw it all. They also saw me passionately talk about starting my own company. Sending my first invoice. They saw me paint the walls of our new apartment all by myself after their bedtime stories and goodnight kisses.

Most importantly to me, I continuously asked them how *they* were coping. There was room for my children's grief, fear, doubt, excitement, joy, and whatever they were experiencing too. They were told that they were not responsible for my feelings or behaviors. They were perfectly welcome to whatever they experienced. I would no longer be that little girl who sucked it up and carried the world on her shoulders. Nor would I be the mother who taught my boys to do the same. We embraced it all and talked about the willingness to fully feel life as it is. I finally took my own medicine and started walking what I had been talking about.

Working with Mountain Carriers

Today, I am now the chief rock'n'roller of my own company. (Yeah, baby!) I get to choose what I do, who I do it with, and who I do it for. I work as a therapist, educator, writer, public speaker, motivator, and wingwoman with ONE mission: *helping people become the person they most want to be while creating their most authentic lives.* Every day, I talk to people who are caught up in surviving rather than living, are held back by fear and self-doubt, and are sucking it up and not wanting to be a burden to others. They are people who feel alone in their pain and in this world. Many are stressed out and completely overwhelmed. Many are busy running from their own feelings while simultaneously taking huge responsibility for the feelings and behaviors of others. I meet people who are afraid to get real or be vulnerable and brave. Like my parents and myself, many are taught to not show weakness, never ask for help, and not show themselves vulnerable. Basically, I work with many mountain *carriers* who are now learning to start *climbing* their (damn!) mountains instead.

I had a small epiphany during a beautiful conversation with a friend— an esteemed colleague and personal superhero. She told me about the impact she saw me having on women within my larger community and how I seemed to be a role model to many females. After untangling myself from massive imposter syndrome thoughts, from shame, fear of rejection, and other psychological tigers and bears, I finally connected with a deep sense of finding a more significant purpose inside my already glowing passion. I knew that my soul's call was fierce and fabulous female empowerment. Rock on, sister!

I started noticing and remembering how my own behaviors of "too much," "chatty," and "dominant" were perceived very differently when displayed by my male peers. I saw that for many women, it seems like the messages we receive from the world around us are that a woman's voice is somehow less important or that being strong, powerful, and outspoken is just not appropriate or attractive for a woman. Today, I meet numerous women who are held back from living their full potential by compelling beliefs about their own strength, capabilities, worth, importance, beauty, and competency. Many women also experience a lack of confidence and courage to be who they want to be and to stand up for themselves when needed.

Starting My Movement

In 2017, I started the Fierce, Fabulous, and Female movement, where I give empowerment workshops for women and offer my therapist colleagues training in how to do the same. The foundation of my work is Acceptance and Commitment Therapy (ACT). ACT is a unique empirically based psychological intervention that uses acceptance and mindfulness strategies and commitment and behavior change techniques to increase psychological flexibility. That basically means contacting the present moment as it is and then changing or persisting in one's behavior depending on what the situation affords to move in the direction of one's chosen values. It's about doing what really matters to you in flexible, workable ways.

I am thus completely passionate about writing, coaching, and teaching courses on the topic that downright sets my soul on fire: how we, as women, can step into fabulous fierceness so that we can live our most authentic lives and be the change we wish to see in this world. How we can break free from the shackles of "being a good girl" and having to be perfect, how we can give authentic voice to what we are truly experiencing, master bravery, speaking up about things that matter to us, having vulnerable conversations and connecting deeply with ourselves and with others in fierce, compassionate, and kind ways. All of this is based on techniques backed by science.

As previously mentioned, we will all inevitably come into contact with pain and suffering in our lives. There is no way of bypassing this premise of the human condition. We feel rejected. We feel alone. We feel fear. We get sick. Others get sick. Loved ones die. We feel sad. We carry grief. Relationships crash. We feel insecure. And. The. List. Goes. On. Now, I am not saying that "life is just sh*t!" Oh no. Not at all. I am saying that life is *also* sh*t and that feeling good and being happy is just not possible all of the time. In fact, it might be the pursuit of happiness itself that causes suffering. Let's read that again: *it might be the pursuit of happiness itself that causes suffering*. Yes, sweetheart. Chasing "feeling good" and running from "feeling bad" can suck the life out of living our most vital, authentic, and meaningful lives. If you want to, then feel free to pause here and make a list of all of the behaviors you have engaged in to *not feel bad* and see if they are working well for you in the long run.

On my own list, you know I have strategies like sucking it up, talking to a tape recorder, taking responsibility for other people's feelings, playing it small, and staying in personal and professional relationships that drained me completely. I could go on and add: too many glasses of wine, too much food, too long working hours, and yelling at those around me to blow off some steam—all strategies that work somewhat okay here and now to reduce something I don't like to feel. But none of these drove me closer to who I want to be or the life I want for myself, nor the change I wish to be in this world. All of these strategies come with enormous costs for my health, my relationships, my wellbeing, and my soul's calling.

Replacing the "Pursuit of Happiness" and "Not Feeling Bad"

So what the heck are we supposed to do instead? Well, thank you for asking. Maybe—just *maybe*—we could replace the pursuit of happiness and "not feeling bad" with the pursuit of true meaning and fully experiencing whatever thoughts, feelings, and sensations come along with that journey? Knowing intense loss and grief at the age of eight is not what I wished for. *At all.* But it was entirely outside of my control.

What *is* within my control is turning that pain into purpose. I tell everybody who will listen that we all need to take a good hard look at what we are teaching our children. Are we teaching them to suck it up, to take responsibility for our feelings and actions, to not speak up about how they are feeling, and to "be good" and "be perfect?" Or do we teach them to be vulnerable, to be brave, to express themselves, to set healthy boundaries, and so forth? And do we teach them that they are not alone in their suffering, that it's okay to feel whatever they are feeling, and that it's something that we can all learn to carry and not run from? I now see that the pain I have experienced has also let me consider how I wish to navigate in this world and what kind of role model I wish to be for others.

My journey here was not all sunshine and happy dancing, as you know. It took—and still takes me—through the wildest rides over the entire emotional rollercoaster. For years, I was unhappy at work and found myself in various business relationships that overstepped my boundaries in so many ways. I have been bullied and ridiculed. I have been threatened, backstabbed, and laughed at. I have been called MILF (an acronym for "mother I'd like to f*ck) in business meetings, and I have had others comment on my breasts and my appealing cleavage. I have had my ass grabbed, and I have been told to "be a nice girl." I have been spoken over and unfairly overruled in meetings, and I have apologized for so much sh*t that never ever needed an apology in the first place. A boyfriend even openly wondered what others would think if he showed up with me—a loud woman with a wide behind covered in middle-class clothes. And yes, I stayed with that guy.

(Let's take a moment of silence in honor of my lost dignity.)

I have fought for love in fierce, brave, and compassionate ways. I have fought in very ugly, needy, and far from elegant ways. I have yelled at my children, my partner, and my parents. I have neglected essential relationships, been unsupportive of others at times, self-promoted in unattractive ways, and let my body down a billion times. I have lacked clear and compassionate boundaries towards others and towards myself. I did not have the guts to take responsibility for my own happiness, to let go of victimhood, and to step outside of all that and into my fierce and fabulous life—until I chose to do just that. Because that is what needs to be done. One must decide to go for that life. It will not come knocking on anyone's door.

Stepping outside of your comfort zone and going for a mighty, purposeful life comes with a cost, of course. When I was drowning in heartbreak, I was unsure whether I could ever love, be loved, or even make love again. Now, I know that the only thing that I *can* do is love others and not expect anything in return. The gift of love is now given freely and unconditionally. It's not given so that people will love me back, but because I want to be *that* woman—the woman who is loving towards others and myself. The cost is that I am petrified to lose. I feel insecure. I fear abandonment. I fear rejection. I feel scared. But there is no way that I can choose love without choosing the heartache that comes with it.

It took me forty-one years to learn to let go of my Superwoman shield, stand in front of a partner, admit to being vulnerable and scared, and ask for love, support, and a hug. Forty-one years, honey! Building my own company has too cost me countless sleepless nights and lots of hours talking to and taking advice from people who know stuff that I just don't. I am never sure if anything will fly or be well received, but I choose to continuously take small steps in the direction of the life I wish to live and the me I want to be. I will not be chased by fear. I would much rather be driven by purpose and passion. So, sometimes, I might be way less nice than I used to be, but I am much more compassionate and loving.

Of course, this is a tribe thing. This journey was not made on my own. I have a loving and endlessly supportive partner, a fantastic family, the best friends ever, and remarkable colleagues and badass clients. And two phenomenal children. They will fiercely guide me in ways that they might not even be aware of yet. I am blessed to continuously have deep conversations with these young men, and we will show ourselves vulnerable and authentic in these profound connections. They will let me know what they feel, and they have the guts to set clear boundaries. When they are triggered by my emotional states, they will tell me and grant me the opportunity to take that burden off their shoulders and allow them to feel what they feel and sit with them in love and kindness through that.

When my oldest son came with me to a psychology conference, he was asked backstage what—if anything—he admired about his mother. Time stood still, and I was curious to hear what his reply would be. I instantly connected with my fear and shame, and the greatest hits of "I'm such a bad mother" was playing on the loudest volume ever. After careful consideration, he gave the most profound answer: "The thing I admire about my mother is the way she gets up when life knocks her down." (Wiping away tears now.) I could not be prouder of this young man. Together, we turned pain into purpose. My children now know that life *will* knock you down at times. It's the getting up that matters. And that, my friend, is where your power is.

Everyone's journey looks different and is defined from the inside out. For some, it means setting boundaries and standing up for oneself. For some, it is the practice of compassionate and kind self-care. For others, it's stepping outside of their comfort zone and being brave. For some, it's coming to terms with their inner critic. And for others, it's turning "chatty" into "articulate," turning "dominant" into "determined," and turning "too much" into "passionate." Yet, for all of us, being fierce and fabulous and living a mighty life with purpose involves learning how to move past fear, self-doubt, and dependence on others' approval. It means listening inwardly to what is calling us and starting to honor that call. I am here to support women (and men!) through the process of defining what fierce and fabulous means to them and of realizing that vision. It's all about turning pain into some kind of purpose. It's certainly about the way you get up when life knocks you down.

My Thoughts on Pursuing Your Purpose

If I could kindly and lovingly offer you three pieces of advice for you pursuing living your purpose, it would be these:

1. *Don't believe everything you think*. Your mind will probably offer you a million reasons why you're not ready, not good enough, not smart enough, not brave enough, or not [_____] enough. I invite you to persevere and keep at it while taking those thoughts with you. Notice how you can have your thoughts—don't let them have you. You can freely choose which thoughts you let navigate what you do and which ones you don't. Is that sometimes hard? Yes. Is that possible? It is.

2. *If you don't change anything, nothing changes*. We all know this, but sometimes we nevertheless keep doing the same thing while expecting different results. If you want to change your life, you will have to make other choices and make room for the discomfort, fear, and insecurities that might show up as you do this. Change can be painful. It can also be totally worth it. Choose to practice willingness to feel what is there when change is painful for you.

3. *The world needs you and your voice*. Yes, baby. There are probably many people out there doing what you do. But no one does it as you do. You don't just go to *any* concert, do you? You go to a *specific* show because you love how the artist or the band is playing and jamming. Find your voice and

your purpose and take the damn stage. Your mighty life is waiting for you to join it.

Rikke Kjelgaard is a licensed psychologist, author, and expert in Acceptance and Commitment Therapy (ACT). She is a celebrated motivational speaker whose teachings have inspired thousands of people around the world. Rikke runs her own company in Scandinavia and is the creator of the Fierce, Fabulous, and Female movement.

You can meet Rikke here: www.rikkekjelgaard.com - and start your Fierce and Fabulous journey here: www.fiercefabulousandfemale.com

Navigating From Slum Life to Healing Others

By Rachael Masaku
Kenya

I am Rachael, thirty-seven years old, born and brought up in one of the dingy, low-income, prone slums of Nairobi Eastland's Kenya, known as Korogocho. I am the firstborn of five, all girls. Life in the slum was not easy and will never be easy.

It's always against one's wish to be brought up in such an environment. The environment is dingy, volatile, lacking all the social amenities—the few available are dilapidated and malfunctioning. My poor parents could only afford the housing in the slum due to their meager income. They picked this slum due to its proximity to the market where my mother sold fruits and cereals and where my dad worked as a carpenter.

I still count myself lucky because, despite my parents' meager income, they managed to squeeze something out for me and my siblings' education, though partly it was also paid through volunteers who would sponsor needy children in the slums. I grew up so naïve. For the eight years of my primary education, I was in the slums. The primary school was only five hundred meters from our house until I went to high school, and I wasn't exposed to the outside world. As a family, our life was solidly in the slums—besides living within the slum, my parents worked within the slum, and we were schooled within the slums. We never left the slum to go to town. My mother was so strict; we always stayed at home when not in school or with my mother in the market. The only day out was going to church, which was also just in the neighborhood.

While living in the slums, I always dreamed of living a better life outside, but the way and how I never knew. Due to poor hygiene resulting from poor sanitation, I have suffered typhoid since I was ten years old. I have received several treatments for typhoid, but it kept on recurring, especially when I was in high school to the extent that it affected my studies. I would be at home for a month while studies were ongoing in school; hence I lagged in my academics. I don't remember not having a headache or stomach ache throughout my life in high school, despite always being on medication. The pains became an everyday part of my life when I was in high school.

Finally, I got relief from my longtime suffering after homeopathic treatment. My dad's friend happened to come upon a clinic, a new project in the neighborhood. He told him about it, and then my dad asked me if I was interested in visiting the homeopathic clinic to try and see if they could treat my typhoid, which was chronic. I heeded my dad's advice and went for the treatment in the clinic, which was run by an American yogic nun called Didi Ananda Ruchira, whom I've never forgotten for her contribution to my life. I was mesmerized with the treatment administered to me (I was asked many questions about my medical history, what other conditions I had before etc.), and I was given tiny white pills to take (medicated globules).

Three days after the treatment, my persistent stomach ache and headache stopped. It was unbelievable to me after all that long-suffering, and I was cured in three days just like that! The treatment aroused my curiosity, and I went back to the lady who treated me for further consultation to learn much more about the homeopathic remedy she gave me. After a detailed explanation, I developed an interest in learning more about this mode of treatment. This is how I got introduced to Homeopathy, and I joined the homeopathy training, which the same clinic was offering in the slum. In the college, they incorporated reflexology and massage as part of the course. So after the first year, one could decide what they are best at and pick the right path for continued studies.

As I took my homeopathy course, my director advised me to take reflexology seriously, even though my main focus was homeopathy. I graduated and successfully passed my class in the three categories, i.e., homeopathy, reflexology, and massage.

After my graduation, my director repeatedly asked me to do reflexology on her. She seemed to like it since she kept asking me to work on her, and she referred several people to me, including the volunteers from overseas who used to visit our college. All of them gave positive feedback to my director about my reflexology and massage. I wondered why she kept on picking me to work on the volunteers as many of us did the same course. The volunteers would tell me I have excellent hands, and at the time, I did not understand what they meant. After gaining experience through working on volunteers and some other few referrals, my director continued to refer more clients to me at the new clinic entrusted to me after my graduation.

I earn a living by offering an alternative treatment to my clients through homeopathy treatment and reflexology. I have a clinic where I do consultations and also do home visits. Most of my clients are in Nairobi, and they prefer to be visited in the comfort of their homes. 70 percent of my clients prefer home visits, and 30 percent come to my clinic primarily for homeopathic treatment. The home-visit process is a bit taxing because I have to drive to different homes to do reflexology. I got all of my clients through word-of-mouth referrals, which is the only means I have earned my living since school.

Since I started this practice of alternative treatment, I have come to feel like it was my calling, and I feel so good when a client tells me their health is better or they are improving due to my intervention. I get surprised at times when I get clients from very far out of Nairobi as well.

My Vision

I envision alternative treatment as one way for the future in terms of health, especially since it's affordable, accessible, and readily available. It's also natural without side effects, and it does not involve machines. In many cases I have handled, I have seen my clients getting better. Some of my clients confess having tried other means of treatment but failed to get better after spending lots of money. As I move along, I have gained more experience and continue to gain more and become better today. My clientele is increasing as well, and I may not accommodate the growing number of my clients. I plan to train more people to refer some of my clients to them and grow my practice while serving more people. With reflexology, I limit the work I can do per day since I am using my hands and energy, so when I train others, I may help create employment or income for the younger generation in the future. I am also thinking about how I can popularize the practice in the rural areas of Kenya. I dream of starting alternative health services in the village. Natural healing methods can be so helpful to the older generation since their immunity is going down, and more chemicals in their body may do more harm to them. In the rural areas, they only know that conventional medicines are what heals. Without tablets and injections, they don't believe one can heal, and they are so naïve about the effects of the same. In my practice, I also give more holistic health advice, including talking about a healthy diet and daily lifestyle depending on the condition that I am trying to address.

Perseverance

Naturally, I am an introvert, partly because I came from the slums and was not exposed to much of the world. My self-esteem was very low. I didn't know what to do or where to start from when I began operating a clinic close to our residence in the slum. In the slum, they depend on donor support, and with their meager income, paying for my services was a big challenge despite me coming from the area and charging according to rates. So those who would pay, maybe one dollar, were patients who were so desperate for a cure because they had suffered for a long time without proper treatment or went for other treatment that never helped them; hence they turned to me as the last option.

Operating in the locality I grew up in was not easy, as some people would come to me for treatment without money, so desperate and hopeless. I couldn't send them away. I treated them without pay and went further to offer them something to eat, maybe a fruit, since I also did not have money and their situation was so desperate. Despite the financial constraint, I had to pay the clinic rent, which was so hard to realize through my service in the slum. My director kept on chipping in to pay the rent for the clinic to keep on running, even if we were not making any profit, so I took it as a launching pad for my practice and didn't give up due to the frustrations I faced.

We applied for funds to support our work as a project in the slums and got it, but it was short-lived and came with challenges. Criminals raided the clinic twice and made away with money and personal belongings from the patients and foreign volunteers visiting the project. This was a significant setback for me since patients were scared to visit my clinic after the incidents. I still did not give up. I started a small support group for desperate women with health issues, and the number grew from six to twenty. I supported them through small donations from well-wishers and some of my wealthier clients in the up-market areas where I was doing home visits. I was buying the group members' nutritious vegetables weekly, making some concoctions for their immunity, like cabbage mala, a friendly flora. They were so used to painkillers that destroyed the friendly flora, most of them would come with issues of candida, especially ladies.

I later got married, but my husband did not live or work in the slum, so my expenses continued to rise as I commuted further to manage my practice. The project in the slum could not sustain my demand, and I never wanted to burden my husband financially since he was also just struggling to make ends meet. When I approached my director for financial support, she was accommodating, and she would give me advice on what I should do.

One day she challenged me and told me, "You know what, you need to stop working in the slum and try the upmarket. You can't be born in the slum, live there, then work there." She challenged me to go out and try for upmarket (wealthier) clients, and she even told me, "I know I can't afford you, decide on the days you will work at the clinic and when to do the home visits." So I decided to do three days for her and three days for home visits. I won't say that it was easy getting my clients, as initially, not many people knew me very well. Also, I came from the slums was not an alluring marketing tactic because it's associated with many negative connotations.

My husband was supportive. He assured me that I could make it. There were many times that I called him to say that I'm giving up on home visits. Initially, I didn't have a car, and I used to use public means and could get so tired because I would walk for long in the sun, and by the time I reached my clients' houses, I was so tired. My husband told me I must have confidence in myself and what I do. Slowly, with time, I started to gain courage and confidence.

My Big Break

The first major challenge I faced in public speaking was when I was invited to a talk show on TV. I freaked out since this was something I had never done before. Once again, my husband came in handy, and through his guidance and support, I managed to pull it through. I presented an introduction to reflexology, how it works, and why you need it for health reasons. My presentation was OK, but I still managed to get several phone calls to set up appointments. Since then, I have never looked back.

I meet different people from different races and socioeconomic statuses in my practice, and they have always been happy and satisfied with my services. I grew in both reflexology and homeopathy. I never believed that I could treat the upper class, considering that I grew up in the slums. I always thought that nothing good comes from the slums. My director pushed me so hard by challenging me to take on different tasks, and my husband would assure me I could do it because he saw my potential. He would ask me to assume that I had a client or a patient. How would you address them? Then I would rehearse as he guides me through how best I could do it. With time I developed self-confidence and would stand before people and address them. I grew to a point where I was now leading training workshops on reflexology and homeopathy. I feel that I am at a level where I can communicate better and do my things independently.

Moving Beyond the Slums

I stopped working at the community clinic in the slum where my practice began since the demand for my services in the upmarket gradually grew. In the upscale, they understood that I did better than in the slums, though I still go back to the slums to give back to the community by offering free treatment there once a month. Some clients would call me so desperate for my help and willing to visit my clinic, but they would be reluctant to visit the clinic due to insecurity. So I had to strive to set up a clinic in a secure upmarket place with parking. I teamed up with my director and opened a clinic where I now do my homeopathy consultations and sell some health products.

When I started my private practice, I faced numerous challenges. Some clients could not pay the amount requested, and I offered my services at eight dollars per hour while others were doing the same at twenty dollars per hour. I used this lower fee structure as a strategy to penetrate the market, but some clients doubted my competence due to my low charges. Since my marketing happened by referrals from the other clients, once they experienced my services, they were happy and had confidence in what I did. So my clientele grew from individual to family members, to neighbors and workmates.

Some clients lived far apart, and I did not have a car. I would walk for an hour between clients and be so tired when I reached my clients' houses. Initially, there were no motorbikes, but thank goodness finally they came, so I could hop on one to visit my clients. I was late for my appointments in most cases, and some of my clients were quite unhappy. I would agree with the motorbike riders to come back for me after fifty minutes of a session, and they would turn me down by not coming or picking up calls. As a result, I would be late or have to reschedule the subsequent appointments.

With the bit of savings we had, my husband told me he would prefer to buy a small second-hand car and that I should also go for driving lessons. I joined a driving school, and after one month, I completed the course. I was to wake up early at 4 a.m. to leave the house with my husband at 5 a.m. when he was going to work, even though my appointments used to be after 8 a.m. I had to persevere in the morning cold in the office, waiting for my appointment time before I drove out. In the early morning, the traffic is less, and with my husband's guidance, I was able to practice driving on my way to work daily, which allowed me to learn to drive. The result was that I was able to keep up with my appointments and clients' demands right on time.

Impact of My Purpose

Since I graduated from school, my practice has been my only source of income. My mother wanted me to be a nurse, but I wanted to be a business administrator since the business was instilled in me when I was still very young. Since our parents brought us up as self-employed people, I believed in making a living without working for someone else. I started with what I had and pushed it further to the level that it now helps support our family, a reality immensely helped through moral support from my husband. The impact of my work is measured by the rate at which I get referrals from my treated patients. My patients cut across all ages and races, and a majority come from the Asian community. This is because the Asian community is more familiar with homeopathic treatment and reflexology. They have more faith in alternative treatment than local Kenyans. All of my family now depends on alternative medicine. I do reflexology for my family weekly and treat them as well as teaching them to eat healthily. For instance, in my house, sugar is only for visitors. None of my entire family consumes sugar.

The Contrast of My Purpose

My past life was in the slum, and it was a hard life. It's a life of desperation, and I never thought I would live the life I am living now. I came from a very humble background in a crime-prone area full of insecurity, rape, and mugging. I couldn't imagine how I was going to bring up my family in such a volatile environment. Due to my background and being an introvert, I had very low esteem, and I never thought of living a better life in the future. We never had running water or a toilet. We used to buy water from the vendors, and we lived in mud houses with corrugated iron sheet roofs. We had raw sewage running past our home in the open.

Since I started my private practice and moved out of the slum, my life has never been the same again. I strived to change my parents' lives as well. My dad stopped his carpentry work, which was earning him very little for so much work, and my mum stopped her grueling fruit vending business after I managed to build them a permanent three-bedroom stone house back in the village in our ancestral land. My father is now a farmer, and my mother is operating her small shop from the comfort of her home. They live a decent life in a serene environment instead of the life and environment they had for most of their life. My mother has arthritis, but I am happy to be managing it with alternative treatment. There was a time when my mother was bedridden for one year. Most of her business partners thought she was going to die. I struggled with my mother's health single-handedly, and through the grace of God, I managed, just by using alternative treatments. My mother is still alive and can do her work back at home.

My Advice for You

1. In life, each one of us has a purpose to fulfill in life. We should always take our time with a very sober mind to think and identify what we can do and where it may lead us to or what we intend to achieve in life. I don't believe in failing. All that we need is focus and proper mentorship. Many of us are blessed with talents, but we let them go untapped and wasted due to the background we came from. In the slum, we see the middle class as the haves, and we are the have-nots. In the slum, we count ourselves as the unlucky ones, which is very wrong. We have to wake up and go for our targets to achieve our life dreams. No one deserves to be poor or suffer pangs of poverty; it's the mindset we have. We all have functioning brains, but at times due to our background, we fear risks and avoid indulging in a new, unfamiliar venture. I couldn't believe I would do this and be where I am today, even more so as a mother and a wife as well.

2. It may not be one's wish to suffer, but life is like being in the boxing ring. As my husband advised me, you must fight hard with lots of courage to come out victorious with your eyes on the target if you want to win. Even if you fall, it does not mean you will lose. Rise and fight on with courage. Before any fight, one must be fully prepared physically and mentally to win the bout. In this spirit, I have kept it up and forged ahead in all my endeavors. Even if I lose, I believe there is always another chance, but one must fight as if that is the only chance. If others succeeded, why not you? You may be failing because you have the wrong approach.

3. Never be discouraged by others' failures. Their failure does not mean you will fail too. We are in a dynamic world; changes happen daily, be ready to change with the world. Obstacles and challenges that come one's way should not be a hindrance in achieving your goal. Achieving goals is always a long journey, and the obstacles may help you achieve better results when you reach your destination.

Rachael Masaku is a homeopath and reflexologist working in Nairobi, Kenya. Growing up in one of the slums, she did not know that she would be of help to society in the future. Her career started right in the slum where she worked for five years with a particular NGO before moving to the upper market where she has established herself. She has served people of different statuses, including government officials, business people, etc. She was once a registrar of the Kenyan Society of Homeopaths for seven years seven years and is currently a board member of one of the NGOs in Kenya. She can be reached through her email at: rachaelmasaku@gmail.com

From a Timid Village Girl to Mother of Thirty Destitute Girls by Age Twenty-Two

By Sharda Nirmal
India

G rowing up in rural India as a girl means limited access to education. Social rights activist and education advocate Nelson Mandela once said, "Education is the most powerful weapon which you can use to change the world." Over their formative years, many young girls are taught this only applies to boys. They constantly witness their inferiority and are affirmed in the knowledge that they do not need education. Because they are expected to marry into their husband's family, leaving their own world and family behind, young women are considered foreigners in their own community. Thus, their upbringing focuses on household chores and caretaking. It isn't honorable to raise their voice or speak up in their own defense—the expectation is to abide by elders with heads bowed down. Being subordinate is constantly ingrained into a young woman's conscience to the extent that it isn't even acceptable to sit on a bed or cot when her husband is around, as that is deemed disrespectful. As a wife, she should sit on the floor, always below him.

As a young girl myself, growing up in a small village in Karnataka, I also experienced this pervasive idea that a young woman's role is centered on the home. Boys had the freedom to express their wants, likes, and dislikes; they could even question their elders. While the boys were encouraged to play with their friends after school, girls were expected to stay home and share in housework and sibling care. Sometimes, even just attending school wasn't a privilege available to many girls in my village, regardless of how much they desired an education. Growing up, I often wondered why such partialities existed and who was responsible for this gender divide. How could we eradicate these norms once and for all? The answer isn't an easy one. It's inherently a paradox—knowledge is critical. To gain knowledge, a quality and comprehensive education are needed. Education can change the world.

To me, education means empowerment. Education broadens one's knowledge of the world and, in turn, expands awareness and understanding of others. Education holds power to change mindsets and viewpoints by opening up different ideas and customs; it provides a vision and motive for living life. Education helps us realize our self-worth and potential, opening up doors that hadn't existed before. When we are exposed to different people and ideas, we explore ourselves and what we're made of, building the foundation to develop a unique personality. When we are comfortable in our characters and confident in ourselves, women can create our own success and inevitably generate the power to transform society.

"Educate a woman, and you educate her family. Educate a girl, and you change the future." – Queen Rania of Jordan

As a young girl, I was drawn to the idea of teaching. I wanted to open doors for other girls to receive a good education and empower more women to be independent and successful. I planned on dedicating time to teaching gender equality to my future students, primarily focusing on honoring and respecting girls and women. I wanted to teach them to dream big, aim high, and have the courage to set and accomplish their own goals. I moved to Mumbai to pursue higher education.

After completing my pre-university education, I began a teacher's training course for primary school students. As I acclimated to this new and hectic megacity, I soon realized that a teacher's role in education was limited to the four walls of her classroom. Our responsibility to our students was simply restricted to academic subjects like math and writing with little room for empowerment and free will.

Change in India was an Imperative and Launched My Purpose

Instead of entering the formal education system after completing my teacher training program in 1998, I joined the organization Community Outreach Programme (CORP). Since its inception in 1977, this NGO has worked to provide a platform for the development and empowerment of women and children in the slum communities of Mumbai. At CORP, I worked with both crèche (preschool) children and children with disabilities. Alongside teaching, I also conducted educational, self-awareness, and health awareness programs with women residing in the Dharavi slums. Through my close work with these women, I acquainted myself with their circumstances and struggles, quickly realizing that whether they are from small villages or big cities, all women across India face oppression in their daily lives. Regardless of location, a woman's role is confined to the home, and expectations regarding education and success are drastically different for men than for women. I could see that change was imperative.

Whenever I saw young girls who were of an age where they should be thriving at school and playgrounds but were instead begging on Mumbai's local trains, it hurt me deeply. I always thought about how I could help them. In 1999, I had an unexpected meeting with an Indian-American volunteer named Deval Sanghvi, who visited the Shalom Center where I worked. We connected on a profound level, and we both voiced the need for better education and support systems for girls. As we talked together, Deval brought the conversation to CORP's management, and the idea of opening a shelter home for girls was born. At the age of twenty-two, I married my husband Nirmal in May 2000, and by June 2000, the two of us started the Sharanam Shelter Home for girls in Dharavi as full-time caretakers. (Today, my husband Nirmal Chandappa is not only the house dad at Sharanam, but he is also CORP's Executive Director.)

I remember well the girl I used to be before I found my purpose. I was very timid—a quiet girl who never fought with anyone. I was always engaged in my own work and was always respectful to my parents, teachers, and elders. I was diligent in everything that I did. Back then, the education system wasn't as good as it is today. I had an innate desire to study. I worked hard but consistently scored average grades. Sadly, in Indian society, not only do people decide your worth by your grades, but so do our institutions. Very little attention is paid to your background, talent, willpower, or hard work. As an inherently introverted person, I struggled to initiate conversations with people. Part of this could easily be attributed to the old adage of the ideal girl being submissive. But, while I may have been timid, I was observant, always contemplating and analyzing these social norms that encompassed me.

Back then, I was lost and indecisive. I didn't know what my life's purpose was; there were no goals set. To me, setting goals was challenging. The transformation in my life began once I joined CORP after completing my teacher training program. I had worked on my personality and developed self-confidence during the teacher training program.

Along with helping myself, I began helping the women and children of the Dharavi slums. My family and the people of the area I worked in started believing in me and my capabilities. With time, by the age of twenty-one, many people considered me as an inspiration in their lives.

CORP's Shalom Centre for children with disabilities had a hundred children with physical disabilities and visual and hearing impairment. I worked with a batch of sixty children. They were very bright-minded, and they were beautiful. But because of their physical impairments, they were afraid to dream and have aspirations for their future. In 1999, we took the children to Hyderabad in southern India on an educational tour. We visited various sites—Char Minar, Hussain Sagar Lake, Golconda Fort, etc. Upon reaching Golconda fort, the children with fewer impairments began enthusiastically climbing the steps to the summit.

The children with more significant impairments stopped and turned to me, saying, "Teacher, you should go ahead and enjoy the view as the rest of the teachers. We will wait here until you return."

Because of their disabilities, these children never truly got to experience trips or vacations to the fullest. If we took them to the beach, they couldn't run around and enjoy the sand underneath their feet like other children. They had been through so many experiences that sacrificing any kind of fun opportunity was now second nature to them, and they did this with a pure smile. I told them, "Either all of you are coming with us, or I am not going either." After much persuasion, I was able to convince them to climb the steps with me. Even though a few of them had to halt because they genuinely lacked the physical strength needed to continue, the majority made it to the top. Upon reaching the summit, their teary eyes gleamed with gratitude. As we watched the golden sunset, they told me that I was the first person to show such a magnitude of patience towards them over their fifteen to twenty years at CORP. It warmed my heart. I was moved by the children's realization that they harbored the great potential needed to achieve their dreams, which they previously thought they lacked. I was able to show them that life may be challenging, but it is conquerable. I realized there are so many underprivileged women and children in Mumbai, and I want to help them attain a better life. I had finally, indeed, found my purpose.

Standing Up for What I Believe

My personal vision is to live a meaningful life dedicated to the betterment of society. I need to live my life in a way that shows humanity, humility, kindness, compassion, and concern for others—family, friends, and strangers. I hope to help people find their inner strength, and I aspire to live authentically and with passion. I love working with and around people. I want everyone to know love and support. I believe in the "pay it forward" model and hope that in helping others, they will go on to do the same, injecting kindness, thoughtfulness, compassion, and wisdom into our society.

There is no life without its challenges. We cannot experience life to its fullest if we live in fear of failure and hardships. I began working at the age of twenty. During the early days of running the Sharanam Shelter Home for girls, there were countless challenges. Because the girls hailed from the streets of Mumbai, they were not well behaved, and they lacked discipline, manners, and hygiene. They often fought a lot amongst each other. The residents of the building in which our shelter home is situated were not happy about it. They would yell at me and express how frustrated they felt living close to the "noisy," "ill-mannered," and "dirty" girls. I apologized every time for the girls' behavior and politely asked the neighbors, "If your child was to behave in the same manner with you, would you throw them out of your house? Would you abandon them?" Over the years, their attitudes changed. In fact, the most prominent protesters back in the day are now those who support us the most.

When you perform better than people's exceptions, you will be met with the same criticisms had you underperformed. A minimal number of people genuinely root for you and genuinely celebrate your accomplishments. As I started rising up in the ranks, some of my colleagues grew jealous of me. They began gossiping about conspiracies about the project because they thought I was secretly getting a hefty amount of money from our foreign funders. They tried to bully me because they had completed more degrees than me. But I never found an urge to defend myself or engage in confrontation because I believed that to serve people, all you need is love, kindness, patience, and compassion— not degrees and status.

One of our girls from the earliest batch, Sumitra, suffered from mental health and behavioral issues. She especially sought attention from males. Once I had to take Sumitra to the hospital, and we stood at the bus stop waiting for the bus to arrive. She began conversing with the men waiting with us. She told them that I was taking her to a hospital against her wishes and pleaded with them to save her. Thinking that she was being kidnapped, they intervened. Soon a large crowd gathered, and everyone started screaming and shouting at me. I implored that she had a mental disorder, and it was imperative to get her to the hospital on time—if we missed the appointment, then the doctor wouldn't be available again anytime soon. But they weren't ready to listen. They threatened to take me to the police. Around half an hour later, when Sumitra saw the people were getting too aggressive, she got scared that they would physically hurt me. So, she grabbed me tightly, yelled at them for hassling me, and told them to leave me alone. This shocked the onlookers. They finally realized I was telling the truth and apologized for wasting everyone's time.

In your work life, your health is just as important as your will and spirit. In 2008, I had a critical road accident where I suffered severe head injuries and blood loss. My son was six years old, and my daughter was just a year and a half old. The duty of taking care of the twenty-five girls along with our two children fell on my husband.

After a week in the hospital, I asked the doctors to discharge me. I would pretend to feel better and stronger because I was concerned for the children at the shelter home. The doctors had advised me two years off from any kind of stress-inducing work. But to me, this wasn't a viable option; the girls needed me. Unfortunately, the accident changed a few internal aspects of myself. I lost my once-high tolerance level, and little things would irritate or anger me. This was only fueled further because the majority of the girls were in their teenage years. They would rebel and argue with me, quarrel with me, and back answer me—without any regard to what I was going through. My husband, too, remarked that I had been behaving differently and that I was very quick to get agitated. All I wished for was that if only there was someone who understood the pain and what I was going through—who would love me, support me, and take care of me. But I had to look after myself for the next three years, from 2008 to 2011. I strengthened myself by meditating, doing yoga, and, most importantly, praying.

Over the twenty years of my social service, I have seen a lot of transformation and change in people's lives. I regularly work with the women in Mumbai's Dharavi slum and help them in various aspects of their lives. The outlook and vision of these women have completely transformed. Women in their thirties and forties who were previously uneducated and illiterate began pursuing basic level education. They started saving money for their children's education. Many school dropout girls and young women started attaining various small businesses and vocational training and are now self-dependent and self-reliant. They have found growth in status, security, and self-esteem. They are proud to be women.

I have supported eighty girls through the shelter home. Many of the girls have completed their education, are working, and have found independence. They are working in a wide array of fields—accounting, nursing, beautician, hotel management, corporate companies, etc. Some of them moved in with their single parents and live in their native hometowns. The mothers of these girls had brought them to the shelter home with the hope of providing their daughters with a better life. I am proud that our girls, who completed their education through our shelter home and have become independent women, now take care of their mothers.

My Advice to Follow Your Calling

My advice to everyone that wishes to follow their calling and live their purpose would be to first understand what exactly is that goal or calling. Think of what kind of changes you expect to occur and would like to cultivate in yourself and in this world through that purpose. Your vision should be authentic to you.

You then need to act on it. Don't doubt whether you have it in you to achieve your purpose or if you can handle the pressures and struggles that come with the commitment. Don't fear how different your life will be once you embark on the path of your calling. Do not worry about failure or if you will ever fulfill your purpose. Drop a pebble into a lake, and the ripples form themselves. Thus, all you need to do is take that one step. Let the waves of change surge out into this world. All the possibilities, opportunities, and transformations will present themselves to you. God is always with those who practice noble causes and will send help exactly when required.

Whatever you do today, do it sincerely and with diligence. Don't expect anything in return. Because if your expectations aren't met, you will only be met with disappointment. Don't do it for validation, recognition, or status. Be compassionate with yourself. When you are broken down, rise up again. Never stop believing in yourself and your purpose. Always hold on to hope. But above all, do it with love.

Sharda Nirmal is an Indian Project Manager working at CORP India and co-founder of the Sharanam Shelter for girls, Mumbai. She studied sociology and has a master's in social work. She is a strong believer in education for girls and women's empowerment. To her, women with great potential often get marginalized due to lack of support—financial, educational, or emotional. She has been working full-time to support girls over the past twenty years and looks after thirty girls aged three to eighteen years at the Sharanam shelter home. She can be reached via email: sharda.sharanam@gmail.com.

The Resistant Purpose Hunter Unleashed at Half Time

By Dr. Alise Cortez
United States

My purpose is to awaken meaning, passion, and purpose in people, inspiring them to contribute at a level worthy of their one precious life. This calling found its way to my conscious awareness around 2014 when I was forty-nine years old. It lingered on the cusp of my active attention for decades, of course, but as all humans can be so resistant, I was no exception. At that time, I was self-employed, conducting leadership and professional development workshops for corporate clients. I had also just wrapped up an ambitious postdoctoral research project I'd dug my claws into—having been driven to learn how 115 men and women across twenty professions found meaning in their work and how that, in turn, forged their identities. I had planned a trip to India in December to present my research at a business conference, and attending allowed the work to be published in recognition of its academic contribution. In November, I had just finished conducting a workshop derived from this new research for a Dallas-based client. They loved it, and I was feeling high on life in the knowledge that I'd created something useful. Then, on the drive back home from that workshop, my cell phone rang. It was Voice America calling to inquire if I wanted to host my own radio show; a role I'd never considered for myself but that immediately "seemed right." I promptly accepted the offer. My show—*Working on Purpose*—has been on the airwaves since February 2015.

In that coalescing year, I understood magic was afoot. I felt powerfully connected to the universe, and a curious dynamic was unfolding from within me. I was increasingly becoming ever present to my purpose, and while I spent most of my adulthood "looking" for meaning and what I was *supposed to be doing with my life*, the divining rod toward purpose was quietly doing its subtle work. I had simply opted for one right step after the other, feeling its gentle but firm pull tugging me along. Now, when I look back, I can see my purpose slowly revealing itself to me over the course of my life. It's like feeling my way in the dark and trusting that I would eventually find my way. I discovered that the closer I got to the awareness of my purpose, the stronger the pull of it became, and the more energized I was in my pursuit to honor it.

The clearer I became as to my calling and the deeper I pursued it, the more my marriage of sixteen years came off the tracks. The actual process of divorce turned out to be an enormous propellant to launch purpose into a life's expression. I say emphatically that I would not be living my purpose if I'd continued wandering in the apathetic complacency I'd allowed myself to descend into while married. When I look back, I see myself as a member of the tranquilized "walking dead" before my awakening. As I leaned into the transformation of a solo life, I stepped into the clearing that was presenting itself to invent my life anew, on my own terms. I channeled the extreme stress from self-doubt and fear of the unknown, wondering how to operationalize my calling into making a new, authentically expressed life and living.

My Foundational Learning

I invite you to join me in a walk back through time. As you learn to examine your past, if you haven't already, you will start to see that your purpose has been with you from early in life. The first significant point along my path to purpose was in kindergarten in Yakima, Washington. It was about 1970, and I remember feeling as if school happened in slow motion. It was like watching a movie only I starred in, as I was frequently lost in daydreams. One day, my teacher finally summoned my attention by sternly and loudly announcing in front of my classmates, "You are the stupidest kid I've ever had in my classroom!" While I was mortified that I'd been issued this proclamation in front of my peers—including one who I had a terrible crush on, the judgment didn't cripple me or hurt my feelings. I just simply and wholly... *believed her*. After all, she had been teaching for decades, and she was in a position to evaluate my academic acumen and potential.

From that crucial moment on, I went through school with a completely transformed mindset and approach to study. When teachers issued their assignments in the subsequent years, I reviewed their instructions carefully instead of taking my prior lackadaisical approach. Snapping my eyes forward and with full attention to the instructions before me, I'd say to myself, "Okay, now I *am* stupid (while nodding my head vigorously), so I'm going to have to work harder than all the other kids on this assignment." Almost overnight, I developed what I would now consider an "over-the-top" approach to studying that I relied on throughout my elementary, middle, and high school career. It was a time-intensive, systematic approach that mainly yielded A grades. Throughout these years, I never stopped believing I was stupid. This mindset began to fade only as I was about to graduate from high school. Nonetheless, I will always appreciate that teacher for shaking me out of my daze and helping to set me on a path of voracious learning and study. This behavioral tendency became a fundamental part of who I am today and how I would continue discovering my purpose over the years as I worked to realize my potential.

Another enormous awakening toward my purpose came disguised in a request. My parents asked me to begin working for them in their restaurant while I was in high school. I was a timid freshman geek and had no idea the tremendous growth that lay in store for me. I am fully convinced that absent that intervention, I was otherwise destined to become the librarian for our town of 4,800 in Hermiston, Oregon, focused on what I knew best at the time—books and learning. Going to work for my parents changed the trajectory of my life entirely because stepping into the stress of restaurant work, a new and much more confident and capable person emerged. I have thanked my parents many times for goading me into the role, *saving me*. I was so shy and awkward at age fourteen, and it was simply terrifying to have to walk up to tables of people I knew—or didn't know— and *talk* with them. Gradually, I learned to manage the negative emotions of fear, doubt, and shame and replace them with enthusiasm, joy, and pride.

Over the next few years working for my parents and through my academic and extracurricular activities, I came to firmly understand self-efficacy and confidently believe in myself and my abilities. This confidence was also fueled by the success of learning to keep pace with my older, more experienced peers at the restaurant, particularly during furiously busy times when every table was full and waiting times long. None of us could move fast enough to keep up. I became friendly and began injecting humor and, later, showy performance into my service. In a couple of years, I grew to a level where I could confidently and flawlessly approach a table of twenty-five people, verbally receive their orders, memorize them without taking any notes, and bring all the cocktails, appetizers, salads, entrees, and desserts to each person during the meal precisely as they had requested them. My customers were utterly dazzled. I was handsomely rewarded with tips. The four years I spent working in the restaurant with my parents, who I deeply respected and felt honored to work alongside, set me on a path to speak confidently, to present myself comfortably in front of others, and to perform—which set the proverbial stage for the life of purpose I lead today: speaking, consulting, and hosting the radio program. My purpose and its expression were slowly, imperceptibly unfolding.

Building on that foundation, I was presented with another gift, which unbeknownst to me would become a vital catalyst in helping me on the path to becoming attuned to my purpose. That gift came in the form of a job offer in Portland, Oregon, which had been extended to me by

Roland Haertl, who I met while working at a co-op job during my last year of high school. The four years I spent in high school working for my parents waiting tables in their restaurant, which was situated along Highway 395, afforded me contact with locals as well as travelers passing through. People dropped in from really *exotic* places, like Portland, Oregon!— and I learned about their lives, which to me sounded like great adventures in far-away places. I became aware that people who grew up in small towns often stayed with little opportunity to develop themselves because options are usually limited. I desperately wanted something "more"—a theme that would govern me for decades—as I'd now glimpsed the possibility of life beyond our small town.

My Fall from Grace that Saved My Life

Roland's offer gave me my ticket out of the small town and prepared me for something beyond. I moved to the "promised land" upon graduation, completed an eight-month business college certification program, and promptly went to work for Roland as his administrative assistant in his commercial real estate development firm. Roland was a joy to work for and employed behaviors that I recommend today to participants in my leadership development courses. He believed in me and gave me ample opportunities to learn new tasks and ways of working that stretched me and helped me grow personally and professionally.

But then it happened … one day eighteen after months on the job, Roland cheerfully passed my desk on the way out for lunch as he had done countless times before. He threw the door open wide, bounced out of it with coattails and briefcase flying behind him, and called out over his shoulder, "You have to get out of here, go see the world, get an education, *do* something with yourself. But before you go, hire your replacement!" And *wham*, the door shut behind him.

I sat paralyzed in my chair, his words echoing in my ears, feeling as if the proverbial rug had been pulled from under me. Fretfully and with a good dose of shock and daze, I turned it over and over in my mind as I sat frozen in my chair.

"Did he just <u>fire</u> me?"

Quintessentially Roland, he returned cheerfully from lunch an hour later, swinging that same door open and passing through, and began to stride back to his office as if the previous utterance had never left his mouth. I stopped him short of his office door and mustered incredulously, "Did you just *fire* me?"

With something approaching jubilance, he replied, "Absolutely! It would be a crime to keep you here." And so, it was settled. Though it was a tearful departure for me, and I lovingly handed over the keys and materials my replacement would need, I came to understand that the man saved my life. Roland ejected me from the comfort of complacency in a most loving act of generosity and kindness. He catalyzed an opening for me that set me on my path. Without him, I would have never left the job on my own. Roland saw something in me that I simply could not envision for myself. Before he uttered his prophetic statement, it had never occurred to me that I could go to college, let alone travel the world. I grew up with successful entrepreneurial parents who had not gone to college, and the farthest anyone I knew ventured to was Hawaii. By firing me, Roland opened the door for me to continue stepping on my path to purpose. We are still close today, and I stop in and see him all these decades later as I pass through Portland each summer.

It took me a few years to find my way to college, as I bumbled my way through various kinds of work after my time with Roland, trying to find my way (accounting, life insurance sales, advertising, and different other sales roles). But I never forgot Roland's words. Somewhere early in my twenties, I became more present to my purpose and called my mother to share in my joyous discovery. There was just one problem: She flatly denied its plausibility, which squashed me like a grape. In those early years, I couldn't articulate or accurately describe what I wanted to do and be in the world. I didn't quite have the language for it, and I lacked exposure to a closer version of my desired work's expression. I told her I wanted to deliver success seminars, an idea which surfaced from all the self-help reading I was doing (like *The Road Less Traveled* by Scott Peck) and those words to "go make something of myself," as Roland demanded. My mother laughed heartily at my idealized career path because I was so atrociously unsuccessful at the time. I have since come to understand that it wasn't that I wanted to help people be successful as much as it was; I wanted them to live fulfilling, authentic lives that brought them into their best version of being. Which, fast forward, is exactly what I do today. I knew by age twenty-two what I was intended to do—I could hear the calling then. But I doubted myself with the ferocity of my mother's well-intended words, which were meant to keep me safe and on a realistic professional path. It would take me another twenty-five years to fully come back around to that essential grounding into my passionate purpose.

I eventually began my college career at age twenty-four and found it a euphoric journey! Learning and developing my mind continued to be the jackpot at the end of the rainbow for me. Midway through earning my bachelor's degree, I elected to join my then-boyfriend, Arthur, on a move to Madrid, Spain. We spent six months there. Having studied French for two years in college, I built on it and learned Spanish quickly, and we saw much of Western Europe together. It was *just* the ticket for me—elevating me to being a citizen of the planet, feeling meaningfully connected to distinctly different cultures, and reveling in learning from and being lifted by people from various countries. I enrolled in a distance bachelor's program at the University of Iowa and kept up my studies while we gallivanted across Europe.

My Desperate Need to Matter

Then in August 1991, Arthur's company moved us to Rio de Janeiro, Brazil. I was 26 years old and enjoyed a life there that most people only dream about. Arthur and I had the luxury of a daily Portuguese tutor (Patricia) who came to our home to teach us the language and three full-time beloved service professionals: Dalva, our live-in housekeeper and cook, Tamandare, our chauffeur, and Manoel, our gardener. It was a charmed life, and these four Brazilians contributed so much joy, beauty, love, and insight to my life. Arthur spent his time as an executive working for a large oil company there, and we traveled together all over South America. I riveted my focus on completing my Bachelor's and Master's degrees. But still, the insistent and nagging feeling—of not being helpful, of not living up to my potential, only "taking" from life and not contributing to it—would not let me be.

During the last several months living in Rio, I poured myself into making progress on *some* count towards realizing my potential and trying to matter. Those words, "do something with yourself," kept haunting me. I taught English to Brazilian business men and carried on with my university career with work on a master's degree (having graduated with my bachelor's in early 1993), But in an attempt to quell this intense restlessness and hunger that still was not satisfied, I poured myself into ten additional courses that convened weekly. They were: Portuguese, Spanish, hang gliding, ballet dancing, jazz dancing, painting, singing, piano, windsurfing, and professional speaking (in Portuguese). Each of these courses had a different instructor, and Tamandare drove me to all of them. Still, amid that intense quest to learn and do something meaningful with my time, I could not conquer that terrible, empty feeling that I now understand through my logotherapy study and practice as an "existential vacuum." It was a lot like desperately clawing for the ripcord of a parachute but fruitlessly crashing to the ground, having never managed its release.

Though I so appreciated the lifestyle and incredible travel experiences afforded me, I felt that I was a flag in Arthur's wind and desperately wanted to fly my own. Countless times, Dalva found me crying in my office or room. I couldn't explain what was behind my tears because I didn't completely comprehend it myself. (She must have thought, this crazy, rich, white American has everything! How can she be sad?!) But my driving, urgent need to be of service, to make a difference in the world somehow, someway, kept gnawing all the way to my bones. The cry for purpose is persistent, if not terribly inconvenient. During that last year in Brazil, I tripped over a school called Fielding Graduate University in Santa Barbara, California, which was known for its offerings in Psychology, Human Development, and Organizational Development for working adults. I made a promise to myself that, someday, I would attend. Unbeknownst to me at the time, the divining rod was fully functioning, and I was finding my way back home to my soul, as I would begin to study at the school just six years later.

A few years after I came back to the States and settled into working in Portland and later Seattle, I experienced what I refer to as my "early-onset midlife crisis" in my early thirties. I had lived a beautiful and enriching life abroad and was back stateside selling various products and services to make a living. I was comfortable. I had a good life, a lovely home, a decent car, vacations, savings and friends. But the experience left me with, "Is *this* all there is?" At the time, I was selling train-car volumes of baking flour to bakeries and plants all over the Northwest US. It was an account management job that pulled heavily on my relationship skills, but it required few of my intellectual faculties. I wondered if I had navigated all over Western Europe and South America just to do this kind of work and live this simple life? It seemed at the time too improbable and quite empty. Indeed, there must be something *more.* My response to that gnawing feeling once again, desperately trying to get my attention was not to have an affair with anyone at work, buy a beautiful, new sports car, or quit my job and go to India to an Ashram to find prayer and solitude. No, my response was to pursue my PhD in Human Development at Fielding. Mind you, it cost about as much as any other "mid-life crisis" response, but I'm prone to believe I took the best path for me to cure the pain of my ongoing existential vacuum. I thought if I could develop into the person, the vessel that could deliver value to help someone or solve a problem, versus selling someone else's products or services, I might stand a chance at quieting that monster that kept raging inside me, fighting to be heard, seen and expressed.

It worked. That academic journey into the deeper recesses of my mind some twenty years ago was a redirection that also accelerated my path to purpose. It is profoundly essential to me to center myself in the intellectual, emotional, and spiritual realms. Selling someone else's product or service for the paycheck or commission just was not going to cut it for me. What I did not know at the time was that my message and approach to meaning and mattering was gathering steam inside me, and it was *that* that I so desperately needed to share and ultimately sell. I came to realize I simply could not resist the urge to change lives by awakening people to their passion, inspiration, and purpose.

People are My "Product," and Developing Them Is My Service

It was about the same time I started the PhD program at age thirty-four that I entered the Human Capital industry. It was late 1998 in Seattle, and the Information Technology world was booming. I quickly found sales work in the IT staffing industry and realized I'd hit another jackpot at work (after the restaurant business in high school). All those years of selling various products and services, and now I'd finally landed on my product—people! The divining rod was still clearly functioning and directing my life. Specifically, the playing field was people *and* work, the divine intersection for me. I had the great fortune of growing up with parents who were extremely hard-working entrepreneurs—first as farmers, then as restaurant owners. They modeled that work was a noble way of life that gave structure and made a difference in the lives of others. So, here I had "landed"—or better, "opted in," to that voice harkening from within that was summoning me ever closer to discovering and honoring my purpose. I worked hard on the dual path of studying for my PhD many evenings and weekends while working passionately during the week in this career. I reveled in understanding how the IT professionals I worked with chose their careers, what it meant to them to work in the field, and how they were connected to their sense of self (or not) through their endeavors. It was this fervent curiosity that led me to my dissertation research topic for my PhD to answer the question: "What is the relationship between meaning in work and identity for high-performing Information Technology managers?"

This inquiry into meaning in work and identity has been an ongoing, consuming focus since I took up the study for my dissertation in 2003. The resulting body of research yielded five modes of engagement. Performing this research and how it informed my sense of identity and path afforded a vast opening for me in further unfolding my purpose than I understood at the time. It all just felt "right." Though I shared the resulting five Modes of Engagement in many presentations for several years (and people got excited to gain new insights about themselves and their work), the results primarily lay fallow for many years as I did not have the conscious understanding of just what this research and its findings meant to my path to purpose or who I was becoming in service of it.

Another contributing factor along my path to realizing my purpose was my entry into teaching at the university level. As a consultant comfortable in my offerings and enjoying my clients, there was still something missing at age forty-six. It might not be a surprise to you, given what you know of me so far, but I missed the intense intellectual inquiry of my life-long academic career. The whisper kept calling, nudging ... *Come back.* I stumbled on a posting for Adjunct Professors at the University of Phoenix in 2011 and applied. Like the planets aligning, the next turn in the key lock went *kerplunk,* the door opened, and I began teaching that fall. The moment I entered the classroom, I *knew* I had come to a sacred place. You *know* when the work you are doing aligns with your purpose and soul. I loved helping my students, most of whom were first in their families to go to college and who were desperately trying to make something of themselves and be an example to their children so that they too could go to college and earn a degree. Here, they could *see* themselves as capable, competent adults who learned they could contribute meaningfully to the world and who would *earn* that degree. Little did I know that in addition to helping my students realize their potential, the giant inside me was ever awakening. Purpose was trying desperately to take the stage. My academic and intellectual interests could no longer be quelled. The dam had broken. Six months later, I embarked on a research project that I didn't know at the time would definitively anchor me in my purpose and place me squarely in the camps of meaning, purpose, and awakening.

By the spring of 2012, I applied for and received IRB (Institutional Research Board) approval from my alma mater Fielding Graduate University to interview 115 men and women, this time from twenty different industries (not just IT) between the ages of eighteen and eighty to ask the same question—how they experienced meaning in their work and what its relationship was to their identity. This time in the analysis of the data, I thought to look for not just a connection between meaning and identity (that yielded the five "directional" modes) but also the *kind* or *level* of meaning they primarily attributed to their work. With more than 2,800 pages of data to examine and code, it was a true labor of love to complete this post-doctoral research and derive, this time, Fifteen Modes of Engagement.

Nothing Holding Me Back—Time to Fly

Now, we have come back to where we started this story. Fast forward to 2014, when I delivered a workshop freshly derived from these Modes of Engagement to a Dallas client, went to India to present the research results at a business conference, got my work academically recognized and published, and was recruited by Voice America to host my radio show. If ever there was a moment when purpose speaks undeniably, it had to be when those worlds collided within a span of a few weeks. It took stepping in and saying "yes" to all those requests for participation that allowed me to cultivate my passions and for purpose to continue to emerge forcefully.

Strange chaos was about to descend on me, and when it did, I didn't know how to handle it. I'd "stepped into my shine," as I like to say. I knew my purpose and was trying to align my life and profession alongside it. But I felt a severe self-imposed limitation as I worked to integrate this new understanding of who I was in the world with my actual existence as a married woman, mother, and business owner. I fell into a working depression as I grappled with this desire to combine these disparate worlds. The decision was made for me when in December 2015, my nearly sixteen-year marriage ended with my husband saying, "I don't want to be married to you anymore." In those last few months of 2015, I was still functional—going to work every day and getting things done, but I was in a strange auto-pilot fog, disconnected from the world and even my close friends. I was a member of "the walking dead" and was in total need of rescue. I knew I was not living up to my potential or honoring my purpose, and I vehemently *hated* myself for it. What an incredible cop-out.

So when I started down the divorce trail in January 2016, the experience proved to be a catalyzing force that inspired enormous energy, zapping me out of this stage of my life and actively working to transform my heart, mind, body, and spirit toward life-giving passion, inspiration, and purpose.

I cast myself into a big open space of new possibilities where there was all manner of room to reinvent and recreate myself. That's precisely what I did. I dropped fifteen pounds in the first two months of separation, which brought me to the weight I was when I met my husband before marriage. That reduced weight and size have been my constant through to now, five years later—this re-sizing and claiming a life anchored in purpose registered as a recalibration of my entire being. I stepped into life and danced with it in a way I hadn't done for several of the last years of marriage. I *savored* people again and the unique spark they brought to the world around me. I *saw* them and was moved by the constant beauty of people and interactions I witnessed everywhere I went. I showed up differently, and people noticed my light and sought me out. I became playful again, like a curious, precocious child. I saw the world differently—as a vast, open playing field, one in which I could create a life I so wanted for myself.

The self-expression and sense of agency I was exercising were incredibly fulfilling. It was like being fully aware of my place in the universe and dancing with the stars, all at the same time. Out of the pain and insecurity about my future emerged a beautiful opening into what was possible. I had not been much of a spiritual or religious person prior, though I did have an epiphany at age six that left me knowing on some level that I was connected to the universe. I felt that I was entering a new space, *just for me*. It was almost as if I was destined to have the experience of being married, having my daughter, and the life that came with it—and then to move on and keep growing and evolving. I felt I had been given a second chance at life: to create the one I wanted to live and which would make me into the person I so badly wanted to become but so far hadn't yet managed to realize.

An Important Stabilizing Force and Stepping Stone

As I considered how to continue shaping my profession in my new single life, I knew I wanted much more for myself than what I had created up to this point as a self-employed consultant. I elected to join a management consulting firm specializing in breakthrough and transformation in May 2016. I fell in love with the culture of the firm and the work we did. We were strongly linked as a small firm and embraced appreciating each other while helping leaders in Fortune 500 companies transform themselves and their teams to a higher level of breakthrough performance. I thoroughly believe I was *supposed* to come to this firm. Their culture of ongoing individual development and transformation helped me realize for myself more of who I was at my core and the life I was no longer willing to let slip past me. I loved working for this firm for more than two years. I felt myself becoming more assertive, more grounded while simultaneously soaring into a more prominent possibility for my own life than I had ever imagined in previous years.

As my work on the *Working on Purpose* radio show continued, the topical evolution expressed the unfoldment of my consciousness as my focus progressed from passion, inspiration, purpose, leadership, and conscious capitalism. A steady undercurrent of propelling urgency to continue the ascent toward higher consciousness and contribution pervaded me. With it came the accompanying need to contribute my highest and best talents in service of the purpose that kept growing in its clarity. In August 2017, I asked Shawn Anderson (whom I met as a guest on my radio program) if he would consider coaching me, as I knew I needed help preparing myself to fully pursue the purpose that was blasting like a volcano inside me. Ten months later, with weekly calls, it happened. I set sail definitively on my path to purpose in July 2018, when I separated from the consulting firm and went back to my management consulting practice, this time squarely aimed at meaning and purpose. I had finally stepped into and claimed my purpose. Today, I stand as "the Anti-Undertaker," helping people, leaders, and organizations to awaken from the dead and pursue passion, inspiration, and purpose across their lives. As Nick Craig says in his book called *Leading from Purpose: Clarity and the Confidence to Act When it Matters Most*, I had finally come "home."

Once I decided to return to working for myself again, a whole new vista of possibility opened for me. It helped that I'd written my eulogy (as a developmental exercise within the management consultancy firm) and could easily see my life would not be limited to working for another organization without expressing my purpose. Standing in that future and greatly fueled by "half-time" energy at age fifty-three, "Half time" is a concept I learned from Dan Pink in his book, *When: The Scientific Secrets of Perfect Timing,* where he explains his research into football games where the team slightly behind at half time often summon the energy to go on and win the game. Suddenly, it all made sense to me: I was at half time of my own life, but instead of slightly behind, I felt woefully behind where I wanted to be. Realizing this half-time posture proved a tremendous motivational force for me that would propel me through many obstacles, setbacks, heartbreaks, and near misses to launch this new, more refined expression of purpose in my business.

I threw myself into fulfilling a triple promise to be completed by December 2018. First, I set out to draft the *Purpose Ignited* book. Second, I set out to develop my own leadership program, which would reflect a sweep of best practices in leadership, inspiration, and purpose and take into account what I'd learned by conducting my two research initiatives in meaning and identity. I also layered into the program what I'd learned by hosting the Working on Purpose program during those years. The result became *Vitally Inspired: Living and Leading from Purpose* program, authored in late 2018 and launched with a small public, year-long cohort in January 2019, and now customized by the module for delivery inside organizations. Finally, the third promise I kept to myself in 2018 was to launch the non-profit Purpose on Fire, which exists to help people who have discovered their purpose meaningfully launch it into the world. My purpose was officially unleashed and working in the world. I had found a way to operationalize it to make a living. It is extraordinary how the energy, courage, and confidence overtakes us when we discover and release our purpose.

Death Infuses Life with Urgency to Live with Purpose

As I launched fully into living my purpose, a new turn of events would sharpen my focus when my parents passed away, twenty-eight days apart, in January 2019. The experience of losing them both so quickly, creating and delivering both their eulogies, and helping handle their affairs, forced me to fully comprehend that death is a part of life and gives us a particular urgency to fulfill our life's purpose. The loss of my parents as the oldest child felt like a swift "kick upstairs" in the family hierarchy, and I felt an even greater sense of time screaming for the finish. This only furthered my resolve to live with passion, work on purpose, and lead with inspiration.

I continued honing my purpose-led leadership and meaning-infused culture consulting that year. When COVID-19 hit in March 2020, and much of my speaking and program work came to a halt, I used the time to channel my energy inward and get the *Purpose Ignited* book finished (it released in November 2020). I also launched Gusto, Now!, an e-learning platform that hosts leadership and professional development courses in English, Spanish, and Portuguese. This platform finally honors and celebrates the languages and cultures that poured passion, expression, and meaning into me all those years ago in Spain and Brazil, as my courses on it are delivered in English, Spanish and Portuguese. So, I've continued to hone my craft, honor my purpose, and persevere mightily to live it. As my expression in purpose continues, I am now being called to and exuberantly embrace helping companies discover and articulate their purpose. I teach business leaders to develop meaning-infused cultures where people thrive, create inspirational leaders who help people discover their greatness and elevate business to serve at the highest cause.

In the last few years, as I speak to audiences, I often pose the questions, "What are you passionate about?" and "What's your purpose?" People begin to sense their existential vacuum and a desire to create a life of intention with passion and purpose when they quietly realize they don't have an answer to my questions. At that point, the awakening has started. When I work with participants in my Vitally Inspired program or the Grab Your Gusto: Vital Well-Being from the Inside Out subscription learning series offered to companies and their employees, participants report becoming "turned on, from the inside out." They brim with enthusiasm at the life and work they can now envision living. Relationships improve, goals become bigger, energy increases, lives are touched, and legacies are made. It's truly glorious to behold—watching people's very molecules change before my eyes—and fills me with gratitude and an abundant desire to continue my service to the world. So many people need awakening, energized, to discover they really matter and the world *needs* them. I'll never be *done,* never fully retired. I love being an entrepreneur, creating products and services that awaken people to their passion and purpose and help unleash their potential. What a blissful way to exist!

My goal is to touch one million lives by combining my radio show listeners, book readers, and programs participants—to ignite passion and purpose so its vitalizing force ripples through families, communities, and companies across the world. This is a small drop in the bucket, when you consider the world population is 7.9 billion, but I hope it's a catalyzing wave. At a time when the Gallup Organization reports that 85 percent of the global workforce is not meaningfully engaged in their occupation, a sea change is necessary. When people are fulfilled in their work, which accounts for over a third of their lives, the feeling of abundance and gratitude washes over all their relationships and interactions. Fulfilled people are more likely to volunteer their time and energy back into their communities, brimming with gratitude for their abundance. I am convinced we can collectively address many of the problems the world faces today—opioid overuse, depression, suicide—when more people are working from purpose and turned on by their lives through unleashed passion.

My Advice to Pursuing Your Purpose

I'll close with three pieces of advice that I hope will help you more expediently *listen for*, hear, and honor your calling:

1. Listen like your life depends on it (because it literally does). Listen to that steady, persistent, yet usually quiet voice trying desperately to get your ear and direct you to your purpose. I knew in high school I should study psychology (and ultimately later did) and realized in my early twenties just what I should pursue in a calling. Still, I didn't persist in listening and refining the message that was delivered to me. I thought it was telling me to facilitate success seminars when it was telling me to help people discover their passion and purpose and create meaningful lives for themselves. I let my dear friend and mother dissuade me from my path—which is not on her but rather me for not listening intently enough and trusting my wise inner voice.

2. Your path to purpose will continue to unfold. It's like stepping along a well–laid out path. Keep following it. Close your eyes and let your purpose-infused feet do the walking. They will keep leading you to a deeper forest of fulfillment as you persist mightily to live your purpose and find more ways to serve from it.

3. Enroll and accept the help of people along the way. Purpose is not for the faint of heart, and you will need reinforcements and encouragement, just like I did when I reached out for my coach, Shawn Anderson. I wouldn't be who I am without him or Roland who tossed me out of the nest so long ago. Keep reaching, challenging yourself to realize *more* of the magnificent person you are that aches to make the difference worthy of your one, precious life.

Dr. Alise Cortez is the Chief Purpose Officer at Alise Cortez and Associates (management consulting) and Chief Ignition Officer at Gusto, Now!

(a multilingual e-learning platform). She is also an inspirational speaker, social scientist, author, and host of the Working on Purpose radio show. Having developed her expertise within the human capital / organizational excellence industry over the last twenty years, she is focused on helping companies, leaders, and individuals across the globe to live with "gusto" and more meaningfully and purposely experience their work to achieve greater fulfillment and well-being, more impactful results, and work-life harmony.

Alise earned a PhD in Human Development, focusing her dissertation research on the relationship between meaning in work and identity, and later greatly expanded the inquiry to yield fifteen "Modes of Engagement." She has served as a leader in several non-profit organizations in Dallas and knows the value of being a servant leader. She draws her language acumen from her previous residence in Spain and Brazil, enabling her to deliver programs and consulting in English (native) and Spanish, and Portuguese.

Today, Dr. Cortez is focused on enabling organizations to lead from purpose and create cultures of meaning that inspire impassioned performance, meaningful engagement, and fulfillment while encouraging a devoted tenure within the organization. She has helped develop and transform thousands of managers and executives in their leadership along the way. She also helps companies visioneer for a purposeful future by facilitating meaningful exchange among all stakeholders for an integrated and dynamic strategic future. For individuals, Dr. Cortez facilitates a global online community and various retreats to enable people hungry for a more meaningful and purposeful life to create it for themselves. Find her at www.alisecortez.com

Transformed Through Adversity

Taking Up Space, Claiming Power, and Playing Big

By Thear Suzuki
United States (via Cambodia)

On April 17, 1975, the Cambodian Communist Regime led by Pol Pot, also known as the Khmer Rouge (KR), pounded on our door and demanded that we leave our home immediately. They told us the Americans were bombing the city, so everyone had to leave. I was two years old when the KR uprooted our lives.

The Khmer Rouge wanted to turn the country back to an agrarian society, a land of farmers, free of the evils of the Western world. They drove millions of people out of the city, into the countryside and forced labor camps. They persecuted the educated—doctors, lawyers, business owners, military, and police. Christians, Buddhists, and Muslims were also targeted. Schools were outlawed. The KR turned neighbors and family members against one another, and children were turned against their parents. During the four years of their rule, an estimated two million Cambodian citizens—at least 25 percent of the population—died of starvation, disease, and execution.

We spent six years surviving war, genocide, and refugee camps.

Life in Phnom Penh and Labor Camps

Before the Khmer Rouge takeover, my family lived in a village near Phnom Penh, Cambodia's capital. There were fears of violence in the conflict between Cambodia's government and the Khmer Rouge. When they approached Phnom Penh with our village in their path, we decided to relocate to the city. My father ran a small pharmacy. My mother stayed home and took care of five children, two boys and three girls.

When the KR entered Phnom Penh on April 17, 1975, there wasn't panic. Many of us believed it would be good for the country if they won the civil war and ended it. It was difficult in Phnom Penh at the time—there was crime, inflation, and looting. We wanted the KR to come in and bring peace and order.

The KR entered the city in military tanks, waving white flags and shouting, "*We now have peace, no more fighting.*" Shortly after, they changed their tone on the radio, saying, "*No! We are here because we won. We have victory through battle.*" The KR started telling everyone that the Americans would bomb the city, so everyone needed to leave immediately. Still, we could return in three days after they repaired the city. Everyone had to leave the city.

Our family was together when they came to our house. We took only the essentials that we could carry—rice, clothes, mosquito nets, blankets, medicines, pots, pans, cups, and spoons. Then, we joined the mass exodus out of the city. Parents had to hang on to their children's hands, so they wouldn't get lost in the crowd. Even very ill people in the hospitals were forced out. We were less than ten kilometers into the walk when we started seeing people dying. It was like a funeral procession—everyone was walking and crying. Some women gave birth on the dirt road and left their newborn babies. The horrors of the new world were immediate.

Day after day, we walked until dark. Then, we would eat and rest alongside the dirt road. We ate dried fish and rice. My mother cooked what she could when we stopped. And all along the way, the KR would take away our belongings. After a week of walking, we learned that Cambodian money no longer had value. The KR told us that there would be no rich or poor; everyone would be equal in the new Cambodia they were creating.

Therefore, money was not needed. People were literally using it as toilet paper. Every morning at 6:00 a.m., the KR would fire their guns, and we would begin walking again. We had no idea where we were heading. We didn't know what was going on. We just followed the crowd.

After twenty days of walking, we arrived at our first destination, a small farming village called *"Sdoktal."* The villagers agreed to take fifteen new families. Our family was told to stay there, and the other families were sent to other villages. We built our own shelters out of straw and palm leaves on arrival, and everyone had different jobs. The men were assigned to chopping wood, digging irrigation, and planting tobacco. Women grew potatoes and worked in the rice fields, and the older children tended to farm animals.

Four months later, 5,000 families, including ours, were transported on a train to Battambang with vague instructions to find a lake called "Bung Pale." My father and siblings eventually found the lake area, ten kilometers away—an open field surrounded by pure jungle - while my mother and I waited for them to come back for us later. This was a terrifying time for our family because my mother was very ill and needed my father to carry her when we moved. In this lake area, we built our shelter out of tree branches and leaves. For twelve days, there was no food provided. We were told there was porridge in a nearby village where we could go to barter for food. They used this tactic to get our belongings, such as clothes, in exchange for the food we needed. They had us do some minor labor around the lake, which was our only water source but was also getting filled with waste and mosquitos. Within four months, 3,000 families died of starvation and disease.

The remaining 2,000 families were then divided into three different villages. My family was taken to a village called *"Gok-a-ka."* My father, mother, and older siblings walked to other labor camps several kilometers away and often stayed there for two to three months at a time. At the labor camps, they slept on hammocks in the jungle and ate rationed meals consisting of a few rice grains in water. Many died of hunger. Because I was too young to work, I stayed in the village with my maternal grandmother, who also passed away during this period. We stayed in this village for three more years until the South Vietnamese invaded and drove the KR out of power and back into the jungle.

The three days we were supposed to be out of the city turned into four years in labor camps. There were no hospitals for the sick. People were tortured and executed out of suspicion of betraying the KR and for stealing food. There were many stories of cannibalism—people doing the unimaginable to fill their empty stomachs. We had no control over our lives as millions of people around us perished. But during this time, my parents never lost hope. They believed that as long as the earth rotates, this atrocity cannot last forever. They were determined to help their five children survive.

Liberation and Refugee Camps

When the South Vietnamese invaded and defeated the KR in 1979, we were liberated. At the time, my second oldest brother was separated from the family because he had been at a youth labor camp far away from the rest of us. There were still groups of armed KR roaming the country. At this point, my parents had a critical decision to make. We could either go directly to the Thai border to seek refuge or risk a journey to Phnom Penh, hoping that my brother would also decide to do the same thing. We decided to look for him.

It took us six months to get through the jungle to Phnom Penh. We traveled when there was sunlight and rested when it got dark. We looked for food wherever we could in abandoned villages. Shortly after arriving in Phnom Penh, we miraculously found my brother. Someone who knew him told my parents they had spotted him. Separated from the rest of the family, my brother joined other families making the same journey to Phnom Penh by helping their younger children. His journey included being shot at and the KR soldiers using him and others as human shields. It is a miracle that my brother survived, and our family reunited.

A little over a month later, my parents decided to escape Cambodia and seek refuge in Thailand. There was so much uncertainty about our future in Thailand, but they also had no confidence that Cambodia would be a safe country again.

In the Thai refugee camps, many relief organizations came to our aid. There, my family heard the Good News for the first time and converted to Christianity. My father had a vision of a man coming out of a fish's mouth. He didn't know what that meant until one of the volunteers pulled out the Bible and showed him the story of Jonah. After hearing the story, my father felt a calling to share the Word of God with others. From that moment on, my father committed his life to love Jesus and sharing the Good News with others.

Life was safe in the refugee camps. We had shelter, had food, went to church, and awaited sponsorship to other parts of the world. At six or seven years old, I started learning to read Cambodian for the first time through Bible stories and hymns. This would be my first experience of a semi-normal life. Strengthening my faith and having God as my savior and friend gave me peace and hope.

Starting School in America – Help from Strangers

After living in refugee camps for two years, my family was sponsored by the US Catholic Conference, Migration & Refugee Services office in Dallas, Texas. We were relocated and provided with housing and three months of food stamps. With this assistance and our newfound freedom, my parents worked and made a living to provide for us. My father was a janitor for twenty-five years and became an ordained minister in the process. My mother cleaned hotels and worked in a cafeteria. Within four years of coming to America, they had enough money to put a down payment on a small home in East Dallas. My parents provided a stable and loving home. They impressed upon us the importance of studying hard and getting a good education. My parents are my role models for perseverance, resourcefulness, resilience, and courage.

At eight years old, I started school for the very first time in the third grade. With the influx of newly arrived refugee students and their parents who didn't speak English, the school didn't know what to do with us. The principal called a meeting with the teachers, and at this meeting, Mr. John Gallagher raised his hand and volunteered to teach us English. Mr. Gallagher flunked me after my first year and made me repeat the third grade, but he made up for it in many ways. Mr. Gallagher and his father helped my family and many other families rebuild our lives. They bought us a Cambodian/English dictionary, took us to the dentist, and helped my parents do their taxes. During my senior year in high school, Mr. Gallagher nominated me for a scholarship at SMU. He wrote a letter to the university's president at the time advocating for me. Mr. Gallagher is not a famous or rich man with positional power or influence. He was an ordinary citizen who saw families struggling and made the altruistic choice to help them. He extended a hand and lifted up those who did not have the means to do so themselves. In doing so, he made a tremendous difference in countless lives, including mine. Mr. Gallagher opened doors of opportunity for me without expecting anything in return.

Ron Cowart, a Dallas police officer who patrolled my neighborhood, and his wife Melinda were two more people who made a difference in my life. Seeing the struggles and difficulties the refugee families were having, they created a Crime Prevention Exploring Post to help teach Southeast Asian teenagers to keep our neighborhood safe, stay out of gangs, and study for our US citizenship exam. I became a US citizen during my senior year in high school through this program, which opened me to many opportunities.

The examples of Mr. Gallagher, Ron, and Melinda have taught me two important lessons in life. *First*, they helped me see that ordinary people in our communities can make a difference in other people's lives, making the American dream possible. Second, I can play a role in helping others as well.

Early Leadership – Taking Up Space

My rocky start in life meant I had opportunities to stretch and exposure to experiences that other kids did not. Because my parents were focused on making a living and providing food and shelter for us, I learned independence early. Coming to a new country, not speaking the language, not understanding how things worked, and not knowing anyone was disorienting and scary. My older siblings were also trying to figure things out for themselves. In elementary school, I signed my own report cards and field trip permission forms. As I learned a little bit of English, I started translating for my parents at parent/teacher conferences. These early experiences were critical in teaching me both independence and how to ask for help.

In middle school, I was embarrassed to be in regular classes while my friends were in pre-honors. Upon encouragement from a friend, I asked my counselor to change my schedule to pre-honors. Getting on this pre-honors track altered the trajectory of my academic journey. I wanted to join the Student Council in high school, but you had to campaign and get people to vote for you. Though I didn't know if anyone would vote for me, my advisor encouraged me to go for it anyway. I made it in because not enough people ran. In 1990, when the Key Club (a boys-only student club) was opened to girls for the first time, I joined and became president the following year. I organized community service projects, ran meetings, and interacted with senior leaders with the Kiwanis Club. I also served as Student Body President of my high school. I had the opportunity to participate in student leadership conferences. In college at SMU, I studied Electrical Engineering with a Biomedical Engineering Specialization, worked part-time, and joined student leadership

organizations. I enjoyed learning, leading, and organizing student programs and community service projects. Through these opportunities, I
practiced communication and leadership skills. I learned how to bring
people together, resolve conflicts, and raise funds.

Though I had leadership experience from school when I started my
career as a technology consultant, I kept my head down and focused on
doing my individual work. I felt lucky to have a good-paying job, and I did
everything I could to fit in. While I participated in leadership activities
like joining the Diversity Council, I did not speak up much in meetings. I
was unsure of myself.

A few years into working, I was fortunate to meet a colleague who
became my mentor and sponsor. At one particular meeting, this mentor
strongly encouraged me to ask a question. I didn't have one, and I didn't
want to ask a question, but he was persistent. I could feel my body getting hot as my anxiety rose, but since he refused to give up, I had to
work through my fears and managed to ask a question. Fortunately, the
question I asked resonated with others in the meeting as well. After this
experience, I made a personal commitment to engage more in meetings, whether with five or 500 people, by asking a relevant question or
making a thoughtful comment.

I had set my intention to use my voice and to take up more space. Through
this experience, I also learned the importance of listening to a mentor
who can give me feedback and help guide me in the right direction.

Claiming Personal Power

Growing up and even well into adulthood, I lived life without a plan and
went with the flow. I worked hard on the things I got involved with,
but I did not think much about living a purposeful life. When met with
challenges, I just pushed through. At times, I felt incapable, small and
insignificant, just trying to keep up. I was not confident and didn't think

I had much to offer. I was trapped in a victim's mindset, a negative narrative about who I was and what I could achieve. I lacked the belief in my potential.

My husband and I married five years into our careers, and we gave birth to four sons in eight years. Though I was progressing well career-wise, I was neglecting other parts of my life. While I espoused strong family values and wanted to give back to my community, my actions didn't match my values. I spent the majority of my waking hours and attention on work. I neglected my well-being, took my loved ones for granted, ignored my community, and was not present with my children.

I was fortunate to have the opportunity to participate in a year-long women's leadership development program called Power of Self (POS), designed and delivered by Marsha Clark & Associates. I learned the importance of being self-aware, showing up for others, and my role in an organization. I gained clarity surrounding my values and what I needed to do to live and act with greater intention and aligning with my values. I gained the tools I needed to start to change the way I was living. This developmental experience transformed my mindset into one that is focused on growth and making improvements.

I decided to change the way I lived and make healthier work and life choices. An executive coach led me through a process of envisioning what achieving my potential would look like. I worked through a vision of my best self, which included three elements: a healthy lifestyle, an engaged mother and wife, and an impactful leader. To improve my personal health, I focused on getting more and higher quality sleep and regular exercise. To become a more engaged mother and wife, I made deliberate and specific choices about spending quality time with each family member. To be a more impactful leader, I made time to mentor others, develop leadership programs to lift up women in corporate America. I made time to engage on causes I cared about, at my firm and in the community.

I worked hard to change my many years of bad habits. I consulted with a coach, sought out mentors, read books, and listened to TEDTalks about systematically developing healthy habits. I focused on one habit at a time. Within a few years, I was able to make steady, sustainable progress, from four to five hours of sleep a night to six to seven hours, from no exercise to running half-marathons, and from no family vacations to regular time with family and one-on-one time with each of my four sons. The books and talks that were most helpful for me included:

- *The art of being yourself by Caroline McHugh (TEDTalk)*
- *Essentialism: The Disciplined Pursuit of Less* by Greg McKeown
- *The Power of Habit – Why We Do What We Do in Life and Business* by Charles Duhigg
- *Why do we sleep?* by Russell Foster (TEDTalk)
- *How great leaders inspire action* by Simon Sinek (TEDTalk)
- *Playing Big: Find Your Voice, Your Mission, Your Message* by Tara Mohr (YouTube)

I found a way to integrate my community work with the business world. For example, when I created a leadership program to connect and develop female executives, I collaborated with a not-for-profit organization on the effort. The partnership's success led to an invitation to join their board. The CEO of the organization became my mentor and champion. This allowed me to build more meaningful connections with my clients who cared about giving back to our community. I realized that my community work did not have to be separate from my job. Community engagement became my "golf course," where I can partner with and build trust-based relationships with clients.

My firm's purpose is Build a Better Working World. We exist to transform industries, grow businesses, and improve communities. We believe building a better working world is where economic growth is both sustainable and inclusive. Our purpose provides the context and meaning to the work we do every day.

My firm's purpose aligns with my values of inclusion. I engaged with my firm's diversity, equity, and inclusion efforts. I teamed with others to develop a leadership development program to accelerate the advancement of women. This gave me a way to contribute to the firm's strategic efforts. In the process, my professional career shifted and expanded from technology consulting to business strategy and operations to a role as a talent leader and to now serving clients as a global service client partner.

While I'm still progressing and constantly improving, I now have greater confidence to claim my personal power by living and working with greater intention and purpose.

Playing Big

As a purpose-driven organization, my firm provided resources for each of us to discover our 'why' and develop a personal purpose statement. I was asked to reflect back to my younger self and describe when I was happiest and at my best. As I shared the memories, the words I often used were captured: action, courage, impact, and leadership. After many iterations, my personal purpose surfaced, *"To inspire courageous actions in others so they can lead more impactful lives."* Courage is the ability to work through fears rather than the absence of fear. Courage is something that I wanted for myself and for others. Having a clear purpose statement made it easier to share my story with others. I realized it was why inspiring, courageous actions were vital to me. As I gained more opportunities to share my story, I learned to accept my uniqueness, show up authentically and began to see it as a strength rather than a liability.

Before realizing my purpose, I was living a life that lacked intentionality and power. I was worried about not being good enough and compared myself to others. I was afraid to ask for what I wanted and needed. I played it safe and small. But equipped with my 'why,' I am living more courageously, owning my personal power, and doing my best to help improve the lives of others. Being clear on my individual purpose has made me more resilient and has kept me on the right path, to focus on the things that matter most. Living on purpose has made me more confident to take on new challenges and believing that I can figure them out. Living in my purpose has enhanced my well-being, elevated my career, and increased my contribution to the world, inspiring me to play bigger. Overall, I feel more fulfilled in both my personal and work life.

Encouragement

I would like to offer three suggestions for those who want to live with more intention and purpose. *First*, get clear on your values and what matters to you. Clarity will give you a north star to work towards. Develop your personal purpose statement, make it visible, and share it with others to keep it front and center. Share your story. *Second*, systematically take steps to develop new habits that will serve your purpose. Seek the help of a coach who can recommend strategies and tactics that will work for you. Participate in a leadership development program or workshop that will help you understand yourself better and be in a community with others to give and get support. *Third*, collaborate with others to move your purpose, vision, and mission forward. We are social beings, and we can go further when we work together.

Let me end with a brief story. For many years, Nurse Bonnie Ware worked in palliative care. Her patients were those who had gone home to die. When Bonnie asked her patients about any regrets they had or anything they would do differently, the most common answer was, *"I wish I'd dared to live a life true to myself, not the life others expected of me."* I envision a world where all people can feel safe and free to be themselves and use their talents and gifts to help others.

Wherever you are right now, I hope you will decide to take that next step to discover your personal purpose and live a life true to yourself. It is a life worth living.

Thear inspires courageous actions in others so they can lead more impactful lives. She is Cambodian-born, ethnically Chinese and Vietnamese, married to a 4th generation Japanese American, and a mother to four boys. Thear is a connector, an advocate for equity. She enjoys spending time with people to help make the world a better place for everyone.

Thear is a Global Client Service Partner at Ernst & Young with twenty-five years of professional services experience. She serves on the Americas Inclusiveness Advisory Council. She champions leadership development programs that build inclusive, innovative, and courageous leaders for the 21st century.

Thear is a 2019 Presidential Leadership Scholar and most recently recognized as one of the most influential business leaders in North Texas 2021 by DCEO. Thear is active with non-profit organizations that develop leaders and lift others up, including the Texas Women's Foundation, the Dallas Holocaust & Human Rights Museum, the Boy Scouts of America, the SMU Lyle School of Engineering, and the National Asian Pacific American Chamber of Commerce & Entrepreneurship. Thear is featured in President George W Bush's book, Out of Many, One – Portraits of America's Immigrants. Thear can be contacted via LinkedIn: https://www.linkedin.com/in/thear-sy-suzuki/

Fate—Not a Threat, But an Opportunity

By Nadalette La Fonta
France

After achieving and failing, I've committed myself to stand up publicly with authenticity to share the lessons I've learned. My work is rooted in my experiences and expertise and my vision and passion for life. I've chosen to transform from being powerful but hidden to be a role model as a woman, a mother, a sister, and a friend who is eager to contribute and demonstrate by example that every person should have a dream and never give up on it.

Sharing and serving my dream is a huge responsibility, as my words echo for so many people in different aspects of their life. My words are helping them to search for their authenticity, escape their limits and the barriers they have set for themselves. My words drive them to love themselves, have self-respect, care more for their balance, body, health, and lifestyle. I hope that in doing so, they will be happier and then become more caring for others.

In 2014, I became disabled with an 80 percent paraplegic body, which in my daily life still means having to deal with many physical difficulties and chronic pain. It's a complicated situation. If you look at me today, you would think I have an "invisible handicap" because, on the outside, it seems as if I have nothing more than "a broken ankle limp." It is challenging to live with, to be frank.

Why am I telling you my story? Because I want to show you that nothing is impossible. Suppose you give yourself the necessary attention and intention to make it happen.

Wonder Woman Was Born

My name is Nadalette, and I am a mother of three wonderful daughters. I am French, but I had a very active international professional career that lasted over forty years. It may not have been too different from yours. I am one of you. Today, I am a writer, and my first book is the story of a major accident in my life that will likely resonate with some of you. I will begin by sharing some insights:

Becoming a writer had been my dream since my youth, but I never dared to do it because of the fear of succeeding or failing or maybe even family loyalty.

Despite not realizing my dream then, I had a very privileged life as a woman.

My life began in a not so kind way. Even though my family was wealthy, there was a substantial lack of love and care in my family. After being psychologically neglected during my childhood, I decided to become a strong, active, and powerful woman. Whatever happened in the past, I came to terms with it, and I can honestly say I have no regrets. I fully assume who I was back then.

"My beliefs" have been my savior since the beginning and at crucial moments of my life. They have helped me survive. I will come back later to the importance of beliefs in our life. Childhood is the first thing that shapes us, and the beliefs that helped me get through my toxic environment were:

You can't hurt me. I feel no pain. Be quiet. Don't show my feelings. I am Wonderwoman.

Does this kind of thinking resonate?

This is a Good Life—But Is It "Yours"?

When I left home at 18, I thought that money was the key to being free, and from the time I was twenty, I worked as hard as I could to earn an excellent living and climb the corporate ladder at Renault, Apple, Thomson, IBM among others. I felt proud to feel financially secure, especially in the money-making decades of the '80s and '90s, even if that meant sacrificing some of my innermost desires and not being true to my personality. Amongst them, I put becoming a writer to the side, which I thought would not financially allow me to live "with style."

I was a "good girl," doing everything perfectly at work, like a mini-Terminator who had no time for a health problem, including one which would have disappeared if it had been managed properly during childhood—if only I had been part of a typical family. Unfortunately, that was not the case for me. As an adult, I was diagnosed with scoliosis, a twisted spine, which I never admitted was a serious issue. Nothing could stop me or my hyperactive life and drive for success.

I had no time for this health challenge. I had no time for myself. There was no time to be anybody but Miss Perfect, who was tough on herself and others and fun, lively, and speedy. I had a hectic career—communication, marketing, talent management—and a social life that included traveling, partying. I was living life to the fullest. All my body could do was try to keep going, keep up with my frantic pace.

By the time I turned fourty, I was in my second marriage, had given birth to three gorgeous daughters, had a busy professional life, had a busy personal life with many friends and dinner parties. It seemed like I always had one foot on a plane with a suitcase in my hand as I was juggling being highly proactive in a women's network. I loved being totally in charge at home and work.

I had no limits. I multitasked everything by choice, always running at a lightning-speed pace. I thought I was invincible! I had a great professional life—as I thought I wanted

Just to give you a picture: for many years, I was a manager leading teams in diverse projects in complex environments. My work required advising senior management within international missions, in communications roles, at several major companies (Renault, Apple Computer, McDonnell Douglas, and Thomson CSF). In 1996, I joined IBM Europe, where I held positions in communication and marketing before heading up a special talent management unit for France and international operations.

I was—and am still—keenly interested in the management of talent, certified Coach Corporate CoachU, Gestalt, and NLP(neuro-linguistic language programming). I focused on gaining a better understanding of change processes and ways to support individuals and international teams in my functions, coaching and mentoring many women within the company as well as in multi-company initiatives. I also worked as a volunteer.

I already cared greatly about diversity and inclusion, ready to do more personally, joining IBM's Corporate Service Corps program to facilitate the activities of volunteer teams over the world, and then heading off to India myself to work with non-governmental organizations (NGOs).

As a board member and vice president for five years of the Professional Women's Network Paris (PWNParis), I actively supported the creation and development of women's networks and mentoring programs. I participated with the Club du XXIème Siècle in the creation of the first mentoring program for women from diverse, multicultural backgrounds who must contend with a double glass ceiling.

My life sounded good, but I had an inner voice whispering, *yes, it's a good life, but it isn't YOUR life.*

Fate Steps In

I was in my comfort zone, where everything seemed calm from the out-side, but things were going deadly wrong in reality. Because when you are in your comfort zone for too long, you believe everything is a given and that you don't need to question yourself. I have referred to it as the anesthesia of success.

It's usually at that exact moment that fate or destiny makes you understand that if you don't stop to listen or make a change in your life—life will make you listen!

As I said before, I believed that I was a Wonderwoman and could push myself to my limit. That served me well at the beginning of my life, but then that lifestyle quickly enslaved me. By 2014, that belief was on the verge of damaging me forever. My body was fed up with not being heard and respected, and this time, it was going to make me listen and take notice.

My scoliosis—that I had neglected since adolescence—had now worsened dramatically. My spine was now bent to a 73 percent curve because I had never looked after it. I was in total denial and had become so good at hiding it that even most of my close friends, relatives, and even my family never noticed how destroyed my body was or how destroyed I was. In 2014, I was at the end of my rope, and it was entirely my own fault.

I was physically burned out and forced to admit that if I did not want to become a hunchbacked old lady—moving around with difficulty, all bent over with my eyes facing the floor—I would have to accept a challeng-ing operation called an arthrodesis of the whole spine. The doctors had recommended I get this done for over ten years, and the time had come!

This ten-hour back surgery consisted of straightening my whole spine between two titanium rods from my neck to my sacrum. It would all be held together with metal screws. After that, the doctor said I would be as straight as a pole—a gory version of a Madonna corset!

But Then I Went to Jail

I was supposed to be back on my feet, living an everyday life two months later. Except that on October 15, 2014, the surgery did not go well. My spinal cord had been damaged. When they woke me up, the doctors told me I would never walk again, and I was now paraplegic. They told me I had no chance of recovery.

I believed that my life was destroyed. It was like waking up from a nightmare, a state so basic, sensitive, frightening, and unreal. I described the experience in my book *Le Roseau Penchant* (*The Bending Reed,* which bends but never breaks).

I went from being in the driving seat of my own life to now becoming a mere spectator. From independent to totally dependent. From hyperactive to not being able to write or even read—jailed in a hospital bed.

My body and whole being became objects, motionless, fed, washed, monitored, scrutinized, investigated, prodded, and injected. My freedom was limited to what my hands could reach from my hospital bed or a wheelchair.

For nine months in the hospital, I felt like I was no one. I felt like I was no longer a mother, a woman, a wife, or a manager. I felt like I was nothing.

It felt like jail. Then, I gained semi-freedom when I moved from my bed to a wheelchair. I was brought for walks in my wheelchair in the hospital courtyard, and I learned to be more mobile with vertical tables and parallel bars. My body became my master. It decided when I could learn to be upright again, the number of months I would need to learn how to walk again—first, with a stroller, then with walking sticks. Just like a toddler, I had to learn everything all over again.

My family and my marriage were torn to pieces, as I became a burden instead of Supermom. I could not access my house anymore. I had lost all power and legitimacy, and I gained neuropathic pain instead. I became powerless to console my daughters and ostracized from their lives as young adults.

My Transformation

I soon met other people who had become more handicapped than me, who were coping with far worse than me for several years. I learned from their courage and way of looking at life. Becoming handicapped levels out the social playing field and can affect anyone regardless of age, gender, race, social status, or religion.

I never believed that I would never be able to walk again, and every day, I kept on doing exercises, even making small Lilliputian movements. That is how, after fainting many times because of the pain, three months after my operation, I was standing again, hooked to parallel bars. Six months later, I was shuffling slowly with a walker.

When I went home in June 2015, my family was traumatized to have me back in this form. I had to face everything that was no longer possible for me, such as going outside on my own, going shopping, just deciding to go for a last-minute walk, living normally like the rest of my family was, like you.

My city, my house, nothing was adapted to my handicap. I had pain and difficulty moving about, but I was outside at last!

We all went, my family and I—a family is like a community—through all the unavoidable stages of mourning: mourning myself, me as the mother or the wife they knew as well as anger, sadness, negotiation, denial, and finally acceptance.

This new initiation and path to a new life are what I unveil in *Le Roseau Penchant*, and I hope the journey I share with you has a universal truth to help you through whatever transformation you have to face.

Transforming yourself is not necessary. Suffering and going through tough times or harrowing ordeal as mine or becoming paraplegic is unnecessary!

So I like to refer also to difficulty with love. There is no such thing as one type of trauma or test that is harder than another, and each problem should be considered and respected. There is no scale to describe a difficult or traumatic situation like from 0 to 10 when describing pain: unemployment, a relationship break-up, divorce, illness, losing someone you care about, accidents, harassment, or aggression. Each of those difficult situations must be respected.

The only standard way of measuring the impact of a difficult situation is what the individual feels and how you cope with it.

Whatever the difficulty is and whoever feels it, each of us can overcome and transcend it. Here are some of the lessons I learned that I want to share with you:

- Don't resist. Don't hang on. Listen to it and let it go.
- Get out of your old comfort zone. Change the beliefs and values you used to have that are no longer relevant in this new phase of your life. For me, I learned that this was my new way of life. I no longer needed to push hard all the time.

- By becoming nobody, I found my true self. I exist. I am not just alive. In my isolation, immobility, and solitude, all I had left was the real me.
- I had the time, and I took the time.
- I reflected deeply and abandoned my false beliefs, and I nurtured the lonely child within me.

The Writer Emerges

Nothing happens to us by chance: my body had to break to meet myself, the real me. My value system needed to transform. My old comfort zone had become my enemy. When you lose something, you also gain something to grow and evolve. I no longer say that I don't care/feel pain or suffer. I know that when it hurts, it hurts every day, but my pain no longer defines me. I am no longer under the false impression that I am omnipotent. I have lost some capacities, but I have also gained new ones—such as writing. I avoid complaining about my life before. I can't dance to rock and roll anymore, and I never will again. The good thing is that I had danced a lot before, and today, I am learning to enjoy the pleasure of being in water—something that I was afraid of before.

After the first sixty years of my *realpolitik* way of life, since it's no longer forbidden to dream, I have realized the dream I had of my youth. I gave up brutal and intense success for the pleasure of being a writer. My dream was to write, and I have now sold over 3,000 copies of my first book *The Bending Reed, the Story of a Marvelous Operation*. Resilience turned me into a writer with great recognition in the media and from my readers.

This was an unexpected success for a book where the subject is not that sexy, from an unknown writer with a complicated name! I definitely won't need another life-changing back surgery to be able to write my second book! It will be a novel, and how one can shape his or her life will be the main subject to explore.

You don't believe me yet, stay tuned. I have more to share:

That first book was published in October 2017, e.g., three years to the day after my surgery. The nightmare had contained some blessings in disguise, and the first one was to dare to realize my dream to become a writer.

But that was just the first step of Season 1!!

Season 2—Some women's associations requested that I speak about my life experience in their main events. I also focused my speech a little differently, as I built on my own experience before the surgery to show-case how women in business life are eager to succeed, maybe doing so at their own expense. I wanted people to pay more attention to their actual needs. In May 2018, I gave my first speech in front of 500 women, where I received a standing ovation from listeners who were in tears.

I realized then that my age, professional experience, and personal life allowed me to speak the truth, and my truth resonated with so many people. Moreover, the more daring and transparent I was about myself, the more helpful it was for others.

Season 3—Four years after my surgery, I was offered the stage at The-atre Mogador in Paris. It was December 3, 2018; I remember exactly. I spoke in front of 3,000 people for a TEDxCEWomen, and my topic was "Nothing happens by chance." *"Rien ne nous arrive par hazard,"* as we say in French.

Scary? Yes and no! I entered the stage, quite unready and trembling. I was worried I would fall on stage because of my poor walking or that my memory would vanish as I was speaking.

None of those fears happened. My talk went well, and the audi-ence was with me—kind, emotional, and laughing. I leave it to you to watch that TEDx, and now it has subtitles in English and Spanish. But I want to bring your attention to the set of findings I was developing in that pitch about transformation.

The failure of my surgery was an ordeal, but it was also my rebirth, my renaissance. I think this is true for two reasons:

The first is my stubborn character. Not walk again? I never believed that was an option. Never. So, the day after my surgery, I allied with my body, and we began, at its pace, to get me vertical again. Weeks later, I could stand up at a special table made for this purpose. Then, I was shuffling with a walker and then with canes.

This was a renaissance, but it was also a renaissance for me because, at a specific moment, I said to myself: "No, no, no, no, no, no, NO; it's not possible; I can't have my life stolen again."

And this time, I heard my voice. I listened to my voice as it said: "Enough, you had your life stolen at birth; you had it stolen during your youth; then you stole it yourself later on. That's it. No more!"

And then, with this voice that I was hearing, listening to, and respecting, my beliefs that were previously limiting me stopped because thoughts are so simple.

Your beliefs are straightforward. They are a coin, and the coin has two sides.

On one side, you surrender to your beliefs, and you give them power over your life. You don't get angry with yourself because you can hardly do otherwise at the beginning of your life. In that period, they have free rein—they become limiting, become obstacles, become enslaving, and become odious. That was my being all-powerful and stubborn. It was my fear of living and my fear of dying!

And then came the day, that day when I gave myself love, respect, kindness, time, attention, light. That day, I looked at the opposite side of that same coin. Those same beliefs exploded in their splendor. They became strength and desire for life. They became creativity, fullness, and femininity.

Suddenly, I felt like everything became possible. They opened the full range of possibilities and the range of my options aligned—heart, body, and spirit; vertically, physically, emotionally, and intellectually.

And I thought also that was it, and the show was over.

Not at all!

Season 4—In March 2019, the incredible TEDx team released the video on YouTube. I was deeply moved listening to it and already eager to see what I should have done better. I was happy to have some viewers, likes, and so, shared with my friends on my networks—LinkedIn, Facebook, Instagram, Twitter, nothing fancy.

In French only at that time: It reached 1,000 viewers, then 5,000, then 10,000. Before I knew it, it had gone viral with lovely comments on the web and people reaching me out by private message. By the summer of 2019, it had reached 500,000 views, and I was laughing at a friend asking for a million. I am no longer laughing. The talk now has subtitles in other languages, and we are at a 1,800,0000 views.

For the fourth anniversary of my surgery, I headed into the fall of 2019. Season 5!!

That's when I was awarded the prize "ReStartAwards" at the Olympia Hall, the mythic theater of Paris, which has hosted the Beatles amongst so many celebrities.

I gave a pitch on the "Invisible Handicap," standing for care, respect, and attention to the weakest, those who have invisible difficulties, advocating that they all be given full support and help. It is another subject I hope I will have other opportunities to speak on.

What is next? Who knows! A conference in English? Why not another TEDx? I am now fully open to what is coming into my life, and I am full of gratitude. I want to publish a second book, that is sure.

My Message for You

And now, if you ask me why or how I am reborn from my ashes? Here are my messages to you:

- Stay or be accessible in your mind and your heart.
- Believe in tomorrow, but live here and now.
- Go through your grief and leave your old life behind you.
- Have a dream or a project and go for it.
- Decide what meaning you want your life to have.
- Resilience is salvation from victimization.

The change is how I now treat myself: with kindness. As a result, there has been a change in how I relate to others. I no longer need to be perfect. The prince may not be charming, but he is who he is. Either I accept it or not.

- I am a victim of no one, of nothing.
- I have a handicap for sure, but I am not my handicap.
- Life is different, slower.
- I am sometimes still full of anger.
- I believe destiny is real, and I feel grateful.

I can't avoid thinking that listening and respecting our inner voice should be taught in kindergarten. If I had been taught that, I would have avoided terrible health issues, which also impacted my family. I would have begun my true mission as a motivational writer much earlier, and I would have been able to play my role earlier and longer in the world. I would have been able to impact more people on the top of enjoying my freedom to write.

A writer. For many years, Nadalette La Fonta was a manager leading teams in multicultural projects, advising senior management in international missions (Renault, Apple, IBM). Caring intensely about diversity, she did more personally, joining IBM's CSCorps to facilitate volunteer teams' activities and then heading off to India herself to work with NGOs. She has actively supported the development of women's networks and mentoring programs.

2014: Her world collapsed. During surgery, her spinal cord was injured. She went from a world where she was active to a world where she was bound to a wheelchair. It was also the awakening of a writer... and of a new life. Dipping her pen in the well of her pain and anger, but also her vivacious spirit and humor, she left her businesswoman's attire in the closet. She published her first book, "Le Roseau Penchant" (The Bending Reed, the Story of a Marvelous Operation) Ed. Fauves. She is a motivational speaker at many conferences—Connecting Women, Jump, Women's Forum Paris. Nadalette has given in Paris a TEDx "Rien ne nous arrive par hasard" Nothing happens by chance—which, on YouTube, has outpaced 1,800,000 views https://youtu.be/8S8mie3bwtw

She is writing further books: a novel, a family saga over three centuries in France and New Orleans, and a personal development guide. Nadalette is graduated of the Institute of Political Studies, by Corporate Coach U and hold a Master in NeuroLinguistic Programming and speaks English, Spanish, and French. She has received the Prize Resilience of the ReStartAwards 2019 at L'Olympia Paris. Find her at: https://nadaletteauteureetconférencière.fr/, https://www.facebook.com/nadalettelafonta/, https://twitter.com/nadaletteLFS, http://instagram.com/nadalettelafonta, https://www.linkedin.com/in/nadalettelafontasix/ ,https://twitter.com/nadaletteLFS E-mail: leroseaupenchant@gmail.com TEDx Rien ne nous arrive par hasard :https://www.youtube.com/watch?v=8S8mie3bwtw

From Workaholic in a Man's World to Balanced on My Terms

By Mirian Zacareli
Brazil

I still remember my enthusiasm to study in the USA with my brother back in 1974. Our passports were ready, and I was waiting to finalize my visa at the American Consulate. However, my brother went to Los Angeles, California, but I couldn't go for several reasons. I had received a great work opportunity in Sao Paulo on the Board of Directors at an American multinational company, where I had already worked for thirty-four years. The director was my teacher, and I learned so much from him. The company was starting operations in Brazil, and the head executives were all men. At that time, it seemed like having women in leadership positions was still a general idea, but I always kept an eye open and had a good relationship with people from the head office in Dallas, Texas. Time went by, and from Executive Secretary, I was promoted to Liaison between our Administrative and Sales Areas. I was part of the first Female Sales Team, worked with operations, was promoted to manager, and became a Director in Brazil, Chile, and Argentina. It is a company that manufactures chemical products aimed at industrial maintenance.

The Challenges of a Woman in Top Management

I was the first female director in a company in my city, Sorocaba, and I must say, it was weird to see my face on the cover of a magazine and in many newspaper interviews. It was unprecedented! My days were long, and to get professional recognition, I had to show results and earn my promotions. I also faced a lot of challenges and concealed boycotts, but it never intimidated me. On the contrary, it gave me more strength to do my best. I have always taken courses to keep myself updated in different areas. It has always helped me understand dealing with people, understanding that the leader can only reach their targets and objectives with their team through teamwork and effort.

Missing My Family

I used to work hard and traveled so much that when I woke up in the morning, it took me a few seconds to remember where I was. I sacrificed my family life and always had my husband's support, but I lost some crucial moments with my son that I'll never get back. Today, I would do things differently.

The frantic march for results, constant travel, striving to reach targets all seemed to promote a kind of blindness in me, and I felt lonely, impatient, and highly rigid towards everybody close to me, both at work and with my family. I had a feeling that they couldn't keep up with me because I was always moving too fast! I can't say the same about friends because I thought I didn't have any since I never had time for leisure.

It Took Getting Sick to Realize

Among the consequences of working and traveling nonstop combined with sedentary office life, I began to experience an ongoing, intense backache. I had surgery scheduled to remove a herniated disc. I confess, I thought the recovery would be fast so that I could return to work, but the fear of post-surgical complications tormented me. I often cried, but there was an internal force that helped me overcome this critical period. Even though I knew the seriousness of my lumbar spine surgery, I returned to work twenty days after the surgery. I flat-out disobeyed my doctor's recommendations for forty days of rest.

The result was horrible. I relapsed, and I had to be immobilized for forty-five days with risks of more complications. It was so different from anything I had already faced in life; I hadn't been that still since I was in my mother's womb. When I realized I couldn't control everything to be successful, I knew I'd learned an important lesson.

Coaching: The Restart Button

In 2007, I spent some time seeking to understand and make some sense of life since everything had always been reduced to work, responsibilities, and reaching goals. I felt the problem was me, so I participated in some coaching sessions. I didn't like the sessions, and I didn't receive the value I had expected. Still, I continued with several coaching courses hoping to acquire further knowledge and skills in personal, team, leadership, executive, and business coaching.

Then I reached a point of high awareness and self-knowledge, which aroused the sense of other things in life that I had not realized until then. That's the reason I felt empty inside. I could understand the importance of having a purpose and redesign my lifestyle to share my knowledge in a way that could help other people. While I was waiting for my flight at the airport, I observed how other executives kept working on their laptops (there weren't smartphones at that time). They looked like crazy people, and now, on the other side, as an observer, I managed to be the conductor of my emotions and realized that I used to be exactly like them. I asked myself, "How could I be like these men who don't even realize what is around them?" But I had been like them for many years. Starting with these reflections, I questioned what the company expected of me, learned to listen to people more attentively, and wanted to know how I could help them align with our company's purpose.

Courage to Innovate

In 2008, I started a new professional cycle with my own business, KMZ Consultoria e Eventos. For five years, I did mentoring, consulting, public speaking, corporate events, and coaching for executives and expatriates. I was invited to give lectures to inspire new professional careers to graduates at UFSCAR – Universidade Federal de São Carlos in becoming entrepreneurs, Veterinary in USP – Universidade de São Paulo, and Administration at UNISO – Universidade de Sorocaba. I was also invited to give classes in several post-graduation courses, People Management Module, at FACENS- Faculdade de Engenharia de Sorocaba, and UNISO.

I looked for more autonomy being an entrepreneur and breaking barriers in my company with a brighter mission and vision. My purpose was to share knowledge and experiences and contribute to the leaders in the organizations using specific and personalized resources, proper methodology, and tools to awaken their awareness from self-knowledge. Discovering this other side has been more and more surprising, because I realize that every moment is an opportunity to see events from a different, broader perspective, learning and giving value to the situations and their misconceptions, correcting them consciously so that mistakes are not repeated, and making it possible to forge new paths with determination towards my goals and purposes.

Sorority is Required

Together with other female executives, I founded Associação de Mulheres Empreendedoras (AME) Association of Entrepreneurial Women, with twenty members. We had the goal of reuniting women from different industries, sharing personal and professional experiences, attracting and giving voice to the women's community. We helped each other by discussing and sharing our challenges, opportunities, and resilience to overcome difficulties and showcased our diversity as leaders. This union of different voices bore fruit, and we contributed to women's empowerment.

We noted that women, in general, are not united, and due to cultural heritage, we often worry about extra things regarding other women.

I noticed this when I was taking part in a forum about domestic violence. The speaker, a chief police officer, was defending women and presenting a robust proposal to ease the problem. I was in the audience, and I heard a leader representing a community of black women make a comment that perplexed me because it was not connected to the topic in discussion. She mentioned that "the chief police officer was wearing the same clothes that she wore to a past event." That was frustrating to hear, but it helped me understand why in 415 companies surveyed, presidency positions are only 13 percent filled by women, and leadership positions are filled by only 25 percent women in companies whose headquarters are in Brazil or are in operation here. In other words, we don't help each other when we don't value other females' competencies and work because instead, we still mainly talk about external appearance. I feel it also when I write technical articles or when interviews about important topics are published because women comment about my photo and not about the content, signaling that they still are unaware of the importance of life purpose, and instead are rooted in comparison.

My work as a coach for expatriate executives who had recently arrived in Brazil was invaluable in helping them face cultural challenges, the language disconnect between their native language and Portuguese, and the establishment of professional goals, while the spouse remained at home with the children without any professional activity because they didn't have appropriate work visas for employment in Brazil. The experience of seeing how it made all the difference to serve through purpose was terrific. I helped my clients make a mental shift to awaken awareness of the different roles they could fulfil in their personal and professional lives, complementing satisfaction by helping people discover their talents using tools for digital jobs, volunteer work, crafts, teaching another language to young people or handicrafts for the elderly. What made me happy was when a client identified their meaning and found their internal sense of purpose for self-realization that sometimes seemed challenging to express. Remembering those moments of discovery brings tears of joy to my eyes.

The most remarkable moment was when I worked with a Mexican man who had accompanied his wife for her job while he had to take care of the house, school, doctor visits, and other kinds of housework. When I met him, he was feeling confused and unmotivated. He had left his rising career as a journalist to support his wife's career opportunity. After our coaching sessions, he awakened and found out he could apply his skills as a video editor and partnered with a social organization. Together, they interviewed families and produced videos of children's stories that were presented at their birthday celebration. Suddenly, life made sense to him again because he had aligned his purpose and values.

From the Corporate World to Public Administration

I was invited to work in the public sector, and the experiences were spectacular. I was able to learn a lot, participate, and contribute to various projects. One project included the process of creating the social stamp and applying the SDGs (Sustainable Development Goals) in the implementation of georeferencing (a tool that makes important information available to city planners about the main needs of the population, such as health centers, schools, drainage, asphalt and other improvements). In partnership with FACENS [Faculdade de Engenharia de Sorocaba—Sorocaba Engineering College], projects were submitted, defending smart cities' concept to improve the population's quality of life and guarantee sustainable cities by 2050. We won the "FAB CITY GLOBAL" Award in July 2018. For our first project, we adopted the concept proposed by Boyd Cohen, and we thought of the Smart City as the author suggests in his "Smart Cities Wheel." We believe that the Smart City depends on a series of actions in many areas, not only technology, innovation, etc., to achieve this status. After all, the Smart City aims to adopt policies, measures, and investments in an intelligent way with technical support, allowing societal well-being regarding its infrastructure and development conditions. Government, society, and the private sector must be integrated as smart cities must reflect more innovative cultures and communities.

The focus of my work is the development of executive leaders in high positions in organizations who do not realize the importance of their true values because of a lack of greater purpose. My contribution is in the sense that they reevaluate their mindset and assumptions, and, through appropriate methodology and tools, we work together to promote the raising of awareness and self-knowledge so they can find their true purpose. Amazingly, many leaders present themselves in scenarios where they are unaware of what the organization expects from them, especially women who sometimes feel pressured and realize an information mismatch because there was no formal and transparent definition of the desired results. The purpose and dissemination of mission, vision, values are necessary conditions for aligning and engaging people concerning the expectations of their organizations. From that, workers can develop their role as inspiring leaders who stand out because of their teams' high performance.

I want to highlight that it is part of my life mission to do volunteer work where the purpose is to promote actions for the humanization of organizations and conscious capitalism. I am a member of the board and advisor for the BYU [Brigham Young University] Management Society, defending ethical leadership in organizations. We promote various actions that encourage civil society, organizations, and politicians [to practice ethics in the organizations].

Working to develop leaders with purpose requires the dissemination and continuity of applying values, ethical concepts, and transparency in organizations, promoting connectivity and humanizing work processes to increase people's empathy, commitment, and engagement. All of this becomes reflected in their families and communities as the "butterfly effect."

As female executives working relentlessly for results, we sometimes become purely rational, following rules and procedures, delivering results, but sacrificing those on our side and who are part of the mission. When we discover that our reason for living has meaning and that our conscience can lead to the development of talent with a noble goal, we will leave a legacy that inspires others and brings hope to make the world a better place. The meaning of life is incredible! It is highly inspiring to serve by sharing our knowledge and experiences and learning from new situations where cooperation and collaboration are predominant factors in the search for innovative solutions to problems that concern the individual and the community as a whole.

I do not know how long I will live. Still, I am certainly aware of the privilege of enjoying the impact of sharing my knowledge, self-acceptance, personal growth, life purpose, positive relationships with others, "well-being." This feeling of completeness and achievement and autonomy—the feeling of sharing and collaborating with people—makes me happy and increases my commitment to improve and be the inspirational instrument through the example of my actions and attitudes. I can only collaborate if I promote a connection between people if I am connected with myself.

For those who want to achieve their goals, contribute, and inspire other people while making money from this work, I recommend:

1. Consider how you live your life and identify your values, talents, and skills (self-knowledge).
2. Seek help from an experienced expert for guidance.
3. Don't give up on your dreams.

Mirian Zacareli works on leadership and purpose development as an executive coach with KMX Consulting and Events. She has previously worked as a journalist, in marketing, and in human resources. She is one of the founders of Sorocaba Women Entrepreneurs Association.

Mirian Zacareli has been awarded State and Regional Management Quality Trophies. Finally, she is an advisory board member for the global organization BYU Management Society (Sorocaba chapter), which has the purpose of "Growing Moral and Ethical Leadership Around the World."

Find here on LinkedIn: https://www.linkedin.com/in/mirianzacareli/

From Prison to Purpose

By D. Renee Hamilton
United States

November 15, 2005

The lights came on. I woke up at 6:30 a.m. on a Tuesday. This was the last place in the world I wanted to wake up and find myself. It seemed almost surreal to me. I laid there on my back, staring up at the piping that ran along the pale white ceiling. Oddly, I did not feel depressed, nor was I in distress. Instead, I felt numb and in a daze about my predicament. The place looked like an army barrack. Bunks uniformly lined the windowed wall that stretched fifty feet. Dull, grayish lockers stood at attention at the foot of each bunk. A narrow pathway separated the bunks along the wall from sparsely furnished cubicles that included a bunk, a stainless-steel basin, and a stainless-steel toilet. Although there weren't any visible bars, I was not mistaken where I was. The main question that loomed in the back of my mind was, "How did a good girl like me end up here?"

I climbed down the ladder from the top bunk where I slept that first night. I opened my locker and took out a small travel-size toothbrush, a short tube of toothpaste, and a white face towel. I turned and walked up the narrowed pathway that led me into a lobby, where I stepped inside a mop room. The room contained a deep dingy sink and a piped faucet that protruded from the wall and over the sink. Here is where I stood in a drowsy stupor to brush my teeth and wash my face along-side two other women. At that moment, the unfathomable realization struck me that this would be my place of residence for the next fourteen months. My heart sunk to the very pit of my stomach.

I walked back to my locker, where I began to disrobe from the oversized nightgown that cloaked my body like a tunic. My bunk was against the wall, thus, lending me no privacy. The sleeves of the gown hung loosely down my arms, and the hem dropped mid-way my calves. It was not a flattering sight. I slipped on the white bra and orange jumper that I'd been given the day before, along with white tube socks and a pair of blue canvas tennis shoes with no shoestrings.

It was breakfast time, and I was hungry. I followed the narrow pathway back towards the lobby. I walked freely out of my assigned dorm, Building G, into the brightness of an unseasonably warm November morning. The grounds were manicured to perfection, without even a single stray leaf left to lollygag on the sidewalks. Zinnias of various fall colors meticulously embellished the walkways that crisscrossed the compound. From where I stood at the entrance of Building G, it was about three hundred feet to the cafeteria. I self-consciously started the journey up the walkway, completely stripped of any pretense, pride, or dignity. Except for my prison jumpsuit, I was as unadorned as the day I was born—no jewelry, no makeup, no weave—just me.

The next fourteen months would yield all the time I needed to come up with the answer to the persistent question, "How did a good girl like me end up in prison?" I knew *what* I had done to land myself in prison, which was healthcare fraud, also known as a "white-collar" crime, but I needed to understand *why*.

I walked into the cafeteria, which to my surprise, really did look like a cafeteria. It wasn't anything like those movie scenes where inmates sit side by side at long tables eating what looks like slop on a tin tray. Instead, the cafeteria, which was nicknamed "the chow hall," had individual tables with connected seats that resembled the style of what you might see in a fast-food restaurant. The entrées were served cafeteria-style, while some of the sides and beverages were all-you-can-eat buffet style. It was nothing like I'd imagined. I was in no mood for a heavy meal for my first breakfast on the compound, so I chose to eat very little: a hard-boiled egg and some orange juice. I stumbled upon a table for two rather than four, and

I sat alone, feeling like a self-conscious teenager on her first day at a new school. I felt naked and alone as I appeased my hunger pains.

After eating breakfast, I returned to my dorm. As I walked back to my locker, my bunkmate, Ms. Bertha, informed me that I needed to go to the multi-purpose building to pick up my permanent prison apparel. I would be rid of the orange jumpsuit and canvas tennis shoes without shoestrings. In exchange, I would get khaki pants, khaki button-down shirts, brown t-shirts, more tube socks, black steel-toe shoes, and underwear. The inmate in charge of uniform distribution asked for my sizes then plucked out my garments for the long haul. Now I was ready to blend in with the general population and start the orientation phase of my stay. I spent the next thirty days learning all the ins and outs and dos and don'ts of prison life.

I Lost My Power

As the adage goes, "Nothing is ever as bad as it seems." This was certainly true of my experience in prison. The fear of going to prison took a far greater toll on me than the prison itself. The day I self-surrendered to that federal correctional facility, I felt like a wearied and tattered soldier who had been sequestered and terrorized for five years in a war with the criminal justice system. I wouldn't have ever believed in a million years that the scariest part would be over the day I stepped inside those razor-wire fences. There was no longer a need to fear the inevitability of going to prison: I was now there. The day I walked into that prison compound, the grace of God met me. It just enveloped me in its everlasting presence and assured me that I had nothing to fear. It whispered to my injured soul: "You can rest now from your fight and the rat race of your life. Be still, and I will make you whole again."

Then, it dawned on me that my heavenly Father was inside the razor-wire fence *waiting for me.*

The first week in prison was the hardest. In disbelief of what had happened to me, I found myself on the brink of tears a few times—once while sitting with the prison psychologist who showed me some sympathy for my plight and the other time sitting in the medical waiting room. I fought back the tears, and I won each time. The seven-year-old little girl within wouldn't let me have a meltdown, even in a time when I most needed to have one.

I knew I had no one to blame but myself. I realized that I couldn't just blame my co-defendant, my children's father, for being in prison. We'd operated a state-funded substance abuse business together, but greed led us to overbill the state for services not rendered. I never felt comfortable committing these actions, but somehow I felt that my children's father would disapprove of me if I didn't go along with the plan.

I had to take responsibility for my illegal actions. I allowed this to happen by giving away my power. How did I give away my power? I gave away my power when I abandoned the part of me that was strong, ambitious, determined, and proud of what I had accomplished in my life. I also gave it away when I compromised my convictions to keep my man. In doing so, I left myself.

Why did I sell myself out and allow a man to define who I was to become? This was a question that haunted me. I thought that I was stronger than this, but I came to see the truth about myself. The fact was I didn't believe I was this amazingly unique and beautiful human being of infinite value and worth. So, in hindsight, I can see how my lack of self-worth and not believing that I was good enough were prime ingredients for a disastrous meal—a meal that would lure me down the path to prison. When we don't understand who we really are and why we're here, then we will allow others to use us in a way they see fit, whether it's to our detriment or not.

Who am I?

The oxymoron about prison is that it set me free. My time in prison was a time-out from this matrix of a world. The experience allowed me to reconnect to the source of my existence and understand my life's purpose. As the weeks in prison went by, the shackles that had held my mind in captivity started to fall away. Prison set me free to recapture the part of me that I'd lost. I now had all this free time to figure out what I wanted out of life. My inner work connected me to my desires, hopes, and dreams.

I begin to ask myself the questions, "Who am I?" and "What do I want to do?" and as I searched myself for these answers, I started to journal:

> *I'm struggling to become something, and I don't know what it is. I've spent most of my adult years trying to figure it out. At times I thought I'd found it, but all too soon, I realized that wasn't it. I thought I was supposed to become a wife and mother, but that wasn't all of it. Then God let me in on a bit of a secret. God revealed that I don't have to figure it out, that it had already been figured out for me before I was born. All I had to do was take one day at a time and see my life unfold before me. But, God then revealed to me that one thing is required of me and that one thing is TRUST. I must trust my instincts and intuition, the true self in me, to make the right decisions for today and leave tomorrow's cares to God.*

> *So, it is as plain and as simple as trusting God. Yet, this is the hardest thing for us humans to do. How do you trust who or what you can't see? Although I'd heard it all my life, I never knew what it meant to trust God. But in prison, I was faced with two options: trust God or go insane with worry. I was used to being in control, but now I had no control over my life outside the razor-wire fence. Whatever went on with my*

children, family, and possessions had to go on without me. It was difficult, but prison taught me how to trust God. And, amid this trust walk with God came the revelation to my questions, "Who am I?" and "What do I want to do?"

"I am the expressed image of God created to express God's compassion through my unique combination of gifts and talents. My passions will lead me to my calling and mission in this life."

After this revelation, I felt I'd been born again. Now, I had finally found what I'd been searching for—an experience with God and a relationship with my true self. Religion alone was not enough for me. I had been craving some tangible means to connect with God for years. When I looked inward and found myself, I found God in there also. I then realized my true source was God. This was that "Something and Someone" I had lost and had been looking for all my life.

As I progressed in my self-discoveries, I understood the true nature of fear in my life. Fear was the shackles that held me captive. I had been a prisoner of fear. My fear had locked me up and whispered lies to me for so many years. I had so many fears. My inner voice told me, "People will hurt and abandon you, so don't be dependent; men can't be trusted, so don't allow them to get close; sex is nasty and vulgar, so keep your legs closed; vulnerability is weakness, so shun it at all cost." Fear had promised me that it would protect me from life's pitfalls and failures if I would just hold on to it. It told me always to play it safe, never take a risk, and don't trust your heart, for it will lead you to pain. Then, I caught hold to the revelation that not only was fear protecting me, but it was also robbing me of a fulfilling and meaningful life.

Mission Accomplished

Prison had served its purpose. It was the thing that could have destroyed me, but instead, it uplifted me. I came out of prison with a changed perspective about life and how I needed to live my life. While in prison, I learned to take one day at a time and stay in the present. Upon my release from prison, I knew that I had to continue to practice staying in the moment to ward off the anxieties of the future and the regrets and resentments of the past. A crisis in our life usually moves us forward, and I was determined to move forward. I decided that I would not allow the social stigma of having been incarcerated to define the rest of my life. My destiny is so much more than one mistake.

Sometimes, we deviate from the expected blueprint for our life. Going to prison seemed like one of those deviations. I can't say that prison was a path that I had to take to get to where I am now, but I can say that it stopped me in my tracks and got my full attention. We all face opposition in one way or another on our path to greatness. Joseph Campbell calls this path The Hero's Journey. In mythology, the main character in every hero story faces an opposition that threatens her fate and, depending on how she handles the opposition, will determine her destiny. I believe had I not gone to prison, and I would not be as determined to make the most of the present moment and to pursue my dreams. It was in prison that I rediscovered myself.

Sometimes it takes painful situations to get our attention. One of C. S. Lewis' quotes says, "Pain insists upon being attended to. God whispers to us in our pleasure, speaks to us in our conscience, but shouts to us in our pain. It is His megaphone to rouse a deaf world." The prison was God shouting to me, "Wake up! And live the abundant life that I intended for you to live." I believe that had it not been for my incarceration, I would have just settled for a life of mediocrity, which would have been even more confining than physical bars. There's a saying that goes, "Whatever shows up in your life is the answer. Your job is to figure out what was the question." Perhaps prison was the answer to my question: "What is it going to take for me to make my life what it is supposed to be?

However, if you don't define your life, someone else will. They will define it based on your past and their perception of you. To determine your own life means you have to take charge of your destiny, and for you to take control of your destiny, you have to have a vision. During my season of desperation, back in the mid-90s, it seemed that I allowed a man to define my life by relinquishing my power to him. I didn't know at the time that I was born to be a wonderful human being who was worthy of all the many blessings that await us. The path to prison turned out to be a necessary one. It helped me regain control of my life. Once I had the reins back in my hands, I decided to gather all the lessons I'd learned, the discoveries I'd made, and the tools I had acquired and start on a new "hero's journey." That was the yellow brick road that would eventually lead me to a more prosperous life. I was determined not to lie down in a poppy field of fear and self-doubt anymore and allow the wicked witch of rage and anger to control me. I was now wide awake and aware of the destructive power they had wielded over me.

Rise to Greatness

The worm said, "I'm struggling to become something, but I don't know what it is." In its larval state, a caterpillar has no consciousness of its fate or destiny. It does not know that its future is to become something majestic and beautiful. It may see the butterfly flittering around it, yet, the caterpillar has no clue of its progression and evolution to become a butterfly. But, despite the ignorance of its fate, it follows its instinct to move forward. Guided by an unseen force, it inches along, looking for food, nibbling itself plump. Then one day, it crawls up to a higher place to form a chrysalis, hidden as it goes through the process of metamorphosis, still unconscious of what it is about to become.

We may go through years where it seems little to nothing is happening in our life. Still, we must wrap ourselves in a cocoon and let patience have its perfect work in us so that we have been primed for purpose when we do come forth. Unlike the caterpillar, which cocoons only once in its lifetime, we must go through many metamorphoses during our lives. I can think of several times in my life that I have been in my chrysalis: during my college years, during the period of my emotional healing, and my time in prison. Like the caterpillar, we don't always see the big picture, but there is an unseen force at work in us. If we keep inching forward and stay on the path, we will eventually find ourselves soaring high above the trees.

God had a purpose and a plan in mind when He created us, and I believe that plan involves how we are made. We must understand how God has fashioned us for a purpose. In Rick Warren's book, *The Purpose Driven Life*, he uses the acronym SHAPE to describe how we are made or fashioned to serve our purpose. The acronym stands for spiritual gifts, heart, abilities, personality, and experience. He explains how we must tap into each of these areas to understand what God has called us to do on this planet. I'm reminded of this statement that I heard, "The two most important days in your life are the day you were born and the day you discover why." How profound! Unfortunately, many die, having never discovered who they are and why they were born.

After Prison

Toward the end of my stay in prison, God commissioned me to follow three mandates that would propel me into my purpose. I must point out here that at least two of these three mandates are relevant to everyone who reads my story. The first mandate was to raise your children. The second mandate was to use your God-given gifts and talents to make a living. The third mandate was to find a mission that will help uplift others.

These are the three things that I did to get started on my path to purpose. Being available for my children mentally, emotionally, and physically was my number one priority. They were still very young when I was released from prison, and they needed a conscious and present mother. I focused on using my gifts and talents to make a living wage to help support my family by teaching, counseling, and writing. When you use your gifts and talents, your work energizes you and gives you a sense of purpose. The third thing I did was find a mission that brings me to where I am now in my life.

It took ten years after being released from prison to return to the prison to do what I call my mission work: to bring the message of forgiveness, hope, and freedom to women locked down in prison. I do this through a program I developed called The Butterfly Strategy. The Butterfly Strategy is a personal transformation program designed to give women tools and strategies that will help them break free from the mental and emotional shackles they have built around their minds and hearts and help them transform their lives while still in prison.

The work I do inside the prison walls is designed to reduce recidivism and build stronger families directly. I started this mission work six years ago, and it continues to bring me joy and hope, knowing that my labor is not in vain. The whole community benefits when we take care of those who have been marginalized or outcast in our society. I've also become Chair of Baton Rouge Reentry Coalition. We assist those returning to society who are in desperate need of wrap-around services, such as housing, employment, and transportation.

In the wake of mass incarceration, I believe it is incumbent upon me to be a solid and compelling voice for prison reform. To do this, my non-profit organization Simon Solomon Foundation is committed to the fight for equal justice for all and to help uplift marginalized and disadvantaged communities.

Serving from my purpose has brought a dimension of meaning and fulfillment to my life that I didn't know possible. It gives me a reason to get up every morning and greet each day as another opportunity to serve humanity. To quote Dr. Martin Luther King, Jr, "If a man doesn't have something (or someone) that he'll die for, he isn't fit to live." The purpose is about moving beyond the smallness of our individual lives and seeing the needs of others, especially those who are hurting and who are less fortunate.

While the prison was my life-changing experience, that life-changing experience could be a myriad of other things for you. For some people, it is a broken relationship, a divorce, death of a loved one, cancer, loss of material possessions, etc. The list can go on. We all face adversities in life. It's just meant to be, but what matters most is how we come out on the other side of these adversities and how we help others overcome their hardships.

I believe the things that sometimes break us are the very things that make us. If you want to know what your purpose is, then identify what brought you the most pain, that thing that you thought would destroy you. Here lies your purpose. Someone is out there going through the same thing you overcame who needs your strength and your story.

I invite you to consider applying the three mandates I was commissioned to follow, especially if you're searching for true meaning and purpose. I also encourage you to do the work needed to break free from the mental and emotional shackles that may be around your mind and heart. The mental shackles that whisper, "You're not good enough," "You don't have what it takes to make your life better," "What you do does not matter in this world." The emotional shackles of guilt and shame may be holding you back from being the unique person you are meant to be.

D. Renee Hamilton resides in Baton Rouge, Louisiana. She is the proud mother of two brave and intelligent young adults who, during the aftermath of Hurricane Katrina back in 2005, had to weather the storm of being separated from their mom for fourteen months. D. Renee is an alumnus of Louisiana State University with an undergrad degree in Psychology. She is also a graduate of Oral Roberts University with a master's degree in counseling. In addition, D. Renee has held state certifications in substance abuse counseling, school counseling, and elementary education. D. Renee has worked in mental health and education, servicing children and adults since 1990.

The Dark Then, the Bright Now

By Flavia Wahnfried
Portugal

When the phone rang, I knew something was wrong. I got up from my workstation and headed to the meeting room, where my boss was expecting me. But I wasn't ready for what happened next. I can't remember the words she used to inform me that I would no longer be working there, but they hit me like rocks. My mind and heart were racing. In a fraction of a second, my thoughts went from *this is not happening* to *what am I going to do,* as I desperately tried to make sense of things. I remember asking if she had tried to transfer me to another department or any other alternative, and then it dawned on me: this was it. No room for negotiation: not there, not at that moment. There was no turning back at all.

I got up to go and clear my desk, tears flooding my eyes. The harder I tried to hold them back, the greater the pressure to come out. I just wanted a hole to open up beneath my feet. I had to pass some people to go back to my desk, and that was painful. I was devastated, ashamed, lost, and confused. I didn't want to talk, to have that recently opened wound exposed. I was lucky to work with some very close friends who took me to a cafe, where I could catch my breath and try to grasp what was happening.

That was October 2009, in São Paulo (Brazil), where I was born and raised. I was living one of the highlights of my career, expecting to be promoted in a company I admired, with amazing friends, doing work that I believed in, feeling proud of my results and accomplishments. Things were not all rosy, as I didn't agree with some of the guidelines coming from management, but I was not expecting that: *being fired, being made redundant, being laid off.* I couldn't even say the words back then. I had never imagined how hard it would feel going through that. Sometimes I simply refused to go through it; I refused to face reality. There were days that I would just sleep for hours, hoping my pain would eventually dissipate on its own. It did not. Instead, it grew stronger, as I felt even worse for not being able to react, for not getting back on my feet as I believed anyone else would. Every time I drove into the city, I would see those smartly dressed professionals with their badges hung around their necks, walking quickly and confidently to meet their commitments. In my view, they had a reason to be there, a purpose, even if it were just another pointless, interminable meeting. I had none. I felt like an outsider—someone without an identity, who did not belong, who had been ejected and erased from the system.

The Darkness Welling from Within

The only thing I knew at that time was that I did not want to rush back to corporate. It was eye-opening for me to see that my identity had been entirely built on a role, and I was aware I needed space to find out who I was beyond a job title. Replacing one superficial identity with another would not be the solution for me. But the pain and the confusion were simply too severe. An entire year had passed long before I had the chance to tap into my true identity, and by then, I had gone on a negative spiral that had led me to a stage where I had neither the energy nor the motivation to take care of myself. Everything seemed pointless. Not long after, I was offered an excellent opportunity to provide recruiting services through my own company, working from home, paid a fixed monthly fee. This was something I had only dreamed. Suddenly, my self-esteem was back. I felt important, I had commitments and goals to meet, I had a business to run, I could pay for my home remodeling, and I had good reasons to wake up in the morning. It sounds like a dream, doesn't it? And it was, in the beginning.

However, after just a few months, I felt my motivation beginning to wane. I beat myself up for that because I believed I should be happy and grateful for this fantastic opportunity. Consequently, I began to overeat, perhaps in an attempt to numb my feelings and suppress the sense of *lack* that I was feeling inside. Realizing that I was very quickly gaining too much weight, I went to different specialists to fix that problem. I tried other diets and every new medication on the market, just to repeatedly fail and gain even more weight. But I believed something would eventually work, so I kept trying. I enrolled in the gym and joined swimming classes, just to drop them immediately. After a few years, I was very overweight. At that stage, I no longer recognized myself. It seemed that I simply did not have the necessary will to meet my own health needs. Little did I know back then that I was seeking a quick fix for a much deeper problem manifesting in that way. I was attacking every symptom without addressing the real root causes—and, of course, being so hard on myself did not help at all.

My husband and I looked like the happiest couple in the world from the outside—we had our custom-painted Harley Davidson motorbikes, our brand-new car, a beautifully remodeled apartment. The reality was very different: we spent a considerable amount of money on things that just did not fulfill us. In addition to overeating, I bought clothes that didn't fit me or that I never got to wear. When I looked at myself in the mirror, I saw a person scattered and unable to put herself back together. The vicious cycle I was living was tough to break. The more I failed in my endless attempts to lose weight and feel happy in my work, the more I punished myself, and the more I failed. When I reached the bottom of the well, I decided to no longer wait for something to change.

I was the one not allowing myself to be happy, constantly establishing conditions that I told myself would lead to ultimate happiness. There was always a convincing reason for not feeling good about myself, sabotaging my attempts to change the way I operated. At that point, I knew change had to come from a potent source. I desperately needed to reconnect to what made sense to me. Knowing that my work life had always been a foundational pillar for my happiness, I knew I would find essential clues if I revisited every aspect of my career that had lit me up. So, this was exactly where I began the search.

My Guiding Light

I started my career back in 1995, working as an intern for an important multinational in the export and import departments of various sectors, rotating roles every few months. Every three months, I went to the human resources department to deliver my apprenticeship experience and feedback reports—this was where I would truly light up, surrounded by piles of resumes on the manager's desk. All those people behind those paper sheets, just waiting to be seen. The stories behind those printed letters, wanting to be heard. Two years after that period, at the age of twenty, knowing that I could not be transferred to the Human Resources department, I felt an urge to leave the comfort of the lukewarm water of that job. Determined to take the plunge into the unknown, I had quit and traveled to New Zealand, a very unusual destination at that time for a Brazilian student. But I wanted the extraordinary, a place where I could meet many different cultures, practice and improve my English, enjoy nature, and, most importantly, find out more about my true nature. During and even after the decision-making process, I was plagued by my strongest fears: *what am I doing? I should just go to university like everybody else. How could I quit such an excellent, fantastic job with so much stability and a promising future?* Stepping into the unknown was terrifying, but it was also liberating: my will to extract myself from that work-to-home and home-to-work life and find out what else there was to life was more potent, so I went for it. And it has been one of the most rewarding experiences in my life.

I came back in 1998, and it didn't take long after starting university until I was invited to join an executive search firm. One of our neighbors was a partner there, and he came by one weekend to buy a painting from my mother. We chatted for a while, and he told me they were looking for a researcher to go through the resumes they receive, contact candidates, and so on. Coincidence? I don't think so. There, not only did I have the opportunity to connect with the people behind the resumes, but also to help them to embrace the next step in their working lives. However, after a few years working in the recruitment business, I felt my role was to move pieces across a massive game board without really getting to know the people behind those pieces. I wanted to go deeper.

In 2005, I pivoted to a role where I could finally address people's motivations and leadership styles and understand the environments they were generating for their teams. I felt truly alive when I could have one-on-one conversations with leaders to help them know what made sense for them. That had been my last role before losing my job. Revisiting my career trajectory brought me many insights: I was able to connect the dots and understand that the reason I had not been happy with my current work engagement was that I had gone back to moving pieces across the board. I needed to go back to where I had felt a more profound sense of meaning in my work.

Coming Alive

I clearly remember that day in 2014 because it represented a turning point in our lives: after a lot of inner-work and research and driven by my recently found purpose, I communicated to my husband that I would attend a one-and-a-half-year coaching training course. Not only was he caught by surprise because it was an expensive engagement for us at that time, but he also found a very different, confident spouse in front of him. I was determined to make it work, so I did. I hired an assistant to help with my work, leaving me enough time to attend my training and work on other projects. Things began to flow effortlessly, making me smile and showing me I had stepped onto the right path. Although there were ups and downs along the way, I always managed to bounce back by reconnecting to my purpose. My purpose was those once-unhappy professionals with whom I was now working, who were able to reconnect to a deeper meaning of their own and find a new professional purpose. One executive I worked with had "the perfect job" in a small start-up and yet was not happy, and he was beating himself up for that lack of gratitude. After a few sessions, he realized how much he truly valued wasn't being honored at that job. He deeply missed the sense of connection and belonging he had had when working for a multinational company, constantly exposed to different challenges, teams, and cultures. His lack of motivation was taking a toll on his personal life, too. Witnessing this moment of profound breakthrough—and all the changes he made in his professional and personal life on the strength of that—was simply priceless for me. I felt truly alive and deeply inspired when I saw my clients reconnect to their core and find their purpose through meaningful work.

Back home, my husband and I began to feel it was time to release excess weight in our lives. We sold our motorbikes and swapped our car for a cheaper one. We decluttered our house and gave away the things that we didn't use. I worked with a nutritionist who taught me how to make simple, realistic, and healthy food choices without forcing unsustainable restrictions. By acknowledging that our previous reality was no longer serving us, my husband and I could own it and envision and plan our future in this new place of ownership and empowerment. In 2016, the company I had been recruiting for was sold, and all contracts with third parties were terminated. That was our opportunity to embrace our long-held dream of living abroad. Synchronicity showed us that we were riding the right wave. I applied to my dreamed-of second training in coaching at the University of Cambridge and, within a few months, we were moving to London. It was a period of fear, discovery, and profound transformation for both my husband and me—from simple things like looking in the opposite direction when crossing the streets, we were continually invited to learn to unlearn and see things from very different perspectives. I felt like a newborn in an adult body. In 2018, we moved again to Portugal, following the sun and choosing to be close to the sea.

Pandemic-Induced Aspiration

We have evolved from a fear-based decision-making model to an aspirational one, where we envision our future, acknowledge the fears that inevitably arise, and take the steps even before the new path is visible in front of us. We recognize that uncertainty has always been part of our lives, more than we had ever previously understood. The sudden loss of my job showed me that. And this has taught me to navigate uncertainty in a way that brings joy and excitement, rather than hiding inside my protective shell and waiting for circumstances to change by themselves. At the beginning of the pandemic, my husband and I decided that I would be in charge of taking the dogs for walks as he is in the high-risk group as designated within the COVID-19 pandemic. In the beginning, I was anxious, feeling stress build in my body: *Would I have time to go out at least four times a day to do this? Would I be too exposed to the virus? Another responsibility was adding to my already full plate.*

On the other hand, I was protecting my husband, which was the right thing to do. While these thoughts and inner negotiations turned in my mind, my perspective turned to the negative, and I felt frustrated. One evening, I was walking by myself in an empty street. It was only 8:00 p.m., but it felt like midnight. As feelings of anxiety arose, I passed a plant that was beautifully reflecting the light of the street lamp. Without any effort, my focus turned there—I looked at that plant and sensed how peaceful it was. There are no worries about yesterday or tomorrow, just being there, so generous with its beautiful flowers during the wintertime.

That experience was deeply inspiring, and I decided to turn the circumstances in my favor. During each walk, I made an extra effort to let go of my worries and focus on the positive changes that the pandemic restrictions had brought to our neighborhood. I listened to the new sounds gifted by the absence of cars. I could hear the calls of owls and crickets in the evening and birdsong during the day. I even discovered that there are rabbits in a small piece of land close to our house, and each evening I would long to go out and see how many I could spot. How many times had I passed that exact place without ever noticing the rabbits? From an obligation and a burden, my walks were reframed as an opportunity to reconnect to myself. They became my daily space to be playful, amazed, and creative: I swapped my regular route to find different paths and perspectives. Instead of rushing through my walks, I extended them. They became sources of inspiration and creativity, bringing some of my recent most extraordinary ideas and insights.

My Enlivening Beckon

Looking back at that scene where I felt like an outsider watching professionals rushing to their subsequent commitments, my feelings have changed dramatically. Today, I feel great joy to be an outsider, an observer who can help these very professionals pause, reflect on their professional journeys, and adjust the route according to their inner compass towards a more fulfilling work life. In addition, the people I have the opportunity to work with—with their diverse backgrounds, cultures, and personal experiences—keep me continually exposed to different schools of thought, ensuring that I keep learning and opening up to other realities. When the pandemic began, I saw women being made redundant in such disproportionate numbers, and I felt an urge to help. It became a very personal mission to me to help as many women as I could who are facing or have faced lay-off, supporting them to recover and reconnect to themselves much faster than they would on their own.

Losing a job is painful, and it is a very lonely process. However, I see the powerful transformative effect that women can have on the systems around them. I am determined to help them navigate and find the true gift beyond the loss of a job, using it as a powerful fuel towards a more meaningful life—not only for themselves but also for everyone they dearly care about. I believe that every woman who has a healthy sense of self-worth and a connection to a greater purpose can transform the world into a kinder, fairer, and more compassionate place for all of us.

Before finding my purpose, I had never experienced this level of excitement in my career and my personal life—never before had they been so interconnected and nourishing of one another. My purpose guides me in my daily decisions and actions, in my personal and professional lives. As a consequence, the adoption of new habits has come very naturally. I have become my laboratory, where I experiment with different approaches, searching for those that will most positively impact my wellbeing and create a ripple effect that reaches others. In 2019, I intuitively created this image of the best version of myself, a picture of physical, emotional, intellectual, and spiritual health. I connect to it daily, visualizing how it will be, feel, and affect my own life and those of others. I have not set a deadline or a goal, rather *a way of being*. Instead of rushing to reach this new version that truly inspires me, I am savoring the process of gradually transforming into it. This allows me to fail, learn with discernment rather than judgment, smile, and resume from where I stumbled. One of the results is that my body has been finding its balance, and I have been able to let go of more than forty pounds of weight without any stress, hurry, or restrictions—only balance.

Before discovering my purpose, I lived on autopilot, unable to connect with what I wanted, just reacting to whatever happened to me. I was quickly lost in the norm of what was considered the markers of success: a stable job, promotions, a beautiful home, a fancy car. When I began to connect to my purpose in 2014, I finally felt the inspiration and strength to challenge, deconstruct, recreate my reality and define what *success* meant for me. Since then, my purpose has evolved and become more apparent, more vivid, and refined. My focus has shifted from constant worry about my performance and searching for external approval to fulfillment through being of service to others. This meant a powerful shift for everyone, and – paradoxically – my performance improved when my focus turned elsewhere. I feel more alive, more present, and more connected to myself and everyone around me.

My Advice

I believe each of us is trying to find and live our purpose. If you are on the path to find yours, pay attention to the many signals life is sending to you – living with purpose brings a sense of flow, where things unfold in a natural way, rather than having to be pushed all the time. Identify these moments in your life. Remember who you truly are, discover your passions and values, as well as your natural gifts and talents; we tend to overlook them because they seem to come so easily that we take them for granted. Ask yourself what makes you feel truly alive. If you find your purpose but don't know how to operationalize it and make it work in the world to generate money, start by envisioning what your life will look like when you are living your purpose. This vision and inspiration may help you find alternatives within your reach right now, allowing you to take the first small steps towards your ultimate vision.

Take one step at a time. Don't compare yourself to others—compare yourself to your yesterday's self. When aligned to your purpose, the steps you are taking now will bring you to your vision of the future. Remember: your failures do not define you. Often, we do not dare to change because we are too scared to fail and be rejected. Fear kicks in, attempting to trap you in the comfort zone and protect you. Do not let it limit you. When the fear begins to rise, reconnect to your vision and purpose to realign and find inspiration to keep going. Believe in yourself.

Be kind to yourself. Be true to yourself. And ask for help whenever you need it. I hope these insights inspire you to seek and live your life with purpose. I assure you, you will find it truly rewarding.

Flavia Wahnfried is a passionate lifelong learner who works as a Career Strategist focused on helping leaders and individuals across the globe to find more meaning and fulfillment in their careers and lives. Currently, she is on a mission to help professional women uncover their real identity and purpose after losing a job.

Flavia is a Certified Professional Coach from the University of Cambridge (UK) and Instituto Ecosocial (Brazil). She holds a bachelor's degree in International Relations from Pontifícia Universidade Católica in São Paulo. Passionate about different cultures, she is a native Portuguese speaker, fluent in German and English, speaks Spanish at an intermediate level and is currently learning French.

You can reach out to Flavia through https://www.linkedin.com/in/flaviagiselawahnfried/ or flavia@careerinflow.com

Reaching
for Solution

Purpose Pains—But It's Worth It

By Benda Kithaka
Kenya

My name is Benda Kithaka.

For the last ten years, I have consciously lived a life of purpose in cervical cancer advocacy, inspiring others to deliberately pursue wellness and healthy lifestyles as a way of preventing disease and improving their quality of life. I do this using my gift of public speaking, strategic marketing, and communications background to help craft and deliver innovative behavior change communications that will empower others to live their best life now. Through my vast networks and connections, I am hopeful that we will positively impact the lives of others.

My life on purpose began in February 2010. I was at my desk, in a high-flying marketing career, selling high-end cars with ambitious goals, a pretty good salary, including health insurance coverage for my family and me. I was living a good life, and I was a poster picture of success.

Then came that call, literally. I remember it vividly like it happened yesterday. It was a Wednesday evening. We had a planned corporate event that coming weekend, and as head of the department, I had stayed behind to verify the final plans one more time. I am meticulous and take pride in doing stellar work.

The Call to Purpose

My sister's husband called me from the village. One hundred eighty kilometers away, his voice was so clear. He said my sister had cervical cancer. In his own words, he had not eaten for three days, as he wondered if she was dying, how long she had to live, and what he should do.

I hung on to those words in a state of panic, trying to process the thoughts in my head, thinking that I could be losing my sister. Who would be the mother to her little girl? At twenty-seven, isn't that too young to die? See, what I knew of cancer then was that it was a death sentence. When I listened to him, he didn't seem to think any differently.

Even though I was trembling on the inside, I steeled myself enough to tell him that we would find a way forward.

When we hung up, I called my doctor. Late as it was, he picked up. I explained the situation, and he said he needed to see her to make an informed decision. We agreed he would see my sister that Friday. I called back and asked my brother-in-law to bring her in from the village for a doctor's visit.

Two days later, my sister and her husband came to Nairobi. He looked shattered. You could see the effort he was making to remain strong. She looked apprehensive—young but not sure what the future held in store. I was there, covering up the fear gripping me on the inside.

In contrast, the doctor was calm, handling the test results, vital checks, and prescriptions with an efficiency that only doctors know how to do. He explained that my sister was fortunate. She had pre-cancerous cells, but she had been diagnosed very early. He would put her on a treatment plan, and we would see what would happen in the next six months.

I genuinely don't remember this part very well, and I cannot tell you what he specifically said. As he laid out a plan for her treatment, I was holding my breath, stuck with the hope that this cancer might be treated but with the fear that it might be too late.

It took us six very long months with what felt like endless visits from the village to the doctor's clinic in the city. All this time, we hid the news from our mother. I am sure Mother wondered why my sister and her husband suddenly paid so many visits to Nairobi. With each visit, we had a bit more hope. On the last visit, she got a clean bill of health. No more pre-cancerous cells. Sigh! We could now breathe easier.

Six months later, my brother-in-law called yet again. My heart dropped at first, remembering the last major call and its fallout. This time, however, he called with a different set of news—she was pregnant! You could hear the joy in his voice. This was the most unexpected news. Not only had the pre-cancerous cells been eliminated, but she had also recovered enough to get pregnant. I wanted to know more, and I was set to find all the information I needed.

Embracing the Path

With my communications background, I knew that I could make a difference by using my policy, social, and marketing research skills and networks to demystify this disease and arm women with the necessary knowledge to eliminate this scourge. So, I dug in deep, searched the internet, asked critical questions to doctors in my network, talked to others in the cancer space—and soon realized that women were too frequently dying because they didn't know about this type of cancer! Yet, there was enough information available to eradicate the cervical cancer problem.

So I made it my purpose to do something about this sad reality. Not pausing long enough to contemplate what life held in store, I started on this journey armed only with a desire to make a difference in how women perceived cervical cancer. I guess you could say that that was how I found my purpose.

But if you look back on my previous life, it was there to see. I would be the one standing up to bullies. I was also the one who would be running around with buckets of water to put out the tear gas canisters during my campus days. I would be picking up the wounded to bandage them after the riots. I was and had always been ready and willing to come to the rescue of those who were handed an unfair hand. Even at the tender age of twelve or thirteen, I knew I wanted to be a lawyer to defend those charged unfairly. Maybe the practice of advocacy is what the call was about all along, and my journey was just a preparation for the task ahead. The time had come in that call on that fateful Wednesday evening.

I have always been passionate about Africa. Never aspiring to go and work abroad like other youth my age, I always knew I wanted to help set things right in my corner of the world.

Since I discovered that cervical cancer could be prevented, I have always visualized a world where Africa is not left behind in the journey towards cervical cancer elimination. The rest of the developed world has interventions and technologies that make it easier for women to prevent cervical cancer. Other parts of the world have also invested heavily in systems and structures that make it easier for women to take the necessary steps to prevent the disease.

I am working to reach a place where every woman decides a position of power. Power to know why they need to prevent cervical cancer, how they can prevent it, why the need for urgency in taking action and granting agency to decide which measures are necessary to prevent it. Ultimately, I am also working on income-generating programs that empower the vulnerable women that I serve, who come from villages and slums and do not have disposable income, to engage in activities that give them the power to meet the costs of prevention and care.

Recognizing the systemic, policy, and social inequalities that we have to surmount for this vision to be realized, I deliberately take daily actions that bring women closer to the self-discovery that cervical cancer is preventable way before it happens. I want all women to know that they have the power to make this happen. When given to our daughters, we have a vaccine, which has been shown to help develop immunity against cervical cancer. Also, it takes up to twenty years for the causative agent—Human Papillomavirus (HPV)—in the body to change cells into cancer. There is more than enough time to stop it.

My daily actions are guided by my firm belief that I am living purposefully to advance this knowledge and empower women with the facts, to build the knowledge that helps them make critical decisions to prevent cervical cancer for themselves and their daughters.

The decision to leave formal employment and concentrate on this field of advocacy was not a direct path. Even as my sister was going through her treatment journey, I went through a personal journey that exposed me to our dysfunctional healthcare system in Africa.

In June 2010, I was blessed with a handsome baby boy who brought me so much joy. My husband and I had been trying to conceive for over three years, and when he was born, I was overjoyed. He was my miracle baby. However, he was a sickly infant, and we were admitted to the hospital every three to six months during his infancy. He would get high fevers, go into convulsions, and pass out. I would be driving at high speeds with my eldest holding tightly onto him in the back seat—knowing that we needed to get him to the hospital as quickly as possible so that he would be put on oxygen. The medical coverage at my workplace helped because I never had to worry about raising funds for the treatment deposit or fundraising for us to be discharged.

At one point, I was in a hospital bed with my son getting medicine through an IV, and I remember that I would hold him so that he wouldn't remove the needle. But the moment he slept, I would lay him on the bed and quickly switch on my laptop to check on my work, verify that our marketing plans were on course, and address urgent emails to maintain my job and the necessary insurance coverage. I was a wreck, trying to hold a job, nurse a sickly toddler, manage my sister's treatment journey, and keep up the appearances of a woman who had it all together. I could not cope. So I consciously chose to drop the one ball I knew would quickly bounce back: my career. I resigned from my high-flying job to give more time to discover what was ailing our son.

In my first month as a stay-at-home mom and wife, I realized that quitting my job wasn't an excellent idea. I would wake up, organize everyone, make breakfast, drive my eldest to school, come back, and manage the house. In one week, I had finished organizing my home. Next, my focus was on my husband. Honestly, I became a pain— ironing socks, color-matching his outfits, micromanaging his time. I realized if we were going to have harmony, I needed to go back to being busy. So I volunteered at an organization that was doing cancer awareness. Unfortunately, most of their work centered on breast cancer, which was not aligned with my purpose for eliminating cervical cancer. So we parted ways, and I was back to seeking ways to actualize my vision.

Early February in 2012, I met two other women who were seeking avenues to do impactful work on cancer awareness. The three of us—a nurse, a doctor, and I, the communications expert—agreed on the need to demystify cervical cancer. Each of us was armed with a desire to change things. We sat over lunch and strategized how to stop cervical cancer. We needed a formal framework to do the work, so we invited a lawyer to join us. Together, we started Women4Cancer, a Kenyan non-governmental organization (NGO) that works with communities for cervical cancer prevention.

Winding Roads and Detours

Being a curious soul, I was always looking for places to be, things to do, voices to raise, to make it known that we could stop cervical cancer. Purposeful work takes time, blood, sweat, and tears. As I went from place to place to give talks at the community level, it took a lot of personal investment in time and resources.

When I registered the organization, I was also blessed with a baby girl, making us a family of five. I can only imagine the financial strain my work has had on my husband, who was the sole financial provider for an expanded family. I am grateful to him. He has sacrificed many things to shoulder the responsibilities and give me the freedom to reach where I am today, confident that my path to purpose will work.

My children, too, have had to bear their share of the burden. I had not realized how big an impact my volunteering work had on them until one day, my eldest daughter and I were reminiscing about this advocacy journey, and she reminded me how we used to go out for dinners to exotic restaurants, just so that she could practice using chopsticks. She missed the experiences where we would drive out of town simply because we were tired and wanted to unwind. I could see the nostalgia in her eyes, wistfully remembering how long ago we had extra money to burn. The younger ones could not understand; they had never seen that side of mom, who could recklessly spend without worrying where the next penny was coming from. My whole household has heard for the last couple of years, especially after my savings ran out, is, "Where is the budget for this? We don't have the budget. We need to budget." I think secretly they also must call me Mom-Budget.

Over and above the money issue is the inner struggle to come to terms with the fact that I am right where I need to be. See, I always felt out of place, a marketer standing out like a sore thumb in place of scientists.

Two years into my advocacy journey, I was invited as a speaker at a conference. I had just delivered an excellent presentation and was feeling quite good about this achievement when a professor came, voice booming, telling me, "Woman, you should be in a pulpit, not here, where we speak science." Hmmm. Yep. All I could think of was a wisecrack at him, "Well, Prof, since you all don't come to church, we are bringing the sermon to you." Someone giggled softly. I felt the pain deeply. Ridicule, disbelief, conflicted—he had voiced what I always felt: *I didn't belong.*

This feeling drove me to go back to school. This time, I was more deliberate about the course I was taking to understand the science behind cervical cancer and better integrate that knowledge into my communications work.

There were many challenges along the way: a shortage of money, feeling out of place, having personal strife in my family, and strain on my children. The only thing that kept me going was the knowledge that we were making impactful strides. Each time I saw one more woman screened, diagnosed, treated early, and fully recovered was fuel to my purpose. I knew if we could do it for the one, we could do it for others.

The situation was still heartbreaking. Although we were making headway with treatments for one woman at a time, the numbers of women dying from cervical cancer were still rising. Progress was slow, but there was still progress. When we began campaigning to educate women about the realities of cervical cancer, only 2,500 women were being diagnosed annually. By 2015, the number had almost doubled to 4,800 women. It seemed like an uphill task, but I found comfort in knowing that more women were talking about their experiences with cervical cancer when any mention of 'female problems' was considered very taboo not too long ago. More women were now talking about it and taking action.

It wasn't always easy being an advocate for others, especially as a woman who hadn't even had cervical cancer myself. My sister didn't want to talk about her own experience, and she didn't particularly like me airing her business. I prayed that I would find someone who would help me make this disease more personal so that others might better see sense in getting screened early.

Then I met Rose—a phenomenal woman. We met at a radio station when she was there sharing her story, and I was there to reinforce the need for early detection as the solution to stopping cervical cancer.

"Head-to-toe meticulously put together" is what comes to mind when I think of Rose that day. She wore minimalist heels, which complemented her height, a black skirt, and a snow-white blouse that matched her pearly white teeth; big-red-statement-earrings beautifully highlighted her perfect ebony skin. Her entire ensemble echoed the vibrant heartbeat in her chest, which throbbed with her passion for prevention. Rose was a cervical cancer survivor.

Rose had a voice and a story to tell, and she was not afraid to use either. All she needed were communications skills to help her share this story with a resounding impact. I knew I could fix that. I was a marketer; I know story-telling.

We teamed up—Rose, with her lived experience of the devastating impact of cervical cancer, and me, the communications expert, who had read broadly, traveled widely and could challenge the science while speaking of prevention. Now, I had a partner. We were formidable. Radio, TV, community gatherings, pulpits; you name it, we were there. Sometimes, we had no money for fuel, and we took public transport or hitched rides. But she was always with me.

Our message was simple: Cervical cancer can be stopped.

There were places we would go together—churches, mosques, places of worship—to talk to women. We went on radio and TV to tell the prevention story. We only attended an international conference together once. All the other times, I went alone, armed with the knowledge that I needed to talk about it, sometimes with no pocket money to bring back gifts for my kids, sometimes with no money for dinner, relying on the fruit on the breakfast buffet, which I would carry back to the hotel room and have in the evening. All because the conference organizer had sent everything else—tickets, conference meals, accommodation, taxi fare to the hotel—but forgotten that I also needed to eat dinner after the conference.

It was about this time when I started feeling tired of being perpetually broke. I decided that I would finish my healthcare diploma and look for a job in the pharmaceutical industry. Maybe I could then work purposefully while earning an income for self-sustenance.

In January 2017, just when I was done with my studies in health systems strengthening, my grandfather was diagnosed with cancer. He is the one who raised me. I was crushed, and I was determined to get him the best care possible. At this time, Kenya went through a national doctors' strike that lasted over one hundred days. All health services in the country were at a standstill. Even with the strike, I used my advocacy skills to secure his doctor appointments, hospital admission, and treatment. I knew this was not the time to leave the advocacy space. I had just acquired the skills to engage in policy dialogue and hopefully influence better policies for cervical cancer elimination. As a result, we deliberately took the initiative to coordinate other organizations in the cervical cancer space to advocate together.

In committing to the journey, I spent a lot of personal time on advocacy, sitting in technical working groups, volunteering for various committees, and nurturing others. At times, I was overstretching myself. I recall in 2018, for the first time in my life, I faced burnout. I had just been told that I was expecting a child and was put on bed rest. At the same time, my grandfather died, and I could not see myself not attending his funeral. So, my family and I traveled for his burial, and unfortunately, the trip took a toll, and I lost the pregnancy. This was painful, and for three months, I went into a deep depression.

I was planning on taking a break from advocacy for my mental health, but that is when Rose, my advocacy companion, was diagnosed with a cancer recurrence. She was treated and recovered, albeit briefly. For a third time, her cancer came back with a vengeance. This time around, she did not make it. When Rose died, it felt like something in me also died. I was going through the motions, but I was not all there. I was hoping against hope that this would be the part that I was cutting loose. Maybe I would find a way to go back to corporate life and just focus on earning an income.

I felt I had lost myself in trying to help others.

Relentless Pursuits

A momentous day came in October 2019; I hadn't showered for three days—angry that my life purpose in cancer advocacy wouldn't let me go. Afraid, not sure where I would start this new journey I was taking for self-discovery.

Then one of our famous marathoners ran a marathon in record time, showing the world that it is possible to pursue his purpose and win. I watched Eliud Kipchoge run INEOS 1:59 that Saturday morning on TV, with the world cheering him on. My spirit gently reminded me of a promise I had made in 2018. I had promised that I would Climb Mt. Kenya with cancer survivors to discover purpose together.

As I sat on that breakfast table, smelly and sad, I saw my life as a movie unfolding—of places God had taken me, people I had met, things I had seen in areas where health systems worked for their people, and the promises I had made. I was also reminded of a dream I had of helping others prevent cancer by addressing the modifiable risk factors and inspiring people to own their health to take steps for early diagnosis.

To me, the INEOS 1:59 World Record brought back my commitment to advocacy. I remembered my purpose. My one burning desire to eliminate cervical cancer; a reality that was still a dream yet to be achieved. Right there and then, I knew my purpose work was not over.

Defeated as I was feeling, I had renewed hope. Maybe if I pushed myself, perhaps if I embarked on this personal journey to climb Mt. Kenya, I could also redefine my advocacy trajectory. I got up, showered, had breakfast at noon, and with questions still unanswered. I embarked on redefining the route I would take. The critical questions I am still asking are: Is it still only about cancer, cervical cancer, or other diseases? Do I need to add more cancers in the fold?

There is much happening on the global scene. The World Health Organisation (WHO) has called for a global strategy to eliminate cervical cancer. With Africa lagging on so many milestones, I feel a burning sense of purpose to ensure that we can fast-track our response to this call.

I have two daughters. One is in her early twenties. The other is eight, as she often likes to remind me. My son recently turned ten years old. I am bringing them up in a world dealing with many life-threatening diseases. Cancer is just one of them. Many of the risk factors are lifestyle-related. We are also in a grey cloud with the Covid-19 pandemic, which threatens to obscure all other gains made in healthcare. Despite that challenge, there is still hope because the pandemic also highlights how much our health is in our own hands.

Now, more than ever, I am convinced that we can help fast-track this journey towards owning our health within this lifetime. That is why I am working tirelessly to climb this mountain, seeking answers for my purposeful journey and clarity on where to focus next.

I have had my ups and downs. I have seen amazing sights and traveled to many places. The one thing that catches me that fills me with wonder is the aura of people alight with their dreams. There is a certain spark in their eyes of knowing that they are doing that, which sets their spirit on fire.

When others look at me, I hope they see the passion, feel the warmth, and recognize the flame that burns deep in my heart. I hope I inspire them to seek their path and follow it.

Ultimately, each of us has one life, but if lived right, if spent in pursuit of our dreams, we can give others the freedom to seek theirs too. If the path is difficult, let someone look at mine and be inspired to push on.

So, you might be asking, how did I get here, knowing my purpose? If I were to give anyone any advice about finding purpose, I would say that you need Commitment, Clarity, and Connection.

Take Heed

Finding purpose is not something that can be done in a few days, weeks, or months. Going by my story of the ten years it took to get to where I am today, finding purpose is a lifelong journey that can only be done one step at a time.

Commit to pursuing the path you are on, no matter what obstacles come your way. The road to finding your purpose has curves, forks, and stops. Keep going. Through the valleys or the hills, even when you feel like nothing is going on or are overwhelmed by the struggles. Take that next step. Commit that time. Be consistent.

Seek clarity that what you are doing still matters. In 2019, I had to pause when I felt like the path I was on was not taking me in the direction I wanted to go. I realized in that pause that even when you change course or take a fork in the path, you still will end up where you are needed. Your approach to purpose needs you to be clear so that you spend your energies on what is ultimately leading you to find meaning, fulfillment, and well-being.

Connect with others, and choose wisely whom you bring into your path. No, I am not talking about the ones you are obligated to walk with daily—your family, workmates, or neighbors. Here, I refer to the people in your inner circle. The friends you choose to share your path to purpose. Surround yourself with people who inspire you to be better, who are ignited in living their purpose too. Those who exhibit your values and are committed to their path; will never deliberately draw you from yours. They get it—purpose pains. They are committed to theirs. Occasionally they will draw strength from your journey when they are feeling lost on their path. And, similarly, when your candle is burning low, it will help you reignite.

The world needs more people ignited with the passion of purposeful living. I am one. Be one.

Benda Kithaka is an award-winning, world-renowned health advocate by day and a creative-closet writer by night. She thrives in storytelling that inspires others to live their best life now. Benda received her Bachelor of Arts degree in Politics and Government from the University of Nairobi and her Post Graduate Diploma in Leading High Performing Health Organisations from Strathmore University. She also has many certificates and awards in advocacy, published in several peer-reviewed journals, and written numerous opinion pieces for local and international publications. In 2016, she was crowned Cancer Ambassador of the Year in Kenya.

A Kenyan by birth, she is a global citizen who loves adventure and likes to weave stories about people, things, and places she has been to. Currently residing in Nairobi, she escapes the hustle and bustle of the city through hiking, reading, and baking for her family. Keep in touch with Benda via the web https://www.kilelehealth.org and follow her work on Twitter https://www.twitter.com/bendakithaka

Not "Wasting" a Thing—Certainly Not a Life

By Poonam Kasturi
India

I was about twelve years old when I met Buddha and believed that "desire is the cause of suffering." I left that history class and immediately put the idea to the test. I experimented with saying no to a movie my siblings were going to see and experienced the conflicting feelings of virtue and disappointment at not seeing the film. In addition, I was left with a detached sense of examining this state and wondering how such an idea impacted a person's behavior in the world. This is a powerful memory. It has not left me, popping up at odd times over these years since.

Today, I am fifty-eight years old, and this year (2021), my project, company, and social enterprise will turn fifteen years old. This seems an acceptable moment to allow me a pause and the indulgence of walking back to remember my time so far.

Redefining Our Relationship to Waste

If you google my name, you will reach a site called *Daily Dump*. Now depending on which part of the world you belong to, this will mean different things. Some folks would wonder why we chose such a provocative name even. But sitting around a table in 2005 thinking of making waste fun for India, we had to select contrarian and memorable things. We set out to help urban Indians reimagine their relationship with their daily waste, waste bin, and daily act of throwing things out. We wanted them to see how their individual actions could help prevent pollution in our water, air, and food. Our challenge was to get them excited about their sense of agency. We wanted our audience to move away from the idea that waste was yucky to the idea that waste was cool!

To get everyday people to start on this new, unfamiliar journey, we started talking about composting at home! Of course, we did that at a time when nobody wanted to keep waste in their homes for any moment more than necessary.

It was like one expert said to me at that time—a foolish attempt. Another told me that no self-respecting Indian homemaker would compost because it was not clean.

Something in my gut told me otherwise. I went ahead and designed India's first home composter. I was teaching design and sustainability at that time, so I would carve out time to spend prototyping, testing, and making communications material. I believed this was an idea whose time had come. When I would talk about this to colleagues and design peers, I could sense the undercurrent of doubt in their tolerant and polite responses.

Why was I even attempting this? I was not young and starry-eyed. I was over 40 and had enjoyed my time as an educator and designer so far. There was no reason to begin on what, by all counts, was a doomed concept. Like the management, folks reminded me, "There is no demand, Poonam, and only you see a need. Is it even viable to attempt it as a business idea?"

Why did this not deter me? It did not matter because I had reached a stage in life where losing was no longer frightening. I felt I still needed to figure out the meaning of life. Looking around me, I saw people define "purpose" in such diverse ways that it made me reflect and realize that I was unclear about my own "purpose," even if all the things I had done so far seemed to be meaningful, fulfilling, and challenging.

So Daily Dump arrived at the right time for me. It was saying to me that you will find a way to bring sense and wholeness to the contrasting pieces of you through me. It seemed to know that I needed a crucible that would nurture an alchemic interaction for the disparate, isolated ideas of my mind and heart. So it did not matter if there was no demand. What mattered was the gift that Daily Dump offered me—a way to grow into wholeness and perhaps purpose.

Looking back, I can see three different parts of me that were seeking amalgamation into a new whole:

- My commitment to sustainability, environment, and design.
- My curiosity about the nature of reality.
- My stubborn streak of "figuring it out on my own terms."

My Commitment to Sustainability, the Environment, and Design

Coming from a small, sheltered town (Bangalore was small in 1979), going to design school was exhilarating and challenged me to enlarge my mental models of the world. NID was quite radical for that time, and since our profession was in its infancy, we were encouraged to be experimental, which was quite a shift from the education system we came from.

Those five years at design school set the foundation for my interest and affinity for ideas about how design could contribute to everyday lives. We learned the skills of the craft and the different perspectives of the social and political environment in which design takes place. Nation-building was a popular "canteen" discussion, and design for us young students was our "superpower" to creating change and impact. Many great minds inspired us in our time there, particularly Victor Papanek and Charles Eames' emphasis on ecological and social responsibility as the twin pillars of design practice, which has stayed with me over the years. The counterculture movement and thinkers like Buckminster

Fuller and E.F. Schumacher also influenced our design discussions in class and outside.

Coming from an urban area and armed with predominantly Western education, going into villages was also new for me. I remember projects I did with leather craftspeople in a cluster of villages. This was a deeply immersive experience that left respect for my own cultural, social landscape and ignited a resolve to understand this part of my identity.

Like many young people coming into their own at that age, I was also exploring my ideas of the world. What I saw did not satisfy me, and there was no relief in saying, "That's just the way things are." I was moved by philosophy but not to the extent that I wanted to read more deeply. I liked the idea of "karma yoga" (what little I understood of it). It fit into my more practical, "let's be useful" bent of mind at that time. I was puzzled by disparity, injustice, and greed. At that age, I did not know that navigating these to reach a semblance of understanding was to be a journey of a lifetime. It left me with lots of questions but very few working answers. I was unconvinced that change for the "better" was necessarily the outcome of doing "good work." The questions "What kinds of change can design make?" and "What creates enduring positive change?" were the ones that would not be shaken. They kept surfacing and encouraged me to keep seeking answers.

I left design school with a mind and heart that was tuned towards sustainability, ecology, and self-reliance. I was a mixture of a "let's do it" attitude and existential angst of "what does this mean?"

Then, My Life Turned Upside Down

Then I lost my father.

I had watched my father and mother work hard to set up their design consultancy and the manufacturing business. Three of us kids would be there on the shop floor every weekend and holiday to help out. This was a time of learning by being pushed into the deep end. Dealing with deadlines, customers, employees, factory inspectors, and the notion of entrepreneurship all happened on the shopfloor and around the dinner table. We got to deal with the real world of work from a young age and had a ringside view of the highs and lows of being an entrepreneur before it was "cool" to be one. Just before my father died, his most trusted colleague had cheated him, and I saw how that had saddened him. I would talk to him about what it meant to own "something," the sense of a loss of trust, and what the pros and cons of building an enterprise were. Ideas of loyalty, trust, and commitment were no longer black and white. They seemed to have crevices and crusts that made it hard to feel like you could ever fully understand them.

My father was someone who I could talk to about everything. He died young. An artist, designer, thinker, and self-made entrepreneur, he was ahead of his time. He guided and loved us so thoroughly that his passing brought my existential side to the foreground. I was not patient enough anymore. I was also angry and wanted answers.

Plumbing the Depths

I reached out to philosophy, joined a *satsang,* and even went for a ten-day *vipassana* meditation session. The reading reiterated that my questions were as old as humanity. The language had changed over time, but essentially they were the same. Yes, this was not a surprise, but it was also frustrating that I could not see the light at the end of the tunnel, which promised the texts I'd read.

The *satsang* brought to fore the paradoxical nature of the effort to understand something. I became obsessed with questions like "Who understands?" "Who am I?" "Is there a reality that is objective?" "How do I operate in this world?" Again, not at all new, I was told.

The *vipassana* sowed the seeds of something beneficial. It planted in me the first signs of patience—the gentle ability to let things be. My personality was always in a hurry, always wanting things to be black or white, always wanting to get out there and act, and this was a significant gift. But I didn't even see it at that time. The Buddha revisited my world, and in my sessions, I was acutely aware of the anger and frustration of not understanding the world.

None of my questions went away. I was caught between doing, which was a big part of me, and the background noise of not being convinced of the mores of the world I encountered daily. When I would listen to someone who made bold assertions of their point of view, I was so impressed that they had the clarity that emanated from their words and actions. I would then reflect on my state to meet the one thought that surfaced: "One day, I will perhaps understand, and then I will also be clear."

After my father died, I decided to stop planning ahead. So when the opportunity to be part of the team to set up a design school from scratch came by, I was free to accept this. Since I had to teach, it became imperative to learn more, so ecology, sustainability, and design were subjects that I delved into more deeply and engaged with peers across the world in these areas. Teaching helped me hone my interest and understanding of design, sustainability, ecology, and future circularity models. Teaching young adults was very fulfilling, and the side of me that "cared" flowered. I could sense that a part of me was made whole—I was of use. It made me less angry.

I was keen that my courses allow students to explore their relationships with the natural world and the world of work. It was an excellent opportunity for me to construct interdisciplinary courses and bring in experts from diverse fields to teach new ways of seeing and creating. Growing a college from scratch is exciting but also a lot of work with long hours. My involvement was complete, and I had a great mentor and powerful woman who was the director, Geetha Narayanan, who taught me all I know about the joys of teaching and education. I am grateful to have had her in my life and enjoyed those formative years setting up the school.

It took twelve years of intensive teaching and helping the school grow. On the personal front, I had the brutal experience of not "being" fully present for my child while wanting to do my best. Being a mother with a full-time career is hard today. It was harder back then. In the yearning to do your best, you are blinded by unintended consequences. Still, non-action is not an option, so you strive to find new ways to balance your different desires to do your "best." Often exhausted, I would smile and tell myself, "The Buddha said even desire to be the best is not healthy!" The confrontation that my best was not perhaps perceived as adequate was humbling, and further strengthened my resolve to uncover other paradoxes in life.

Stumbling onto Composting

In my teaching, I ran a cross-discipline, collaborative course called Design Matters. We had engineering, design, and science students explore issues in water, waste, and energy. Composting was studied in this course as a possible approach to reducing waste thrown out in the public system. Since it was only a short course, the ideas generated by the group were tested only a short while, and then students moved on to other programs.

Something about composting and the explorations stayed with me. I had visited a landfill site as part of my first project in design school, and maybe that is why waste resonated with me. Whatever the reason, I could not let that go and began prototyping and testing to create a solution.

In *Denial of Death*, Ernest Becker talks about how many of us unconsciously deny the physical "us" that is perishable. We create "immortality projects" that help us believe we will last forever. He says how conflict is natural when one person's enterprise (her immortality project) clashes with another's (immortality project)! When I read Becker, this idea made so much sense. Do we feel a more profound loss because we invest in immortality projects? Is there so much personally invested in what we do that anything that happens to it can destroy or elevate us? Is what we do the only thing that defines us? Can we create without attachment or fear?

I found a similar tension in the college, a clash of ideas of how the immortality project should shape up, and I started prototyping composting ideas.

The timing seemed opportune. One day, I stopped working at the college. I left with no feeling of loss and with a resolve to try my immortality project with a caveat that it was to anchor me in "reality" (which I wanted to figure out).

My Curiosity about the Nature of Reality

"What is reality? Who am I?" The world says these are spiritual questions. I don't understand this definition. If I am alive and want to know who I am and what the world is, these are the most practical questions in my mind. "Spiritual" has the connotation of being dissociated from the world, from the everyday, and that does not sit easily with me. Also, "spiritual" has too many overlapping boundaries with "religion," which makes me uncomfortable.

In searching for the answers to my questions, I met Douglas Harding in his book *On Having No Head*. His ideas made so much sense to me, and I was surprised why we still carried on from the point of view of individual personas and so much anxiety. Of course, I had both an enormous ego and loads of stress which needed work. I resolved that using Daily Dump and all the creativity I could muster, I would set out to find myself and the meaning of my "purpose."

The one rule I laid down for myself was that every time I got angry, worried, or anxious about anything I was doing, I would gently remind myself of Ramana Maharishi's *advaita* pointing—find out who is anxious, who feels anger? I used this journey to find out "my true self," as the Buddha, Ramana, and Douglas Harding suggested.

It was tough going. My biggest challenge was my anger, impatience, and attachment, and my need for "things to be just so." I saw my fear of belonging to the world or the loss of this. It would simply arise in me, and slowly, very slowly, I reached a point where I could distance the fear from the sense of self. Measuring your worth against the media story, network story, or peer story is often a futile and transitory exercise. The goalposts keep changing, and the yardsticks are at best arbitrary. But it needs conviction at a very deep level to stay truly unintimidated and unaffected and yet be appreciative of fresh ideas and perspectives.

For fifteen years, I meandered down this path. Since I began my journey, I have become less angry, more peaceful, not at all worried about the future of my immortality project. I have also deepened my respect for the world and its vast diversity and tremendous energy. I am getting ready to hand over the company to the young folks who have worked alongside me for the past five years.

Have I found my true self, my purpose? I guess what I have found is that I could use my daily acts of doing to allow me to glimpse "myself" and, in effect, my purpose. It's a more contemporary route to seeking "self" than sitting in the Himalayas. As a metaphor, my company was my Himalayan cave.

My Stubborn Streak

Mine is not a conventional definition of purpose. I have a hard time following a traditional route because I have a hard time understanding concepts most people get readily. For example, I was thirty-two when I finally understood that numbers were a concept. I had spent all that time thinking numbers were real. You can imagine my great surprise and awe (and some disgust) at my ignorance! I was in a state of disbelief for a week. There are many such concepts in the world that I have trouble figuring out. I don't understand how money works, imaginary numbers, thermodynamics, quantum worlds, osmosis. The list could go on. So I have hacked my way since school, doing things in a way that better suits my style of understanding.

This trait allowed me to use what I am committed to, like sustainability and design, to help me understand myself.

I am supposed to run a social enterprise. Daily Dump has not been run on any management principles, and we did many things wrong. No self-respecting manager would condone our path. But since I was not out to make the largest, most profitable enterprise, it did not matter. I was more interested in intervening at the best leverage point to help the waste system, and I had a plan.

What did I have:

1. An idea whose time had come but had no demand in the market.
2. An idea that would help grow the importance of self-reliance and individual citizen involvement in urban built landscapes.
3. An idea that would make folks feel reconnected with natural cycles often overlooked in urban lifestyles.
4. A case for getting your hands dirty and bringing dignity to this sector.
5. A case for increasing the circular flows of nutrients.

I had very little money and no appetite for networking and convincing funders. In my head, that was too much of a time sink. I sunk my teeth into the hard work of prototyping, ideating, and how to build demand organically and stay the course.

I outlined a set of principles that would guide the running of the project—be creative, get customers, look after customers, listen to them sometimes, and don't spend more money than you have. In case there is enough money, hire good people and pay yourself less. Be friendly and helpful to competitors and spread the idea, not necessarily the firm. Some folks are going to be nasty, some good. Enjoy both.

I had no business plan, a small team of interns and part-timers who floated in and out, and we grew organically. We were able to achieve the spread of the idea because of our ability to be adaptable (something hardwired plans do not allow), freely share our work, and allow for others to own the solution to solve the collective waste problem. I was stretching the idea of an individual immortality project.

Now, after 15 years of this experiment, a stock check would reveal:

- We designed India's first home composter.
- We have reached the idea of home composting to over 10,000,000 families in India today.
- We nudged the policy from centralized waste management to decentralized practices. Our customers, through individual action, help keep over 60,000 kilograms (132,000 pounds) of organic waste out of the landfill DAILY. This is at no cost to the government.
- Our designs have been copied worldwide, and we have documented over 40 look-alikes as far as South America and Thailand.
- We have helped over 25 potter clusters earn more with our products.
- We have helped put back 50,000 kilograms (110,000 pounds) of compost into the soil as sequestered carbon. We continue to inspire other small entrepreneurs to begin their ventures, and we enjoy talking to anyone who will listen to the ideas of sustainability and design.

Is this going to change the world? No, but this was the only way I could have done it, part–intuition, part–common sense, and driven mainly by my questions to find myself.

If you ask me, "Is Daily Dump my purpose?" I would say it has served its purpose, and I am unsure if I have a purpose. I am wary of putting caring on my sleeve. In my glimpse of reality, it is possible to care deeply without caring for something.

Now it seems like the three loose and different threads of my world have come together and formed a thick flexible cord, which has all the strength of each strand and some more. I am deeply grateful for my version of the Himalayan cave in this lifetime. No, I would not recommend this route to any young person who wants to find purpose. You have to figure out your way. That is the only way of doing it.

Poonam Kasturi is a designer who is creating Swachh Bharat one Kambha composter at a time. Visit her website: www.dailydump.org or write her at: pbkasturi@usermail.com

Woman with Purpose: On Becoming an Advocate for Cancer Services

By Salomé Meyer
South Africa

E quitable cancer care in South Africa and probably in most Low Middle-Income Countries (LMICs) is a dream. Access to health remains a fundamental human right. However, to achieve any of that becomes a life journey once you become part of the quest to work towards equitable cancer care for most people.

In 1996, I lost my best friend and mentor to breast cancer. She was only thirty-seven, and she left behind a two-and-half-year-old daughter. Being with her almost daily towards the end made me feel so helpless and even cheated. Her death seemed senseless. Both of us were young and busy climbing the corporate ladder. We were achievement-driven, people-centered, and focused. Shortly after her death, I mentioned her in a meeting that I was chairing and was asked, "Who are you referring to?" I realized that while she may have been known to me (and others) for her qualities, no one will ever remember you for what you stand for unless you make a meaningful difference. I was faced with that specific question—what will give me purpose in my life? I was about to be promoted, so the prospect of one step up the ladder, more income had to be weighed up against a loss of income and the uncertainty of what to do if I were to be at home 24/7/365? My life partner, twenty years older than me, was promoted and had another ten years of effective service before retirement. Having a more considerable income between the two of us would indeed be comfortable, but we realized that the nature of our jobs and our sense of commitment would drive us apart. We made a joint decision that I would leave permanent employment—with its security of income and all the benefits attached—to pursue a differ-ent life. My friend's untimely death had to have a purpose. That deci-sion led to my discovery of my purpose: serving the cancer community of South Africa to make a real difference.

My newfound career as a volunteer and advocate started small, as a board member at a cancer non-profit organization. Community devel-opment was my forté, and it was indeed a challenge to initiate that mindset change in an organization at the dawn of our new democracy. How does one implement cancer services from a developmental per-spective? As that was the most relevant discussion at the time. This led to the facilitation of an advocacy program in early 2000. That endeavor remains as one of the leading advocacy departments of a cancer non-profit organization today. After my tenure as a board member was completed, I was asked to lead the establishment of CARISA (Cancer Research Initiative of South Africa), a focused cancer research program designed to drive the research into the burdens of diseases. Eighteen months later, I was retrenched with the message that I could not be appointed as the Director of CARISA as I do not have a doctorate! It, however, would only have had a lasting impact if I had allowed myself to believe that having a piece of paper (a PhD degree) is necessary before people will listen to you.

My Journey to Serve

Instead, I decided to turn the experience into an opportunity to re-brand myself as an independent advocate— a person who has her own voice and does not need a CEO's sanction or opinion or be someone who can make a difference. It calls for a strong sense of self and enough commit-ment to know that you can make it out there. It calls for a robust support system at home and the freedom to allow you to achieve your dream. It still does not come with a salary, but I had realized twelve years prior that money doesn't buy you happiness or fulfillment. Leading a basic life with purpose is much more meaningful than a life that chases unrealistic dreams and achievements.

This also comes with sacrifices—as one gets absorbed in the passion for what you're doing and the quest to achieve more. There has been an impact on personal relationships and a limit to time spent with my life partner and family. Hobbies take second place, such as the jewelry making I enjoy. Cancer takes precedence; you become the go-to person because of your commitment and dedication. You are always available—it does not matter what time of the day or night or how big or small the problem is. It is because you are just that person. I would not have it any other way as it fulfills me in my quest for purpose.

When I became involved in the cancer field in 1996, three cancer non-profit organizations registered in South Africa. In 2011, the landscape had changed so drastically that more than twenty-five had been registered. We were fighting the same issues that were identified in early 2000. Nothing had changed; cancer was not regarded as a priority disease, and cancer registration that would assist the government in planning and managing the disease was seriously lacking. The government was shifting the goalposts, saying it could not talk to twenty-five organizations and that it wanted to engage with one voice that would speak on behalf of the community.

This led to the establishment of the Cancer Alliance in 2011 as a collective voice, and I joined as the first independent cancer advocate. I had to make sure that I established my name so that I could use the extensive network that I had built up over the years on behalf of the cancer community and not fall into the trap of benefitting myself, putting the self above the community. Again, that will become who you are and how people will perceive you. Are you someone who works with purpose? If that purpose is to serve and to improve for the sake of others, it will be evident in the relationships that you build to achieve your dream. I soon realized that it was also not a quest for success—but rather a journey to serve.

The Cancer Alliance's focus is also about collaborative action that fosters a mind shift to work towards group goals rather than within a single organizational mission. As the independent advocate, your role is to be the voice of reason for the collective. This takes a particular focus on purpose to ensure that the bigger picture remains the objective. I have set out to become a *"Voice of the Voiceless"* through advocacy and activism. Many people say that there is no such thing and that people need to stand up and speak for themselves. I disagree: systemic human rights discrimination in many societies has led to people being unable to recognize their specific needs. They are too busy fighting for survival on another level.

In the South African environment, advocacy in the health field implies a human rights-based focus. This speaks to your value system.

As a young student in Community Development in the early 80s, I was exposed to the wise words of James Yen, who, as part of the Chinese Revolution in 1920, wrote:

> *Go to the people,*
> *Live among the people,*
> *Learn from the people, plan with the people,*
> *Work with the people.*
> *Start with what the people know,*
> *Build on what the people have.*
> *Teach by showing,*
> *Learn by doing;*
> *Not a showcase but a pattern,*
> *Not piecemeal but an integrated approach,*
> *Not to conform but to transform ...*

This has become my guidance on how and what to do. It frames my purpose.

The Inequities in Cancer Services

Increasingly, I became more and more aware of the inequities in cancer services in South Africa—the jarring divide between the public sector that serves 84 percent of the population and the private sector. It was just a natural progression from advocacy to activism once I became involved in the real issues behind access to cancer medicines. In 2016, the Cancer Alliance joined the Fix the Patent Laws coalition. I became aware of the injustice of cancer medicines being made more readily available to privileged people who have access to private-sector medical schemes but not to the patients in the public sector where affordability drives availability and ultimately dictates whether you live or die.

Part of my involvement in cancer was also to train breast cancer survivors in advocacy. I met Tobeka Daki in East London in 2015. She was one of those women who were denied treatment. She found her voice and became the voice for so many others.

Claudio Schuftan of Ho Chi Minh City runs a weekly blog on human rights issues in which he reminds us that inequality is part of an ideology and part of a political process. It goes without saying that if you are involved in the inequalities and inequities of the health care systems, one has to have a sound evidence-based foundation. This requires research and a sound, renowned network system that you can associate yourself with.

Since 2017, with the publication of the Cancer Alliance's report "Exploring Patent Barriers to Cancer Treatment Access in South Africa: 24 Medicines Case Studies," my purpose has been redefined to the quest for equitable health for all.

While my belief system drives me, I also have to make sure that I do not alienate people and thus have to learn to listen and take the needs of others into account. Positive relationships dictate whether you achieve your objectives—even if you are on the opposite end of the (political) spectrum from those who have to work with you to create a more equitable system.

My daily life is taken up with my focus on Access to Cancer Medicines. Having to fight a system to make sure that all patients have equal access to life-saving oncology treatments is ultimately also about distributive justice. It means that one must persevere, irrespective of the setbacks. I have learned to have patience, as equal access does not happen overnight in a short time. Instead, it takes months of systematic focus and strength to make sure that you keep your eyes on the ball. It takes a supportive enabling environment to maintain your focus. That also requires nurturing your relationships with those who are significant in your work and personal life.

Through the Cancer Alliance, I am proud to say that I have been instrumental in securing access to lifesaving treatment with trastuzumab for women with HER2+ breast cancer in the public sector. Today, women in most public sector treatment facilities and the private sector have equal access to this life-saving treatment. In two specific provinces, this is still an issue. This again will require dedicated focus. Trastuzumab access was coupled with the successful development of a breast cancer policy. When asked why a policy was needed, the argument of equity and sustainability formed the basis and led to the further development of other cancer policies to ensure just that.

When we started the Access to Medicine campaign, my naivety had me thinking that I would achieve access to at least four cancer medicines in two years. It's now three years later, and we're still fighting for equitable access for lenalidomide, a lifesaving treatment for patients with multiple myeloma. After three years of dedicated attention, we can still only say that generic access is now possible. This still leaves the public sector without affordable access to this medicine. It will take at least another twelve months before this can happen. In the meantime, one must remain positive. Patience pays off, as does being consistent and focusing on the systemic issues that must be corrected to ensure equity for all. One can achieve success in the long run. The adage "When you commit, you build hope; when you keep it, you build trust!" is very appropriate in advocating for equity and justice.

Who I Became Along the Way

Looking back at my twenty-five years of advocacy since I identified the need to make a meaningful difference, I can say that I have grown immensely. At first, it was just easy to focus on a small group. However, having to impact a national scale is a far more significant challenge and purpose. The ability to build relationships and positively maintain them plays an important role.

Being an advocate or activist is not to say that one is involved in the conflict. It is the opposite. Being conflictual will get you nowhere. Being assertive is associated with a forceful personality—one can easily scare people away with being too aggressive and uncaring. Being trained as a social worker and coming from a lineage of care workers (nurses, social workers, medical doctors, occupational therapists) is also part of who I am and how I was brought up. I had parents who allowed me to grow into my own and become a replica of them or conform to what they wanted. I have surrounded myself with many people that influenced my life positively over the years—friends, family, whether locally or globally, as I firmly believe that no one is an island. We need others to shape and fulfill us, irrespective of age, sexual orientation, creed or ethnicity.

At the age of sixty, I am faced with another challenge: to make sure that what I have set out to do and achieve is a meaningful legacy that can be taken over by any person who has a purpose and who has the same interests and passion that I have. It's not about creating another me. It is instead to empower someone that can take over the baton successfully.

Having children was never part of my relationship, and it was a personal choice and sacrifice that I made twenty-five years ago. My work became my everything in life, and it gave me purpose. Like guiding a child through life to become an independent being who is caring and will honor human rights, I have the vision that this "child" will continue long after I am gone.

Although I never had the privilege of being a mother, I played that role for my friend's daughter, whose death inspired me to live my purpose after she died. When my friend's daughter was 18 years old, I became more involved as a surrogate mother. Left with no parents and having experienced a disastrous childhood, she was faced with going into adult life with no reference system, no self-esteem, no value system, struggling with an eating disorder. Over the last ten years, it has been my daunting task and privilege to become her reference person, to guide her to become a whole person who can live life meaningfully and independently. She will always have the disability of mental health, which will plague her for the rest of her life, but she is far more able to manage life's curveballs now than she was a couple of years ago. Today, she is a qualified speech therapist who has chosen this career path as she wanted to serve with purpose.

Not all commitments have a happy ending, and I have learned not to take it personally if things do not work out the way I had hoped. This was brought home to me when another friend for whom I played the role of reference person and go-to person for nearly eighteen years tried to end his life. His attempt was unsuccessful, but the person he was and the life he had ended on that day. I discovered the reasons behind his decision, and it was frightening to realize that he had only shown me a part of himself. For me, it's another lesson and a reminder to make sure that your own house is in order in terms of decisions of life that have to be taken if you are not able to do so. It also implies that you will make peace with the fact that your life's journey can end at any given time. Make sure your mental well-being remains your number one priority in life. No one but you is responsible for the happiness in your life. Money cannot buy that. Living life honestly and with true intention can indeed be the key to happiness and a life fulfilled.

My life has been an incredible journey filled with challenges, opportunities, and emotional well-being, fulfilled by serving with purpose.

Salomé Meyer became a qualified Social Worker at the University of Pretoria in 1981, obtained an honors degree in Medical Social Work from the University of Stellenbosch in 1982, and an M.Soc Sci from the University of Cape Town in 1988. Since then, she has specialized in community development and worked at the local, provincial, and national levels of government for fifteen years. Specifically, Salomé has twenty-five years of advocacy experience in cancer, focusing on cervical and breast cancer, policy development, advocacy toolkit development, and access to cancer services. She is a member of the Women's Empowerment Cancer Advocacy Africa Network (WE CAN) and lives in Rondebosch, Cape Town, South Africa, with her life partner, Faan, and labrador, Skollie. Salomé is a keen gardener and cook, and she spends her free time doing various craft forms and jewelry making. Contact her at: https://canceralliance.co.za/

Confidential: Surviving Cancer Twice

By Udie Soko
Zambia

Discovering My Purpose

My cancer journey began when I was twenty-three. In 1988, I hit the job market after attaining my BA in Public Administration at the University of Zambia. I was fortunate to find a job at the Ministry of Foreign Affairs.

However, several months before my graduation, I noticed a small lump—the size of a grape, on the right side of my neck—which, out of fear, I ignored. It was only in 1989, after catching a nasty cold from a workmate that caused unbearable pain in my neck, that prompted me to seek medical attention finally.

The lump, which was now the size of half a golf ball, had fairly quickly multiplied in size and was now also on my left side. After an initial inaccurate diagnosis of tuberculosis of the lymph nodes, two biopsies confirmed that I had stage IIB cancer of the lymph nodes.

Devastated and shocked, with no clue how the disease would forever change my life, I began treatment. There were no cancer specialists in Zambia, no dedicated cancer center, a severe shortage of chemotherapy drugs, and absolutely no radiation therapy available. But I was one of the lucky ones. Through what I now know as divine intervention, I was assigned to the diplomatic service through my former employer to West Germany, where I successfully completed treatment. In 1990, I heard the sweetest words, "You have no more cancer." While cancer had left my body, unbeknownst to me, it had, however, left an indelible mark on my soul.

Subsequently, I was promoted at work and transferred to the United Kingdom. I finally came back to Zambia in 2000. What struck me upon my return was that most cancer patients' fate had not changed much since I'd left eleven years ago. The same despair, ignorance, stigma, and imminent death were rife. There was something wrong with that picture, and I knew I had to do something to help make a difference.

After volunteering for six years at a local cancer organization that focused on supporting children with cancer, I had a deep conviction to set up my organization that would not only help children with cancer but men and women as well. I knew that starting such a venture would involve more than mere passion, so I applied to the American Cancer Society to attend training at the American Cancer Society University (ACSU). In 2006, I became the first Zambian to attend ACSU, culminating in the World Cancer Congress held in Washington DC, which serendipitously is also the city of my birth. During this time in America, I knew that making a difference in the lives of those affected by cancer was my calling. For the first time, I finally realized the magnitude of the beast I had conquered and came to terms with the loss, anger, rejection, and pain I had unconsciously associated with it for over sixteen years.

A bit of a back story about my name Udie: I was born in America on November 11, 1965, the same day Ian Smith, the Prime Minister of Southern Rhodesia (now Zimbabwe), declared a Unilateral Declaration of Independence (UDI) from Great Britain. My father who was Zambia's first Ambassador to the United States and also a patriot decided to name me UDI. My father's decision can be traced back to his ancestry. He was Ngoni by tribe, part of the mighty Zulu Kingdom of South Africa, once led by the mighty King Shaka Zulu. Besides being legendary warriors, the Ngon's are also known for naming their children after what they consider a significant occurrence. My mother, somewhat perplexed, suggested he add an E to make it a name rather than just letters. Fortunately, he agreed, even though my birth certificate bears the letters

UDI only. Ironically, in many ways, my life reflects my name in that I am independent, resilient, and an outlier. As I grow older, I would also like it to symbolize leaving a legacy of positive transformational change.

My Vision for Living on Purpose

I returned to Zambia, bolder and more persistent. I began to ask myself earnestly, "What if I set up a cancer organization that touched millions of lives? What if I could set up a cancer organization that allows people to talk about cancer rather than hide in shame? What If I could set up an organization that could help other cancer patients and caregivers continue living productive lives?"

So I did! I founded the Zambian Cancer Society initially as an online resource the following year with hardly any resources. In 2009, the organization relaunched the mission to holistically improve the quality of life and patient experience for people living with and beyond cancer. This is no mean feat considering that cancer was and still is often referred to as the killer disease in Zambia.

By now, the cancer landscape had improved in terms of increased access to treatment primarily due to establishing the only cancer hospital in the country. However, this state-of-the-art Cancer Diseases Hospital is staffed by less than thirteen oncologists serving 18 million people. In terms of the rate of incidence and death, the figures are alarmingly on the rise. When the Cancer Diseases Hospital opened in 2006, it saw less than 100 new patients that year. Zambia now records more than 12,000 cancer patients annually.

Navigating, Perseverance, and Overcoming Cancer Twice

Cancer, one of the most feared and deadly diseases globally, has visited me twice—uninvited on both occasions. In 1989, I was diagnosed with cancer of the lymph nodes, otherwise known as Hodgkin's Lymphoma.

The following year I was declared cancer-free. In 2015, a few months shy of my fiftieth birthday, I was diagnosed with early-stage breast cancer. I am currently on hormonal treatment and responding well.

In Zambia, the five-year survival rate of any type of cancer is less than 30 percent. This is mainly due to late diagnosis and difficulties accessing treatment. The fact that I have survived cancer for over thirty years is not lost on me. It's another reason to count my blessings!

Treating cancer has been difficult for me. I have the scars to prove it! To get rid of the cancers, the doctors have had to remove some of my body parts. During my first cancer, doctors removed my spleen. This was a precautionary step. In Germany, the doctors told me that research had shown that Hodgkin's lymphoma often recurs in the spleen. So, by removing that organ, we would significantly increase my chances of it not coming back.

Later in 2015, doctors removed my left breast. While I have begun the process of reconstruction, I have not completed it. I am not sure if I ever will, as every year that passes, the desire for an implant dissipates. I am in my mid-fifties now, and wearing a removable breast prosthesis is no longer such a big deal. However, every day I look at myself in the mirror, I am reminded that cancer took away one breast and knew that it could come again and take away the other.

Leaving a Legacy

When we created the Zambian Cancer Society, the one thing we were sure of is that our efforts would be patient-centered. It was established to support cancer patients and their families, irrespective of age, gender, or type of cancer. The Society's purpose was guided by the belief that no one should face cancer alone. In a country where cancer is still shrouded in mystery and fenced in silence, we are the voice of the voiceless. Because myths and misconceptions—fueled by damaging cultural and spiritual beliefs—are rife, our mantra is "breaking the silence on cancer in Zambia." In doing so, we help create life-saving awareness. We are also pioneers in creating evidence-based, culturally sensitive local content about cancer using multimedia platforms. This information is not only in the official language, English, but also in the seven main local languages as well.

One example is a radio drama series we created in 2020 called *Tisamala,* meaning "We Care" in one of Zambia's main local languages called Nyanja. Its origins began about three years ago when a friend of mine, Ellen Banda-Aaku—a multi-award-winning writer, editor, workshop facilitator, radio drama, and documentary film producer—and I began musing over the idea of creating a radio drama about cancer. We had worked on several cancer projects before, so we were treading on "familiar" ground. Unbeknown to us, what we thought was merely a dream started to take root in this fantastic universe where powerful thoughts become things! Then the dream sprouted! In 2019, the Zambian Cancer Society won a highly competitive SPARC MBC Challenge (Seeding Progress and Resources for the Cancer Community Metastatic Breast Cancer Challenge) grant from the International Union for International Cancer Control (UICC).

Through this grant, we created Zambia's first radio drama about breast cancer. Radio was our media of choice as it is the most popular and the most accessible to most Zambians. *Tisamala* is set in a fictitious breast cancer clinic. The storyline is intended to be entertaining and educational, not only to provide factual information in a compelling and digestible way but also to dispel the myths and reduce the stigma associated with advanced breast cancer.

Endorsed by the Ministry of Health, the thirteen-episode series aired in 2020 through a privately owned Christian radio station and the country's national radio. Collectively, they have an audience of more than nine million listeners.

Apart from being aired on radio, *Tisamala* is also accessible via the Zambian Cancer Society's podcast on our website at www.zcs.co.zm. With Season 1 successfully completed, we are currently looking for partners to support the creation of Season 2.

The year 2020 will go down in history for several reasons, probably most of all for the COVID-19 pandemic. I often hear the phrase "new normal" a lot. Ironically, this is a phrase I have lived with for over thirty years. What do I mean? For cancer patients, a cancer diagnosis means your life, for better or worse, will never be the same. We try our best to adjust to the "new normal" of forever being on medical surveillance being observed for recurrence, new cancer, side effects of treatment, and even death from the disease.

One of our strengths as the Zambian Cancer Society is our creativity— our ability to create something out of nothing. 2020 presented another excellent opportunity to do just that. A few months before October— commemorated nationally and internationally as breast cancer awareness month, my team and I began discussing what activities to undertake. We considered that what was meant to be our eighth annual Pink and Blue-Ribbon golf tournament had been canceled due to the pandemic. Additionally, due to the uncertainty of how the disease would pan out, we ruled out organizing any other physical events.

During one of our brainstorming sessions, we recalled an idea called the *duku* challenge, an idea mooted over three years ago that had not seen the light of day until now. I explained to our new members that the idea was to encourage people to wear a *duku* (headscarf) in solidarity with breast cancer patients, many of whom lose their hair when undergoing chemotherapy treatment. The more we talked about it, the more excited we got. We believed the timing was perfect, as many things were aligned: an increasing number of people were using social media, the cost of data had decreased, there were fewer cancer awareness physical activities—so we thought it could potentially become a lead activity. We were so convinced that we declared that October would now become *Dukutober*—a blend of the words *duku* and October.

To participate, all one needed to do was take a picture of oneself in a *duku*, post it on their or the Society's Facebook page using the hashtags #dukutober, #dukuchallenge, and #zambiancancersociety.

The idea was simple, cheap, and potentially could be done by anyone anywhere in the world. Plus, you could post as many pictures of yourself as you like throughout the month.

We launched the *duku* challenge the second week of October 2020, and wow, did it take off with more than 3,000 participants globally eventually taking part. A few days into the event, we realized that wearing a *duku* was more than just about wearing a headscarf, as many pictures were accompanied by heart-wrenching posts. It represented the life of someone impacted by cancer not only in Zambia but worldwide. What started as a humble breast cancer awareness activity "to get your *duku* on" quickly transformed into a movement. A movement that is more than about breast cancer evidenced by the tidal wave of candid stories about participants' experience with different cancers and why participating in the *duku* challenge was so important to them.

For some, it was in celebration of surviving cancer; for others, it was in honor of caregivers—our unsung heroes. For many, it was in memory of one or several loved ones who had succumbed to the disease. Each person told a unique story with heartfelt emotion. As expected, primarily women took part, but it was heart-warming to note that some men came on board too. One male participant wrote, "I don't think empathy is gender restricted, so I might as well take part. I stand in solidarity." A female participant said, "I have done this duku challenge for mum who was diagnosed with cervical cancer mid this year and for myself as a breast cancer survivor."

As the challenge gained momentum, we were thrilled to see some companies join in by *duku*-ing up at work! It was an excellent team-building exercise! We also saw, with awe, ladies going for various cancer screenings motivated by the duku challenge. How awesome was that, because early detection and effective treatment help save lives!

No one was more amazed than us to see this simple concept trend primarily on social media, but it also got its fair share of publicity on traditional media. Since then, we have applied to trademark both dukutober and *duku* challenge to raise awareness about breast cancer and use it for fundraising as well in subsequent years.

My Life Before and After Cancer

Much of my life has been intertwined with cancer in one way or another, either as a patient, survivor, or advocate. Since cancer struck me at a fairly young age, I cannot say how my life would have panned out without the disease, but what I do know is that throughout my journey, there have been several times when I doubted whether I was living according to my calling of supporting other cancer patients and their families. Not surprisingly, these moments of doubt usually manifest when I am going through a trying period of great uncertainty.

One example is when I was diagnosed with breast cancer in 2015. When cancer struck me again, I was blindsided. I was shocked and devastated. I felt God had let me down. I wrongly thought that I had already "paid my dues." So, what was up with dealing with cancer again? As the treatment process progressed from weeks to months, my spirit splintered. I put my prayer life on hold. Out of duty, I still attended to cancer matters of the Society but was going through the motions. I became fatigued and wanted to be in my own space. Beyond battling the harsh side effects, I felt empty. I thought I had run my race and wanted to put fighting cancer on the back burner. I was still alive yet felt dead inside.

I subconsciously started to withdraw from life. After several months, I realized I was slipping into depression. It was coming silently and stealthy—just like cancer. Fortunately, I had the wherewithal to notice and knew that if I did not get a grip, I would eventually become chronically depressed. At the end of November 2015, I made a conscious decision to retake control of my life. I joined a gym and hired a personal trainer. I also reached out to God. Additionally, I gave myself an unofficial middle name—Favour—because I had seen the favor of God in my life again! Bit by bit, through exercise and spiritual growth, my sense of worth and purpose returned.

The invisible thread to the Society was being stitched back. My life had color again. All was not bleak. Over a couple of weeks, I went through the Society's bank of pictures, newspaper articles, letters, and social media posts. It was an uplifting experience, reminding me how far we have come and how much good we had done. Most importantly, we still had work to do!

Advice for People Who Want to Live Their Life on Purpose and Still Earn a Living

1. Start with the *right people* who believe in your vision.

When we started the Society, we did not know exactly step by step what we were going to do. We learned for sure, though, that we would support Zambians affected by cancer irrespective of age, gender, or type of cancer. We knew that we had to take a holistic approach and come in at the point when a person hears the dreaded words, "You have cancer."

All I knew is that we were going to do *something*. The *how* and *what* details would work themselves out. I went on to hire my first staff member, who would ask every weekday morning, "What are we going to do today?" To which I initially had no idea how to answer. We had no weekly, monthly, or even yearly plan. When I hired her, I decided that she should only work half a day. After two days, she said, "No, let me work full time. I know the pay is low, but we are just starting, and as we find our feet and grow, you can look at increasing my salary."

Within a month, I went to see a doctor who I knew had been working in the cervical cancer space for some years and talked to her about the Society. She advised me to go to the then-female cancer ward at the only public university teaching hospital and see how we could best help. We took her advice, and over several visits of speaking to staff and patients, we decided to donate toiletries every month. We dubbed these "hope baskets" and dutifully delivered them over the next few years. Remember that the right people are more important than the exact plan. Plans may change as you go along, and having the right people with you makes it easier.

2. Begin where you are with what you have.

Action has a wonderful multiplier effect. When you prove yourself faithful in the small stuff, God is happy and gives you more. If I could turn back the clock, one thing I would have done from the outset when setting up the Society would be to integrate financial sustainability into the plan. Yes, it is excellent to get donations and occasional grants, and it's all exhilarating in the beginning. But the idea that "every little bit helps" is a dependency mindset. It does help to a certain extent, and it's easy to get complacent until reality hits when that donation does not come when you expected it to arrive. Not to mention COVID-19!

With hindsight, we should have acquired tangible assets from the get-go. We should have invested in land and safe shares. We have learned from our mistakes and are playing catch up with our first land acquisition on the horizon.

3. Build Powerful Local and International Networks

A few years after we set up the Society, we became an international cancer organization member. While membership is discounted for organizations from low- and middle-income countries such as Zambia, the annual membership fee is still rather steep for us. After three years, we decided to withdraw our membership. Thankfully, a doctor friend of mine urged us not to. She underscored that membership benefits outweigh the costs, even if the services are not immediately apparent. Heeding her advice, we continued our membership.

Eventually, we realized that the organization offered excellent opportunities in various areas, including advocacy, capacity building, and fundraising. It dawned on us that we had simply not taken advantage of the opportunities. We had been passive, thinking that magically by being members, we would get stuff like grants without writing a compelling proposal. So, we changed our mindsets and began seeing ourselves as an equal partner—a member of worth. We began participating actively in events, signed up for funding and capacity-building opportunities, including grants. Success began to show up, catapulting our mission's trajectory 100-fold. We now have the privilege of accessing expert groups, which include high net worth private institutions and companies.

Closer to home, the Society sits on several national and local cancer working groups and committees. For example, we are a National Cancer Control Technical Working Group member, the Non-Communicable Diseases and Injuries Commission, and the Zambia Non-Communicable Diseases Alliance.

In 2019, one of the country's leading private hospitals set up the Udie Soko Support Programme in my honor—in recognition of my hard work and dedication to the cancer cause. This program, which the hospital solely runs, helps support the most vulnerable cancer patients with state-of-the-art cancer care.

At the beginning of 2021, I decided to reinvent myself and took the initial step of becoming a certified health and fitness advisor. With this knowledge, I will inspire women to lead healthy and active lives.

I firmly believe that each of us is special—that we are designed to thrive in whatever it is we have been called to do. I know this to be true for me and that my life is a gift to others. The bible says in the book of Joshua chapter 1 verse 9 says: "Have I not commanded you? Be strong and courageous. Do not be terrified. Do not be discouraged, for the Lord our God will be with you wherever you may go."

Udie Soko is a survivor of both cancers of the lymph nodes and breast cancer. In 2009, she founded the award-winning Zambian Cancer Society (www.zcs.co.zm). It was established to counteract the silence, shame, stigma, and isolation that often surrounds the disease by providing information and support to patients and their caregivers irrespective of age, gender, or type of cancer.

Udie is a World Health Organisation Patient for Patients Safety Champion and sits on multiple national committees on cancer and other non-communicable diseases. She has received several accolades, including the Udie Soko Support Programme named in her honor by Medland Hospital and an I Am Equal International Women's Day Award.

Udie holds a BA in public administration and an Honours equivalent Chartered Secretary qualification. She is a certified breast health educator and a health and fitness lifestyle advisor. Udie lives in Zambia, and she is an avid 5km runner and amateur golfer. She is also a founding member of the Eagles Toastmasters Club. Her website is www.udiesoko.com

Awakening to Life as Not Granted

By Sandy Beky
France

I feel so blessed to live and work for my purpose. In concrete and simple terms, I do so by setting up leadership labs in business schools and corporations. I made the deliberate choice to work for both the academic and the corporate worlds, involving today's and tomorrow's leaders (currently bachelor students in their third and fourth years). It brings a lot to my mission to be able to navigate between those two worlds and enrich each one of them with the learnings coming from both sides. With either community, we dissect, observe, and question the current state of leadership. We explore and debate the next leadership practices and what it takes to transform them to bring the most adequate responses to the multifaceted challenges the world is going through. Leadership has reached a glass ceiling, and its transformation does not just mean adding or removing features. That transformation is about creating a new form of leadership.

The manifestation of my purpose is to invite existing and future leaders for a transformational journey that will take them to build teams, organizations, and societies based on new forms of relating to oneself, others, and the world. In doing that I find deep meaning in opening a space in their minds and hearts where they will let a new meaning-making system emerge by exploring the consciousness they place on everything they think, say, and do.

I strongly believe that the evolution of human consciousness is the most effective lever to operate the foundational shifts the current world is calling for. It requires that we tell ourselves another story about who we are (our being), who we are with (our interconnect-edness), and what we are capable of together (our shared power) in order to enact that story.

Being core to my purpose and the construct of a new meaning-making system is the foundational principle of interdependence. It has become vital to helping leaders reconnect to that principle which links the past, present, and future and exists across both time and space. Interdependence has nearly become an unnatural process because of years of separateness where the silo has been the predominant mode of thinking and perceiving reality. Many leaders go public with a call to change the way their nations and organizations conduct politics, business, financial affairs, etc. If the call for action can be posed inside the current paradigm, the shift can only occur if the action itself is thought of and implemented from outside that paradigm.

It is our consciousness that distinguishes human beings as the highest form of life on this planet. That's the very reason why I decided to make conscientiousness the starting and focal point of my work.

My Tri-part Purpose Discovery Process

Arriving at my purpose was an eventful discovery process. It started when I was a child and can be summarized in three words: multiculturalism, bee lover, and circularity.

I come from a multicultural family where the values, traditions, languages, and behaviors of Northern hemisphere countries (France, Sweden) and Southern hemisphere islands (Madagascar, Reunion, Mauritius) are intertwined. The beauty of having multiculturalism in your DNA is that you think in multiplicity. You are out of linearity, out of the silo mentality, out of separability because inside yourself you are a mosaic of differences. Holding that diversity means that you need to connect all dimensions of it and make them speak and act together, so you can find and create inner harmony. Ignoring one dimension of that multiculturality, neglecting it, means that you let one part of yourself suffer and die.

A second childhood element also contributed to the discovery process. My parents both had executive jobs, yet they were very close to nature. My father would spend his Saturdays meticulously designing his rose garden while my mother would take care of her beehives. I loved roses, yet I was truly fascinated by bees. I found it amazing that such little insects had created a system that had never failed nature.

Circularity is another legacy of my childhood. I grew up in Madagascar where extreme poverty led people to give multiple lives to every piece of glass, plastic, metal, fabric. Every day, through dozens of examples, I witnessed the famous quote "nothing is lost, nothing is created, everything is transformed," attributed to Antoine Lavoisier, the father of modern chemistry. That was (and still is) the paradox of a developing country like Madagascar: the daily confrontation of the most basic yet creative forms of circular economy (industry ecology, repair, reuse, recycling, upcycling) and, on the other side of the spectrum, unimaginable levels of pollution and the massacre of biodiversity.

After my childhood and teen years in the Indian Ocean area, I moved to Europe when I was eighteen. I studied, worked, traveled, and lived in different places in the world. I worked for multinational companies, had global positions, and was a certified Six Sigma Black Belt and Project Manager Professional. In the midst of that, the past resurfaced. We were reaching the end of the new millennium's first decade, and it felt like the childhood times were knocking on the door. I landed in the diversity and sustainability department, and there waiting for me were beekeeping, circular economy, and diversity. I often say that the mission of that job—raising awareness that we only had one future and we needed to balance profit with people and planet—was the springboard for my future role as a CEO ... Conscientiousness Expansion Officer.

CEO – Conscientiousness Expansion Officer

To bring that message forward, I spearheaded several employee engagement programs including:

- circular economy educational sessions and workshops. While I was rediscovering a philosophy and a way of doing things that had been for many years, although partially, part of my life in Madagascar I was nonetheless officially introduced to a framework to rethink the take-make-waste economic system.

- corporate beekeeping and turning the rooftops of the local headquarters of the multinational I was working for into a refuge for honeybees, which were no longer thriving or surviving intensive pesticide exposure in farming areas. This initiative reconnected me to the crucial pollination role of bees in the global economy and the survival of humanity.

- diversity programs to accelerate minorities' career development and to ensure greater inclusion at the tables where key decisions were to be made

That role was a double awakening to social justice awareness and sustainability awareness. It then became obvious to me that leaders were the key interpreters of how and to which extent a nation or an organization would undergo significant cultural change and transformation to meet sustainability ends. The one thing that distinguished leaders, being accused of acting a branding show or giving a cosmetic response, from those embracing change from a holistic and systemic angle was the maturity level of their conscience and the role it played in their decision-making, risk evaluation, impact assessment, and all subsequent behaviors and actions.

After eighteen years in different global roles in multinationals, I felt the need to spread my wings outside of the corporate world. I pined for sustainability to bloom outside of the boundaries of a department. I yearned for it to be everywhere, and more particularly, I wanted to grow the space it occupied in human minds. I decided to explore adult psychological development. In the early 2000s, my passion for human development led me to study and certify in Enneagram and Neuro Linguistic Programming (NLP). The next step for me was to learn how to help individuals embrace ever-vaster mental horizons and develop advanced leadership capacity. I also decided to pursue a certification in Circular Economy with the aim of relating leadership and circularity to develop a style of management, out of linearity, out of the silo mentality, out of separability.

Since then, I have thrived on promoting the vast possibilities offered by a leadership that would fully grasp the long-term value of all forms of capitals (human capital, cultural capital, social capital, health capital, natural capital, industrial capital etc.), make them speak and act together, as well as realize that when one or several aspects of that multi-capitalistic view of the world are severely ignored or neglected, the entire system suffers and eventually dies. I feel fulfilled when they move from a fragmented way of understanding the world and start integrating its material, technical, societal, and spiritual layers. That happens when they realize that the problem is not a knowledge or a skill gap but a knowing-doing gap. It is key for leaders to distinguish the fundamental difference between what they know and how they know what they know. My work is focused on that "how" which is actually the container of the knowledge, not the knowledge itself. Together, we explore how to enlarge and make that container as wide as possible, not to add additional knowledge but to use their existing knowledge in many more contexts and see the interdependencies between them.

Developmental Action Inquiry and the Circular Economy

In my interactions with managers, leaders, students, developmental action inquiry plays a key role. Developmental action inquiry is the systematic discipline of inquiring into one's actions, to augment self-awareness about the thinking process, the value system, and the whole mental structure that encapsulates and precedes any action we perform. That developmental action inquiry step allows leaders to realize that they usually have all the knowledge they need. It's how they view the world and how that view is mentally configured that potentially creates the disconnect between what the adequate, fair, altruistic, sustainable, human-centric, environmentally friendly, etc. action should be and what they actually do instead.

The inquiry I guide them into creates new representations, new mental associations, new neural circuits. By systematically inviting them to interrogate the meaning they give to a situation, they learn how to dive into the deep structures of their purpose in life, their experience of being, what needs they act upon, and what ends they move towards.

Developmental action inquiry is also a powerful inner transformation method to revisit their relationships with power, linearity, duality, and immunity to change. Going into how they define power and form relationships with it is instrumental in understanding how they decode the overall relationship between humans and nature and therefore make sense of high-priority topics such as climate change, energy transition, and circular economy.

The principles of circular economy are also an integral part of my approach. By breaking with the model of a linear economy, based on a non-sustainable take-make-consume-discard pattern, circular economy has a lot to teach us in many other fields than product design, waste management, and recycling. For many years, I have been a strong supporter of circular economy principles being applied to leadership, people management, human resources management, career development, professional mobility, and lifelong learning. In the form of transactional and emotional disengagement, high rates of unemployment, the world of work is currently creating an enormous amount of intellectual, emotional, physical, and financial waste.

Individually and collectively, people represent a vast reservoir of skills, talents, and appetite to learn that call for the rules of the world of work, the legal framework governing it to be revisited in order to better recycle, redeploy, reuse all the soft and hard knowledge available.

Sri Aurobindo

In my work as a developmental leadership practitioner, I am of course nourished by the multi-decade research materials from a very large community of leaders in that field. I am also profoundly inspired by all the writings of Sri Aurobindo, the Indian philosopher. The way he speaks about human beings entering into communion with the rest of their environment completely resonates with me and transpires into how I bring this whole approach to leaders. Sri Aurobindo posits that a man's or a woman's "higher light of illumined consciousness can be either obstructed, inoperative, or work with occasional displays or intermittent glancings as if from behind a veil." Taking full accountability of fixing the suffering caused by social oppression and inequality as well as the suffering of natural systems caused by human activities, demand for more and more leaders, whatever field they are in, to start lifting the veil up. In 2019, several global movements such as the Business Coalition for Inclusive Growth, the new statement on the purpose of a corporation signed by 181 American CEOs, the Fashion Pact, and other ones, have brought hundreds of corporate leaders together for a pledge to act. Beyond the pledge, citizens, voters, consumers, and employees expect unadulterated sincerity that is worth their trust.

That means transforming leaders into people who not only understand the complexities of technical domains, whether it be marketing, music, or mathematics, but who also primarily develop their mental complexity and continually display the ability to deal with an increasing diversity of perspectives however contradictory, ambiguous, and uncomfortable they can be. I live my purpose and make the world slightly different and better each time a leader I work with makes the decision that he or she will learn to walk that path towards inner transformation and come to the discerning conviction that sustainable development is strongly tied to human consciousness development.

Sri Aurobindo refers to that journey as a supramental yoga practice. This world needs a profusion of supramental yoga teachers and followers. That's the only way we are going to break that leadership glass ceiling and stop imposing the hegemony of one perspective and nurture perspective-pluralism instead.

As leadership is reshaped, it also paves the way to:

- rethink the higher educational system and foster the development of leaders with another consciousness and frame of mind, seeing their roles as actualizing positive change in and for the world.
- entrust those purposeful leaders to shape an economic model that rests on four pillars (people, planet, partnership, and prosperity) in order to create shared value for both the non-living (physical matter such as mineral resources) and the living world (plant life, animal life, human life)
- run this economic model using governance through consciousness principles
- create a worldwide community of citizens holding shared responsibility in being daily change agents at the service of the well-being of the Earth.

I have to admit that when those existing or future leaders cross my path, it can make theirs more difficult, at least at the beginning. I come into their lives and ask them to revisit their assumptions, to question their vision of themselves, of others, and the world, to take a step back and look at what happens in their minds before they go into action and to decide on the proper one for today and tomorrow.

I know how difficult it is to do all of this. I have been there myself.

Going Against the Grain

Throughout my career in the corporate world, I have heard numerous stories from female role models describing the perfect boss, the perfect mentor, the perfect husband who all made it possible for them to achieve a successful career. I did not have exactly that. Whether in my personal or professional environment, I lived in a white, usually male-dominated environment. So like most members of minority groups, I did not avoid conscious or unconscious gender and racial stereotyping nor the cognitive and behavioral bias going with it. My way of coping with that was being unpredictable and making choices outside the neat labels people wanted to give me as a woman, as a black person, as a person not educated in France, as a suburban wife, etc. I did things they did not see coming, or better said, they did not want to see coming. I went back to studying at forty. I went part-time despite what it meant, financially speaking. I left corporate life behind and started my own company. I chose a field of expertise few people knew about. I became the president of a large professional women's network. I was a speaker at the Global Summit of Women in Sao Paulo, etc. Doing things people had never imagined you do can inspire admiration. However, it can also cause resentment, envy, anger, and violence especially when you deal with people who need to think that you are only capable of being who you are thanks to them and want to convince themselves that you will remain in a submissive position. So it takes inner strength to hear but not take in every word of the protecting voices saving you from making a mistake, the deceptive voices hoping you will make a mistake and fail, the guilty voices wondering where that real you (that they have actually never taken the time to really know) has gone, the humiliating voices incapable of anything else than criticism to deliberately sap your self-esteem.

I had to lift the veil covering my own life and face the fact that I was masquerading as the happy wife with a great job who was living a perfect life in a residential community while behind closed doors the real story looked much less glamorous. That facade lasts until the curtain falls on your own show, and that can happen in many unannounced forms. Illness is one of them, as it strongly signals incongruence with your true self and calls for tough but unavoidable decisions. The deep-rooted aspiration to create for my daughter a world governed by healthier and more sustainable relationships gave me the courage to write a new story for myself.

It took me about four years to mature the idea of transitioning out of a permanent job in the corporate world and operationalize my purpose to make it work. What I am sharing hereafter is what worked for me in preparing for that change of life.

My Life Post Corporate World

The first year, I worked with a professional coach. I wanted to plan everything like a perfect certified Project Manager. Her advice was powerful and so valuable. She told me to start with doing nothing. Her recommendation was to let go and create the space for my other self, the one who would live by and for the purpose to emerge. She invited me to connect to that new identity. We prepared for the moment in that encounter when I would meet my fears and hidden vulnerabilities. It was equally painful and blissful to reconcile all parts of myself and make one decision that will engage me into another phase of my life. The day

I made the decision that in the near or distant future I would go and live my purpose, it became my main focal point. I looked at everything through the prism of that purpose.

I then worked part-time during the following three years. I wanted to put some physical as well as mental space between myself and my job. I wanted to have time to study, to research the field of my purpose, and read as much as possible. Working part-time also meant earning less and revisiting some priorities in terms of needs and spending. It is important to put oneself in an entrepreneurial mindset and prepare oneself financially by saving money as early as possible. Having a financial safety net will make money one thing less to worry about when you start living your purpose. However organized and prepared you are, unexpected and unplanned things will appear.

Meditation was also a daily companion. It helped me remain connected to the quintessence of my purpose whatever the external environment would throw at me.

I realized afterward that those four years were my own version of the awakening journey I am taking students and corporate leaders through when working my purpose today.

Since I set out to live and work my purpose, I have surrounded myself with a first-class team. They are a group of people who make my life easier and richer from many points of view:

A selected circle of family members and friends who, no matter what, will never fail in their presence and support.

- A coach for myself who has been such a precious ally when mountains had to be climbed, meanders had to be avoided, curves had to be negotiated, straight lines were the only way.
- A network of virtual mentors who truly energize me: Deepak Chopra for his inspirational meditations, Brené Brown for her

fascinating work on exposing one's vulnerability, Thomas C. Corley for his very pragmatic insights on rich people's habits, and Robin Sharma who says the following about any transformative change: "Change is hard in the beginning, messy in the middle, and gorgeous at the end." In my experience, change has definitely been worth it.

When I am asked what it looks like to live my purpose and what has actually changed, the answer is quite easy and straightforward. There is one huge difference: my job today is a lot of hard work, yet every cell of my entire body is passionately drawn to it.

Like many others who spent years in the corporate world, I heard over and over the expression "bring your best self to work." Yet, I still remember countless situations from those years when some people wished I had forgotten my best self at home or recommended I switched it on silent mode and had it ride along with mainstream thinking. Today, I can truly say that I am bringing the real me to work. I don't need to know whether it is my best self. Knowing that the version of myself that I bring to work today is deeply connected to the child I was is more than enough to create an immense feeling of gratitude.

Another Urge to Matter

In 2019, I arrived at another crossroad in my life. Beyond my work with academia, corporations, and individuals on a personal development journey, I felt the urge to give my purpose a wider societal expression. I launched HeHop Help for Hope, a non-profit organization at the intersection of who I was, what I had gone through, and who I have now become personally and professionally. HeHop's purpose is to contribute to the reduction of violence behind closed doors, bring back hope to victims that they can end the violence spiral, and restore faith in the judiciary system.

Worldwide statistics show that the vast majority of assailants are men, and victims are overwhelmingly women. As sadly reminded by António Guterres, Secretary General of the United Nations, on November 24, 2019, a third of all women and girls experience psychological, physical, or sexual violence in their lifetime. Violence perpetrated against women is as common a cause of death and incapacity as cancer and a greater cause of ill health than road accidents and malaria combined. HeHop provides a free-of-charge blockchain integrated application allowing victims to collect tangible, highly secure, and tamper-proof evidence of abuse, enabling the judiciary system to enforce the laws, provide reparation to survivors, and stop the perpetuation of impunity for assailants.

Maya Angelou once said, "Hope and fear cannot occupy the same space, invite one to stay." HeHop has set itself on a mission to power the judiciary system and society at large so fear changes sides.

Selected through 168 projects, HeHop was first presented internationally in October 2019 at the Croke Park stadium in Dublin, Ireland, for the Social Innovation Tournament, organized by the European Investment Bank Institute. Winning the first prize of that tournament marked the beginning of another endeavor in changing mental representations rooted in unequal power equations. Another story about rebuilding the relationship with who we are, who we are with, and what we are capable of together when sharing the power to enact that story.

Sandy Beky spent eighteen years in the corporate world as a Learning and Change Management professional. In 2015, she founded KyoSei Solutions Lab (www.kyoseilab.com) to promote new levels of conscientiousness in the way leadership and corporate governance are driving business decisions. In 2017 she created a Leadership Lab and a mentoring program within a business school to explore next leadership practices with future leaders.

In 2019 she founded HeHop Help for Hope a non-profit organization (www.hehop.org) whose mission is to leverage blockchain technology to turn media files (photo, audio, video) into legally valid and traceable evidence. Sandy is also active in promoting female entrepreneurship and has been a member of the French ministerial delegation at various editions of the Global Summit of Women (Paris, Sao Paulo, Warsaw, Tokyo, and Basel).

She is the co-author of eight books, white papers, and reports (on mentoring, networking, well-being at work, circular HR, social media & relational intelligence, social media & innovation, climate change). Sandy is certified in developmental coaching, circular economy, and corporate social responsibility. She lives in Paris, France, and works in English, French, and Italian.

The Quiet Helper Grows into a Healer to Lift World Leaders

By Dr. Valerie Nkamgang Bemo
United States (via Cameroon)

My purpose is to nurture and inspire leaders, especially those from developing countries who face adversity, to change their mindset to help create healing and thriving for the world. My goal is for everybody to have the opportunity to live a peaceful life and be resilient.

We all face adversity, and it is up to each of us to decide how we react to it: deny, cope, or thrive. When facing challenges and troubles, I believe it is an excellent opportunity to reflect and grow, thus embracing each challenge as a gift from God. Often, our fears surge, and we embark on anger, noise, and destruction. I am that ear, hand, heart, a presence to guide, challenge, and encourage self-discovery of that light inside each of us.

Over my years working in global development, I strived for system change through thoughtful and innovative projects, and each time I had a positive outcome when I focused on the leaders versus the things or the whole system. I saw the difference between communities, organizations, countries, and/or continents that one person, a leader operating in as their authentic self with love and compassion.

My dream is to see transformations in Africa and Asia through their own forces with authentic and charismatic leaders who build a system based on culture and people versus economic and political gains. I want to focus on leaders that will drive that change.

This has been a life discovery that I am still unpacking. I was born in Cameroon to a high-middle income family where both my parents were highly educated. However, my wider family was a mix of modern and highly traditional members. Like many places in Africa, society and community play a significant role in our life and are usually intricately influenced by religion, education, traditions, and economic status. I was the fifth of six children, and from an early age, I have always been the one there whenever somebody was in need. I helped the neediest child in my class, gave my food, stayed at bedsides when somebody was sick, helped in the kitchen. As far as I remember, I wanted to be a doctor, and most of my toys were linked with medicine: stethoscope, injection, microscope, etc.

I became a medical doctor, and I focused on healing the body. I enjoy the interaction with patients, exploring their stories, and finding a solution. Immediately into my practice, I took more time with patients asking more questions about their life, engaging the reason they are sick. For example, one lady from a poor neighborhood, barely able to get food for her family, arrived with insomnia and general pain. I started by asking how her life was. She responded by telling me that everything was fine, except she wanted to sleep better. Then, I asked about her work, kids, and husband.

After a moment of silence, she burst into tears, telling me that her husband left her, her son is in prison for what the father did, and she just didn't know what to do. Instead of prescribing sleeping pills that would have been logical treatment, I spent thirty more minutes with her, just listening and challenging her that it will be worse for her son if she cannot cope with the situation. Then, I gave her some muscle relaxers. Three weeks later, she came with a big smile to let me know that the situation was resolved. When I asked about her husband, she laughed with tears. She finally faced the reality that he was the problem, and from the moment she let him go, she started sleeping well and found a solution for her son.

After that experience, I started spending more time with my patients. Unfortunately, that didn't put me in a good relationship with the hospital administration. Fewer prescriptions were coming from me, and I took too long, which limited the number of patients I could charge per day. Despite that, patients were willing to wait for my availability instead of going to another doctor. I remember arriving some days at 7a.m. with more than thirty people waiting and seeing patients non-stop until 4 or 5 p.m. That was my encounter with a new path as a doctor: we can also engage with emotions. Following that, I entered a master of public health program to find a way to help understand the cause of the disease and find solutions for people. I want to find lasting solutions and not just apply band-aids.

Dealing with Death

My mom died. As a kid, I was a big introvert with few friends. I was silent and didn't open up easily. Due to bullying from my siblings, I closed myself off more every day, barely talking and focusing on reading, nature, and creative activities like cooking, baking, singing, drawing, sewing, sports, etc. My mom was the only one who was able to understand and communicate with me. I left home at nine years old for boarding school. When I was eighteen, I left Cameroon for Côte D'Ivoire to attend medical school. In Côte D'Ivoire, I connected with a family who welcomed me like their daughter. I found a new home and family with closer relationships with the kids than my siblings. My only connection with my true self was my mother, who was always able to read my heart, even when I was just pretending everything was okay. Each year, when the school year ended, I was eager to go back home to be with my mom and feel that unique place of love.

When I was twenty-three years old, my mom got sick and passed away only three months after the onset of her illness. She had been diagnosed with cancer. Being so far and almost being a medical doctor and not doing anything or even being there with her during her last days was painful. I traveled back home for the funeral and left the day after her burial, as I had an exam. I kept the pain deep in me, never expressed it, and continued life as if nothing had happened. It was almost as if she was still there, and I was just not talking to her. The first year I went back home on vacation, the reality hit me hard. For the first time, I felt the big void she left. I stayed busy finishing medical school and buried myself in work even more. I avoided going home for vacation for three or four years, pretending to be too busy with my career. I had lost the only person who was able to help me surface my pain and confront it.

It took me ten years to cry over that loss. This happened when I was in a crisis area with many atrocities. Playing sports, I had an accident where my Achilles tendon ruptured. I had three surgeries. After the third surgery, the surgeon mentioned that I may not recover completely or regain full mobility. I was on crutches for six months, but my physical ability was essential for my work. I was scared and lonely with no one to talk to. I missed my mom so much that I cried alone for hours one day, finally accepting that she was gone. That's when I knew I needed to find what she saw in me. I started back on my spiritual quest.

HIV/AIDS Medical Experience

I started my career working on HIV in Africa when no treatment was available. Back then, announcing an HIV-positive diagnosis to a patient was a death sentence combined with shame and rejection from family and community members. Most patients I had were already at a late stage. Usually, they had already been abandoned by family and were without resources to even be able to get minimum treatment. I realized at that time that sometimes just entering the room with a smile, holding a hand, sitting with them, and talking to them about their life was enough to lighten their faces. However, facing death every day without support to handle it started to take a toll on me, and to protect myself, I realized that I was becoming insensitive and was losing myself.

I noticed my interactions with friends and during sports competitions were different.

After a year, I decided to change my career path to avoid dealing with so much death where I could not provide a solution.

Taking Care of My Father

In 2000, I came back home to Cameroon to visit family and spend time with my father. I had just finished a year-long mission with Doctors Without Borders in a rural region in Kenya. I was taking a two-week break before going on a new mission. Upon my arrival, I realized that my father's health was not good. After a few exams and analysis, we found that he had cancer. It was already advanced, and he only had a matter of months left. I decided to drop all my assignments and stay to take care of my father. I spent quality time with him, but I barely slept, not knowing if he would make it to the morning. I saw him degrade physically, but I was there taking care of him and making sure he had people and love around him. Four months later, my father passed away in my arms. I tried so hard to be present and suppress my emotions that I was frozen for almost two months after the funeral. Again, I managed to get out of the hole by finding that space with God with support from friends and family members.

Working in War and Disasters

In my global development work, I accepted a position to work in Sierra Leone during the war. In this case, I felt I could support people affected by the conflict even though I was putting my life at risk. I encountered people and heard many stories of thriving through adversity. This is one fantastic story among many: one day, I was walking in a refugee camp when I saw a man sitting in front of a tent singing and looking so happy. As I engaged in conversation with him, I asked him why he was so pleased. He told me, "Why not be happy? I am here with my wife, our three kids, a roof over our heads, and food to eat! Many families were not as blessed as us!" He made me rethink my life philosophy and be grateful for what we have, and just breathe.

I became a natural optimist, training my mind to see the positive side of each situation, even if it was only 1 percent. I have met people who had lost everything: their home, job, family members, and who were living in refugee camps without even knowing how long the situation would last. Yet, they always had a smile, were willing to help each other, would welcome you and share whatever they had. Since then, I have worked and been engaged in many significant crises in the world: Liberia (civil war), Côte d'Ivoire (civil war), Chad (refugees), Democratic Republic of Congo (civil war), Indonesia (2004 tsunami), Haiti (earthquake), Greece (Mediterranean migration), Jordan (Syrian refugee camps), Lebanon (Syrian refugees camp), Bangladesh (Rohingya refugee camps), COVID-19 response to just list major ones. The story is always the same, no matter how dramatic the situation is. Human beings are resilient and can rise and thrive. The key determinants are love, hope, faith, compassion, and forgiveness. In the community, you always find a leader (teacher, doctor, mother, religious leader, etc.) who believes in life to maintain the hope alive and being of service for his community.

Dealing with Racial, Gender, and Social Inequality

I am a Black Woman from Africa who doesn't speak English as my first language. Growing up in Africa, being black is not an issue. You don't even pay attention to the color of your skin. However, being a woman already sets you apart as less than many limitations and few opportunities except being a good wife and mother. Luckily, I have a good role model in my mother who fought to give me space, an education, and a career.

One story I remember is when I was around thirteen, my mom and I played basketball on Sunday at the university with other women. I heard comments from people that my mom should be ashamed to be seen in public playing with her daughter, but my friends admired our relationship and thought that I had the coolest mom. They loved visiting our house, and usually, we spent more time with my mom. The other figure to define me was my father, who always told us that we should pursue our dream and be sure about what we engage with as there will be many hurdles, but if the goal is deep in our heart and we want it, there will always be an angel that will support us. This is the secret of thriving through adversity.

My first realization that the color of the skin matters started in Africa. In that situation, the problem was "not having white skin." My first mission with an international organization was in Kenya, where I was the only black expatriate working there. We lived together and shared the same house and food. It was also the first time for many of my coworkers to have a black person not as a servant but as someone sharing the meal with them. Based on some of the behavior and treatment I faced, it was shocking that people who came to serve didn't see me as equal, forcing me to work ten times harder to demonstrate that I deserve the opportunity. Then, I reached America, and I realized since I am Black, I still must work ten times harder to barely made the mark.

Spiritual Connectedness and Discovery

From my young age, I have always been closely connected to God. This has allowed me to listen to that inner voice while making some life decisions. Over the last 20 years but more intentionally the previous eight years, I actively engaged and searched for spiritual discovery through reading. As I travel extensively, I purposefully explore other religions and cultures and visit historical monuments to understand their essence. Again, the same truth emerges: crisis and calamity happen, but human beings thrive in adversity, and leaders play an essential role in either destruction or reimagining.

I served for two years in an advisory group to the Fetzer Institute to help define love and forgiveness in different professions. I represented the health sector with 16 other members. This group quest led me to understand the choices we make as individuals define our truth. The concept of forgiveness was new for me, and the interdependence with love while highlighting the importance of self-love started with forgiving ourselves. It opened a new field of learning for me, looking at the many ways leaders are operating through fears that could be changed if introduced by the concept of love and compassion. As we looked at examples in the world, again, the big thread was the role that one leader can play to change his or her community from chaos to hope.

Two years ago, I participated in a Growth Summit in Arizona. I didn't have many expectations going there, and I was just happy to be in a sunny place outside of Seattle in October. Surprisingly, it led me to what I was looking for. The room was full of thousands of successful people who were guided to mindset change. As I was doing the exercise myself, I realized the big difference it made in me. That is when I noticed that this type of support is not provided in most developing countries. When the support is available, it is only accessible to a small, elite group, and it is not adapted to the context, culture, or traditions.

It became clear that everybody deserves the chance to access that kind of enlightenment to help their mindset shift from fear to growth as a leader. That shift could be one of the critical solutions for poverty reduction versus the current global development agenda that focuses on technical issues, donations, etc. I then committed to engaging in the field to provide growth opportunities to leaders in the south and create a multiplier effect on development. I signed up for leadership coaching training. As I got my certificate for individual coaching, I developed a curriculum for group training. I conducted the first training last year to twenty-three middle-level leaders from ten countries in Asia and Africa.

My global exposure to multicultural, multidisciplinary work, the experiences I endured have all helped shape my purpose to support leaders in facing adversity, healing, and thriving.

My vision is that leaders from the southern hemisphere have the self-confidence to stand up for what they believe will benefit their people. I stand for inspiring them to have the vision and strategic leadership for system change. This is approached through a growth mindset, cultivating love, compassion, empathy, and selflessness.

I envisioned a world with the opportunity for these leaders to move out of the inferior position and embrace collective local ability, culture, and knowledge in a world where everyone will live in peace and harmony. I want them to be able to move:

- from a culture of receiving to that of giving,
- from victim to mastery,
- from follower to leader,
- from cultural prisoner to leaving the box,
- from uncertainty to seeing the possibilities and being part of the solution,
- From passiveness to actors who are solution makers.

Coming from a culture where a woman should be married and have children, my extensive traveling and living in various countries have constantly meant that my culture has labeled me as a renegade. Even during my professional career or when I was at the top of my class in school, my professor and colleagues thought I should be a teaching resident or professor. My family hoped to make lots of money and even offered to build me a private practice. There was disappointment around me when I decided to drop a well-paid, respected career to volunteer with Doctors without Borders in a remote village without a salary. For three sleepless nights, alone, I retreated into prayers, thinking about my mom's words:

always encouraging me to follow my heart and assume my decision. With all odds against me, in addition to my trust in God and my deep feeling, I was so scared of making mistakes. My consolation was to give myself a year to try the experience because I could still revert and return to a well-designed life and career. Three months into the work, I had the clarity that I had made the right choice from my heart, which will be my new path. This brought me to more fieldwork in more rural and remote conditions.

Many months later, I realized that focusing on healthcare was not addressing the critical needs of people if other aspects were not looked at, like access to clean water, livelihood, or access to food. I broadened my scope of work to embrace agriculture, sanitation, nutrition, and financial services. Most of my friends and family members believe that I was lost and wasting all my education. Today, the breadth of knowledge is now an advantage and aspect that helps me engage more holistically.

The other challenge I faced from my family is that my broader view of spirituality is different from religion. Although I am Christian, I am open to learning from other faiths and cultures, which is usually believed to be a sin by my family.

Today, my listening ability has systematically drawn people to me for advice, guidance, and support. My friends and colleagues worldwide will call or reach out every time they are in a challenging situation.

Across continents, I have supported leaders from countries, international organizations, the UN, and local organizations not only to transform the developed world, but now I am intentionally supporting their personal growth.

As a global leader in the humanitarian sector, I supported the system change for local ownership and innovative approaches. I was involved from the beginning of the COVID-19 pandemic. I worked with both the Gates Foundation and the Leaders in Africa to prepare the continent for the eventuality that the pandemic reached Africa. The initial effort prevented Africa from experiencing the catastrophic death that we see in other places.

Three Pieces of Advice

I have for individuals who ache to live their purpose but don't know how to operationalize it and make it work in the world to make money at it:

- Listen to your inner voice and reach for your dreams. Consider adversity as a gift and opportunity to grow.
- Be your authentic self and adopt a posture of curiosity, and consistently seek to learn.
- Always act with love, empathy, and compassion. Assume the good intentions of others.

Dr. Nkamgang Bemo is a distinguished leader, motivational speaker, coach, and mentor and an internationally recognized expert in global health and humanitarian response. Born and raised in Cameroon, educated in France and Spain, Dr. Bemo has established a strong reputation as a cross-cultural connector and thought leader. Her ideas and reflections are inspired by her multicultural lived experiences, a multilingual education, and spirituality. With over 20 years of experience as an international development practitioner, she has worked with communities, governments, local and international organizations to strengthen systems and empower leaders to create lasting social change.

On behalf of the Bill and Melinda Gates Foundation, Dr. Bemo has worked with poor and vulnerable communities worldwide, especially those impacted by natural disasters, disease outbreaks, and conflicts. Examples of her work include leading the Foundation's global humanitarian response program such as Haiti earthquake, West Africa, Ebola outbreak, cyclone Idai in Mozambique, investing in programs to strengthen the capacity of local and regional humanitarian agencies to better respond to emergencies, supporting the design and implementation of sanitation and health programs for Rohingya refugees in Cox's Bazar, Bangladesh and Syrian refugees in Jordanian refugee camps, and co-leading interventions as part of the Foundation's Africa response to the Covid 19 pandemic.

Throughout her work, Dr. Bemo's approach is grounded in a commitment to and passion for solutions that will shift mindsets and remove institutional and systemic barriers to empower individuals and groups to create locally grown solutions. She brings an abundance of optimism, energy, and authenticity to her work. As a team leader and facilitator, Dr. Bemo cultivates an atmosphere of playful creativity and innovation, a sense of adventure, and collaboration.

Dr. Bemo received her MD from the University of Côte d'Ivoire, an Epidemiology Diploma at the University of Paris, and her MPH from Madrid Autonoma University. She is a certified trainer and coach.

From Intergenerational Trauma to a Path of Purpose

By Dr. Mavis Tsai
United States (via Hong Kong)

Through my nonprofit organization—Awareness, Courage & Love (ACL) Global Project—my purpose is to grow and nurture a world-wide network of open-hearted change-seekers who strive to meet life's challenges through deepening interpersonal connection and rising to live more true to themselves. This task is essential because there is a significant public health epidemic of loneliness and social isolation. A wealth of recent scientific literature has shown that people who lack social connection suffer impairment of numerous bodily systems, from immune to cardiovascular, and face an increased mortality risk equiv-alent to smoking fifteen cigarettes per day. I am serving anyone who longs for more closeness with another human being. My vision is to help alleviate the global epidemic of loneliness and social isolation by creat-ing ACL chapters in every city and country to reach anyone who desires richer, more meaningful relationships.

My discovery process involved paying attention to what felt most true to me at every level of my being—my gut, mind, heart, spirit, and soul. This opening to what felt true had guided me many times in my life, but never as much as when I had the privilege of spending a week with spiritual author Marianne Williamson in her workshop "A Course in Miracles."

My most inspiring takeaways were:

1. People, events, and experiences don't happen to us by acci-dent. They happen for a purpose. In every situation, we need to explore how deep we are willing to go and take the next step into our depth and creativity.

2. Part of the work that we need to do is seeing others as their best selves. In that shift lies the complete healing of the human race.

3. Prayer/meditation is the medium of miracles. God is not a belief—it's an experience. The path of light is opened by the consciousness of a human being whose mind becomes a conduit for the spiritual impulse. It's essential to focus on service rather than ambition.

4. We must connect and act upon our greatness to save the planet; what we work for must be a gift for future generations. We need to become vehicles for transformation, to become what our hearts know we are capable of. We can live life in two ways— react, or live out of a vision of what could be. Significant social change happens because a small group of people has a different idea that fosters the human race's betterment and evolution. We hold in our hands the future of humanity--if we don't do everything possible to intercept our current patterns of global destructiveness, the amount of human suffering is unimaginable. How amazing that we are living at this critical time. No other generation has had the fate of humanity in its hands. The only way we can be happy is to know that we lived for the ages. Susan B. Anthony devoted her life to the 19th Amendment, women's right to vote, but did not live to see it happen in her lifetime. Her soul, however, must tingle every time a woman goes to the polls now. What will make your soul tingle after you pass from this earth? Proclaim to yourself, "I stand in the light of my highest possibility."

Coming into the Course in Miracles workshop, I believed in a higher power, but not in God per se. So many atrocities have been committed in the name of religion and God that it was something I stayed away from. When people asked me about my divine beliefs, I'd say I was spiritual but not religious. Being around Marianne all week, listening

intensely to her words, engaging in prayer with her, I felt more connected than ever—more connected to myself, to others, to Marianne,
and to her God, which is a non-denominational God. As she said, God
is an experience, not a belief, and this week I was filled with more light,
love, and guidance than anything I'd ever experienced before. One of
the most moving experiences I had was on the last day when we all
prayed together, and I asked God how I could be of service. The message
I received was, "You are on the right path. You need to take Functional
Analytic Psychotherapy and its principles of Awareness, Courage, and
Love to all corners of the world. You will reach an audience that no one
else can because you are comfortable both in the world of academia
and of the general public. Others can feel my (God's) love through you,
and I will guide you." I received that message almost fourteen years ago,
and I have been living that mission ever since.

My Vision with Purpose

With me living and serving my purpose, individuals who seek authentic
connection will find similar others either in person or online via the ACL
Global Project. By practicing ACL, we aim to nourish human connection at
all levels of life's experiences. Every individual has a complex life story full of
anguish and joy, disappointments and hopes, vulnerabilities and strengths.
Although our lives are unique in their specifics, we share many life experiences in ways that bind us with the unseen ties of family in its broadest
sense. Sharing our most authentic selves strengthens us as individuals and
communities; connection goes beyond our human relationships to encom-
pass affinity with all living beings and the planet we call home.

My nonprofit organization is guided by what is in the best interest of
those we work with, and we are privileged to share journeys of exploration, connection, and growth with whoever crosses our path, whether
it's for an afternoon, a few months, or years, or a lifetime. We collaborate with partners from all cultures and walks of life to learn languages

of love committed to inclusivity for all. We welcome feedback, skepticism, and questions.

My Challenges

I carry deep-seated anxiety that comes from intergenerational trauma. My parents endured over a dozen years of war in China, first with the Japanese, then with the communists, with bombs randomly dropping close by. "Tao Lan" was the term they used to describe escaping from war with only the clothes on their back and whatever they could carry by hand, in addition to my brother and sister, who were toddlers at the time. My father was an MD who held a high-ranking position in the government, similar to the US Surgeon General. My mother was a nurse. They were precisely the kind of people the communists wanted to decimate. Most of their friends were tortured, killed, or committed suicide. My mother engineered an escape right before the communist takeover in a small plane flying chickens to Hong Kong, and I was born in freedom. I believe in the impact of epigenetics; it feels like I carry my parents' trauma in my genes which resulted in a deeply rooted sense of fear and lack of safety.

The fact that my parents often woke me up in the middle of the night with their vicious fights exacerbated my deep anxiety. As a six-year-old, I would calm them down and get them back to sleep. Amid all this strife, my dad doted on me; he taught me to expect men to cherish me. My mother was stoic, but I've never questioned her love for me. In this environment of intense parental conflict but great love for me, I developed my skills to soothe, love, and bring out the best in others.

I attended a rigorous, very competitive Chinese Catholic school in Hong Kong, where students were ranked in class, standing on every report card. I was competitive and worked hard to attain the number-one ranking, but I was highly stressed as a young child. It took me decades to overcome my competitiveness with others and to focus instead on collaboration.

My mother went back to work as a nurse at age fifty to emigrate to California from Hong Kong. I was twelve and struggled with a sense of social exclusion in an all-white school. I worked as a waitress in a Chinese restaurant the last two years of high school and four years of college at UCLA and honed my social skills as I was given immediate reinforcement via tips for my ability to connect.

I received excellent mentoring as an undergraduate, then as a graduate student at the University of Washington. The death of my beloved advisor Ned Wagner to a heart attack when I was twenty-three, in many ways, is my most painful loss because I never had a chance to say goodbye. My first three publications were with him, and it took years for me to overcome a feeling of sadness at seeing my name in print.

I started dating my husband Bob Kohlenberg in January of 1979 when I was a third-year graduate student. He was a faculty member and a little over years older than me. My parents forbade me to see him because he was older and divorced. I was too good of a Chinese daughter to outright rebel against their wishes and didn't argue. A few months later, I wrote them a long letter about how they had always trusted me and that I wanted them to take the risk of trusting that I knew in my soul that Bob was meant to be my life partner. I invited them to come up to Seattle to meet him, and I will always be grateful that they kept an open mind and eventually welcomed him into our family.

Bob and I started creating Functional Analytic Psychotherapy (FAP) in the mid-1980s based on the influential work I was doing with my clients that focused on the authentic in-the-moment connection in the therapy room. Because our theory is based on radical behaviorism, FAP has been rejected by many therapists who have adverse reactions to what they perceive as a mechanistic approach to therapy. On the other hand, we have been dismissed by behaviorists who criticize our approach for not being faithful enough to behavioral concepts. The concepts of "Awareness, Courage, and Love" (ACL) which are user-friendly terms that have been translated from the technical language of FAP, have caused painful conflicts between me and some of the earliest core trainers of FAP. By listening to my divine guidance and my inner drummer, my heart also has been broken. After all, I've chosen to part ways with some of our dearest friends and colleagues who objected to how we were bringing FAP to the general public because they believe we did not have enough scientific data. Our approach, however, is novel and is based on collecting data as part of the dissemination process.

My Impact

There are now ACL chapters in 104 cities, 29 countries, and 6 continents (North America, South America, Asia, Europe, Australia, and Africa), and the program is rapidly expanding. I conduct experiential trainings over Zoom once a month on Sundays for these international leaders, and they then take the protocol of the month to their local groups.

Thousands of people have attended our meetups. I'm so moved by how they've been impacted—here is a sampling of their written feedback capturing the essence of their ACL experience that has touched me the most:

- *"This experience was like lending life to each other for a short moment and embracing them with love with heaven and hell inside of them ... I thought it was impossible to contact joy at this moment, but I was able to. So I'm very grateful for that (a participant with terminal cancer).*
- *The separation that we usually create around people wasn't there and I felt experience of being one ... everyone had the opportunity to have a say and to be heard ... this is a safe place where magical connection WILL happen ...*
- *Gratitude for the healing power of connection. I am not alone. I feel much freer facing my fear. It's more challenging to hide.*

- *Shortcut to candor, speaking what's true—an opportunity to peel away layers of identity (judgements, labels) to connect with the deeper judgments.*

- *ACL meetings always remind me who I am.*

- *Deep sharing—humans are more alike than different and more alive when recognizing that … opportunity to notice how vulnerability feels in my body and practice moving forward while allowing it to be.*

- *It was an experience of intimacy in a safe space...Being seen was a blessing.*

- *I went through a huge range of emotions and found that people don't run away when I show them. I feel so much love!*

- *It was essential for me to reconnect with myself.*

- *Environments like this meetup are scarce in daily life—when I try to interact differently with people I already know, I feel so alone. Here I have such a different experience.*

- *ACL creates new possibilities for me in living. These meetings are helping me to develop my self-love. It is incredible how feeling well treated by strangers. I started treating myself better—a sense of peace and connection with the world, and even the Universe …*

- *Thank you for helping me finally feel my heart and listen to my needs …*

- *Awareness, courage and love seem to me a powerful way to help transform this hurt world ..."*

One of our participants, Anne Gulyas, wrote a powerful blog about her experience. Here is an excerpt: *"Connection … is the whole reason for existing at all, and I know that I am not alone in this belief. Yet, despite the central importance of connection for me. I found myself adrift and excruciatingly isolated. I might have continued in this manner of "living" until my passing were it not for a friend who invited me to Mavis's*

ACL meetup group. In this very first group, I experienced a reconnection with myself and my purpose. So powerful was this "awakening" that I have dedicated myself to the mission of ACL: facilitating individuals in deepening interpersonal connection and rising to live more true to themselves ... I no longer wait for the universe to provide me with the chance meetings that somehow become memorable. Now, I create and share the extraordinary." [Anne is now the Chief Operating Officer of ACL Global Project].

Before Discovering My Purpose

Before I discovered/lived my purpose, my life was beautiful in many ways, but I often felt a nagging sense of unrest that I wasn't doing enough, that I wasn't fully manifesting my gifts in service of the world. Since I've been living my purpose, I feel a sense of expansive connection with the universe and with my soul. I don't want to paint a picture, though, that it's an easy path to live one's purpose. I sometimes feel weary. I sometimes feel overwhelmed. I sometimes feel inadequate. I sometimes feel envious of people who can kick back, relax, and watch TV. Living my purpose is a calling and conviction that I choose to recommit repeatedly, and the rewards of seeing the positive impact I can make on other people's lives far outweigh the sacrifices. Living my purpose enlivens my spirit beyond words.

My Advice

1. Build your spiritual practice. Carve out time daily to meditate, to connect to the divine, to listen deeply to universal guidance, to your higher self. Whatever you want to call this connection, it is with something much more significant than yourself; and your calling or purpose is much grander than yourself. Cultivate a sense of both being grounded into the earth, being open to the heavens, and channeling a voice that feels sacred, which

expands your ordinary consciousness towards love and human betterment. Spiritual practice will help you get out of your way as you combine personal humility with clarity for how you can serve humanity with your gifts.

2. Face your fears directly, move towards what frightens you. Think and play big. Courage is being willing to take a risk in doing something important when the outcome is uncertain. To succeed, you have to be willing to fail, to tolerate ambiguity. Strive for what's important to you even if your voice quakes and your body quivers. Do you have an invisible shield that you carry to keep you safe? If so, notice how it also keeps you blocked. What would happen if you allowed it to dissolve a little bit? Is there something that you are feeling called to do but feel afraid to? Are there gifts that you know you can share more with others? Your vision precedes resources. If you think big, it will often lead to significant resources in the future.

3. Ask for radical honesty agreements with as many people as you can who you believe have your best interests at heart. One of the hallmarks of life-giving relationships where individuals grow is giving and receiving honest, caring, loving, authentic feedback. So if we are feeling hurt, we learn to say ouch, without blame or attack, but simply this is how I'm feeling. We ask for what we need. We practice acknowledgment by looking for the good in others and praising it--"I notice this in you, I see this in you. I'm amazed by what you just did." Honesty means that you say yes when you mean yes, and you say no when you mean no. One can only feel the freedom to be expansive when one also feels the liberty to observe limits, to say no, this isn't for me right now, or I only want to share this much. You enter into the expansiveness of possibility through the honoring of limits.

4. Invest in yourself. Go to conferences, network with others who play big. Buy books, go to workshops and seminars, pay for

therapy or coaching. There is an essential distinction between an expense and an investment. Doing what it takes to make yourself better is an investment.

Mavis Tsai, PhD, is a clinical psychologist and senior research scientist at the University of Washington's Center for Science of Social Connection. She is the co-creator of Functional Analytic Psychotherapy (FAP), a treatment that harnesses the power of the therapeutic relationship to transform clients' lives. She is the co-author of five books on FAP (some of which have been translated into Portuguese, Spanish, Japanese, Italian, Korean, and Persian) and over seventy articles and book chapters. She is a recipient of the Washington State Psychological Association's Distinguished Psychologist Award in recognition of significant contributions to the field of psychology. She is a Fellow of the Association for Contextual Behavioral Science. As Executive Director of the Nonprofit Organization "Awareness, Courage & Love Global Project," she trains volunteers to lead chapters in six continents to create a worldwide network of open-hearted change-seekers who strive to meet life's challenges through deepening interpersonal connection and rising to live more true to themselves.

Visit her website: www.livewithacl.org

Finding Purpose is Often an Intense Journey

By Neelam Chhiber
India

I started my professional journey around the age of twenty-two. In 2020, at the age of fifty-eight and after thirty-six years, I have finally started internalizing the philosophical ramifications of the question "Who am I serving?" Being academically qualified as an industrial designer, I have always believed that design thinking resonates with problem-solving. I identified the problem as my primary focus during my work life: the *stark poverty faced by most communities with valuable, traditional skills.* I started my journey by engaging and serving people who appeared to have much less than me and who belonged to underserved communities but were uniquely talented with untapped potential skills that could bring sustainable opportunities and income to them. Geographically, I first started my exploration in rural India and eventually moved to the global sphere as that just seemed natural.

Initially, learning how to serve people through my work and projects drove me forward during my early career. However, I now realize that in 1994 when I co-founded Industree, it was a step for me to serve myself and my core purpose in life. I say this because, in my spiritual individuality, I see service to others as service to "self" that helps us to live in the sense of wholeness. My experiences in life have served as my learning ground for my quest for wholeness and have helped me emerge as a person who likes to balance philosophical and pragmatic approaches. This is why while it has been essential for me to *do* something, it has been equally significant that I do something meaningful in living my life.

My academic qualification allowed me to engage with artisans and the craft sector in India, which has complex and cumbersome dynamics. My decades of working in the industry as a stakeholder has made these dynamics part of my professional existence and work delivery. Briefly magnifying the scenario of the vast and diverse ecosystem in which I have operated, statistics are conclusive about why my life purpose was focused without any urge for a shift or a bifurcation into anything else. Analysis of sector experts and seasoned stalwarts states that the Indian artisanal sector comprises roughly 200 million lives of the country's 1.3 billion population. Globally, this figure is more than a billion people with artisanal skills and knowledge that has been transferred intergenerationally for centuries. Most artisans live in positions of serious vulnerability, on less than five US dollars a day wages, with four in every five people living in rural areas.

The acute crisis emerging from the scenario is the risk of extinction of traditional knowledge of skills and practices these artisanal communities retain as part of their traditions. The low priority of development and progress of these communities for macro policymakers and development charterers has resulted in the status quo for years in this disadvantaged community when solutions lie within reach. If the sector remains non-progressive with regressive business practices, modern consumerism will eventually be devoid of its traditions and vibrancy. Machine-made mass products have already replaced a critical base of human ability built on the rich accumulated wisdom of centuries, handmade production full of cultural content. Yet, these handmade skills are gradually being recognized as a valuable asset for the growth of the *Next Regenerative Economy*. This recognition has been further encouraged by the COVID crisis and is driven by a narrow vision and pathway to economic growth. In contrast, mass consumerism has our planet gasping for survival.

Artisans as human capital assets are at the heart of the new emerging producer-centric economies, be it the connoted as the circular or the regenerative economy, due to its vital sustainability aspect. The emergence of new economic systems and their growth is a relatively slow process. Still, the pandemic—COVID 19—has successfully created large-scale disruption in the conventional methods, creating unique opportunities to speed up the next economies' development. Disruption will continue as COVID19 cycles continue, but fast-tracking adaptive and re-assertive old traditional best practices into new age emerging systems can take advantage of the crisis and replace the insufficiencies of the existing systems.

The Instinct to Commitment to Serve "Better"

With the year 2021 declared the International Year of Creative Industries, increased attention on the revival of this creative sector with appropriate global and national policies can impact eleven of the seventeen Sustainable Development Goals laid by the United Nations. Upholding and replicating progressive frameworks from other sectors could affect billions of artisanal producers and their enterprises with sustainability. As a social entrepreneur, I foresee the impact of good global policies and platforms on billions of artisanal producers across communities in the Amazon, Africa, Asia, Europe, Australia, and regions within the American continent. We must remember that until the industrial revolution just three to four hundred years ago, these communities produced and consumed sustainably for centuries before they were disrupted. Only if we can reimagine the revival of artisanal businesses and their successful operative practices that can be authenticated—by examples such as reviving indigenous wheat and bread made from it in the UK or artisanal recyclable plastic made from orange peels in Spain and Mexico—can we lead to a blend of old and new knowledge that holds immeasurable potential in sustainability and survival.

Circling back to my purpose in life, it came to me organically and gradually. *Today, I am satisfied that I instinctively adopted a goal that offers me the ability to have no regrets when I breathe my last breath.*

If I trace back my temperament to my childhood, I can see my evolution of being born to be independent and conform to excellence. As my mother often recalls, during my infancy and early childhood, ever since I became physically independent, I insisted on doing everything myself and always resisted any external help. Similarly, as in India, education and academic performance are synonymous with achievement and success. I needed to study hard and do well as my default mission. I dreaded unwanted psychological consequences if my performance and scores weren't the best in class. My mother had to step in with ways for me to manage any situation if this possibility was foreseen. During my higher education, I decided to become a design professional. I made this decision in the meditative state of mind of a seventeen-year-old who stared at a night sky filled with stars while sleeping outdoors on the terrace. During this time in the 1970s, I was based out of Ahmedabad. I decided I did not want to spend the rest of my life serving the ill to get better as a doctor but would instead serve the healthy to live better. Opting out of the medical field, it was clear that I wanted to help in a less defined way. I had apparent creative leanings, so the other options were design and architecture. Both had professional parity in terms of concept and imagination, but instead of *architecture*, *design* offered more open-ended pathways. While *architecture* meant designing spaces, d*esign* represented problem-solving, as that's what I interpreted from the brochure of the National Institute of Design. Thereby, my decision and journey into design education enabled the process of continued self-discovery step by step until I was hit by full-blown existential angst at the age of twenty-one. I often wondered why life was not seamless. It bothered me that there was a divide between academics or the pursuance of a professional training program and life in general. My young mind was bombarded with questions such as why work was oppressive, why we couldn't enjoy life wholeheartedly, why we need a break from work to have fun, and if our forefathers also felt like this?

My Quest for Better

Eventually, as I started practicing my profession, my assignments took me to Indian villages on rural site visits, where I noticed people's natural way of being. I observed the limited division between their daily lives and work. It was almost impromptu that *I decided to explore how we produced and functioned as an economy for centuries* before the Industrial Revolution. My thesis project allowed me to engage and work with extremely remote tribal communities deep in central India. My travels and work brought me directly and unchangeably to my purpose that I could commit and stay true to. Suppose I aggregate all the events of my life from growing up to being an entrepreneur and now trying to be a community voice. In that case, I can affirm that success intrinsically always mattered to me but not in terms of material possessions.

My time traveling through life and experiences led me to frame a vision of my purpose that I want to live but leave behind with some milestones that can lend to its progress and fulfillment. The vision that I have is about engaging with communities of people who need better clothes, better education, better food, and better lives and help define *better* means for them. I also ask if we could arrive at a better deal for all. Could we better include caring enough for the planet and not polluting it with chemicals or putting out dangerous carbon at the root of the struggle for its health? The pathway to a better deal has constantly evolved for me. As perceived from the lens of our global village, the core quest remains *connecting communities of consumers who want to buy more local and healthier with producers who make them as directly as possible*. These consumers and their links may already exist but are still a tiny part of most economies. Connecting people who are makers and producers with users can help society become whole again, despite our geographical divisions.

It is invaluable to reconsider how socio-economic and eco-culturally diverse activities of producers and markets existed on the planet for centuries. They catered to day-to-day life, but this economy has lost its sanctity in modern times, leading us to compromise fundamentals. It is commonly believed that when we make anything with our hands, our left and right brains flow in seamless conjunction that bears the fruits of good health, peace, and joy. In alignment with this belief, what if we shifted our consumption models to those that promote the production of handmade items to collectively contribute to vital Sustainable Development Goals such as SDG 12: Responsible Consumption and Production, SDG8: Decent Work and Economic growth, and SDG 13: Climate Action?

There are processes and systems wired into our being that are in grave danger of alienation. As such, an extension of my vision encompasses building a supportive ecosystem that can serve as a toolkit for agency for everyone to feel empowered to do something, become something, and feel the love for life that allows us to fulfill our simple wishes. Over my years of work with Industree, I have kicked off the formation of this ecosystem focused on supporting women and youth in rural areas in India and across the world. The ecosystem will eventually help under-served people achieve their potential to become economic actors who can further emerge as entrepreneurs by using production or livelihood practices that already exist in their communities with a modern thrust that makes them viable to cater to the demands of markets and con-sumers who have a pressing urge for sustainable production, consump-tion, and cultural equity.

Overcoming Adversity Strengthened My Resolve

Other than these aspects of my journey, another tangent is equally important to mention. Being born as a woman anywhere in the world is not easy. In India, specifically, when I was growing up, girl children moving into their adolescence were expected to be beautiful. As I belonged to the North Indian community, I was also expected to be light-skinned, which I could barely keep up with since I was always deeply tanned for not conforming to the custom of not being out in the sun. The comments I received about my skin color often resonated in my head, though they didn't come from my immediate family. I rebelled against societal stereotypes where girls were expected to receive an education, get married, and raise children. My parents' full support allowed me to grow up to be an individual who was authorized to do precisely what she wanted to with hardly any pressures or expectations until my late twenties when society applied the pressure of finding a suitable boy for marriage.

Apart from the social challenges that reflect societal stereotypes, another incident during my academic phase of professional education deeply impacted me. I was barely twenty, so my mind was impressionable. During this period, I was close to a full-blown meltdown—caused by a deep sense of the degradation of my self-worth, which was initiated by some thoughtless comments by a senior faculty member about my abilities as a student. The feeling of depression that settled in me stayed for over three years. It was nevertheless a surprise that the same faculty was the most effusive in his positive comments about my graduation project a few years later. However, during my graduation years, I tackled my loss of confidence through the encouragement of another faculty member who motivated me to hand weave in the textile lab. I was finally cured of my self-worth issues with my two-or three-year-long stint deep in Indian villages working with communities during and after my graduation project. Building my path—and my very infinitesimally small role in resolving and tackling the critical issue of India's poor in its villages—was foundational for the onset of my keen sense of purpose. This sense of purpose finally restored my faith in myself. As I set out to work, it was vital for me to experience firsthand how our oldest communities functioned, which provided me with clarity to refocus on my goal with laser-sharp intensity. The articulation of the goal and the activities to achieve them have evolved since I was a twenty-two year-old student. Still, the evolution has always been guided by the spirit that

I became a part of being an active participant in something larger than myself and more extensive than the close confines of family and friends.

Navigating my life through time and space, I am experiencing life as explained in the Vedic Culture of India, which states that a human lifespan is divided into twenty-five years each. There are four phases—Brahmacharya Ashram, Grihasthashram, Sanyasashram, and Vanaprastha Ashram that correspond to life as a student, house-holder, retiree, and renouncer, respectively. After my student life, I navigated the life of a wife, mother, daughter, and daughter-in-law, along with being a full-time entrepreneur. I experienced my next significant internal change during my early thirties. In the mid-90s, after Industree had started, I suddenly began waking up in the morn-ing with a hollow feeling in the pit of my stomach, and gradually, I stopped waking up happy. I woke up without feeling joyful in the morning for the next 22-23 years! It was caused by the uncertainty that I had plunged myself into. However, as with the other events I mentioned earlier, this issue has also been resolved, and now those feelings have diminished.

Yet, when I look back at the challenges that I lived, I can't even begin to describe those that surfaced because of having a super competi-tive, achiever personality. When combined with motherhood, I was responsible for raising two sons, staying supportive of my spouse while looking after aging parents who lived with us and of whom one was terminally ill, followed by aged in-laws moving in. Life looks so fulfilled today when I see the same wonderful spouse by my side, live with a thriving one-hundred-and ninety-year-old parent and in-law, and two sons who have educational degrees from the very best global universities and have emerged as great individuals in their own right. The daily challenges of navigating life and purpose seem to be in the fuzzy past, though the stress of time did leave behind an imprint in the form of vertigo attacks, once every four years. My secret navigational toolkit contains a non-negotiable yoga practice, alongside constant pursuance of spiritual matters, followed by a practice of hard work and service, and finally, "love for all." Above all, I was gifted with an intuitive "don't care a hoot of what others think" attitude that descended from my mother, as well as being tutored in "unrelenting acceptance and support" that came unfailingly from my husband. My two sons gave me the ability to love unconditionally, and for these gifts, I shall be ever thankful.

INDUSTREE'S Contribution to the World

The critical impact I have made is as a role model for a few struggling individuals and looking for solutions to help them navigate their way forward. I often share the core approach with everyone because I am who I am because I was influenced by people I lived with, worked with, learned from, read about, met, and continued to meet. Everyone is different, of course, but very often, we all are also so similar. Each one of us cannot hope to make a dramatic tectonic shift in society, but every drop of our endeavor makes a change somewhere. I see this in all who work in Industree to make it what it is today and what it has the potential to become. Thus, despite whatever the organization or I may have achieved, it will always be a drop in the ocean, and it's the continuance of a legacy that matters.

The Year 2021 is the "International Year of the Creative Economy." It is an opportunity for Industree to spotlight its network of 175,000 creative producers in India, with whom work has been in progress and expanded projects making headway in Ethiopia, Puerto Rico, Hawaii, Sri Lanka, and many other nations. Another feather in the hat has been the seeding of "Flourish"—a 100 percent producer-owned brand and global e-commerce portal. Similarly, "PIE" is a global technology platform for Inclusive Entrepreneurship that aims to offer an ecosystem the first mile to enable their sustainable production practices to reach global consumers worldwide. PIE is also a community-owned effort. Apart from these new efforts, entities like GreenKraft, a collective of 2,000 women producers, are a daily reminder of the substantial impact of Industree in Tamil Nadu in India and Tibeb Shema in Ethiopia.

Women in rural India and Africa walk to work or work from home, earning their families' sole or significant incomes. Our work through Industree has shown that economic contribution leads to social gains. Women start playing critical roles in the community where their voices are heard. Their contribution in the labor force is rising as they are emerging as entrepreneurs and can speak up for themselves and many other required subjects such as their girl children, nutrition, education, and violence.

I Took the Road Less Travelled

The contrast of my journey from where I was to where I have arrived has been fascinating. As a young girl, I could never understand how the aim of many of the people was to look good, dress well, go out in the evening for a movie, have a nice dinner, and go to bed. I admit reading Germain Greer's The Female Eunuch had an impact on me. I have never been particularly feminine in that sense and was always influenced more by men than women in my life, so I could never sense that I was/ am a feminist. I thought I was pretty gender-neutral. The only female role models I had were a couple of older aunts and my grandmother, who were all very hardworking, selfless, humorous, highly tolerant, and independent women. All my life, I never had a feminist point to make, except to be left alone to do what I wanted. What I wanted to avoid the most was "the" appalling situation to ever be in—living without a purpose.

I had a general plan for my life since the early years of adulthood. At least I was clear about choices I would not make. One of the books I read as a teenager that resonated with my thoughts was Colin Wilson's The Outsider. It helped me not feel alone and belong to something even at 15 to 20 years. I learned that many others also feel like a fish out of water in their general, societal existence. When I go back and look at why I sunk so deep, post some criticism from a figure of authority at the age of twenty, I decipher that it could be simply because I was direction-less at that time. The projects that I was doing at design school were an attempt to fit into more accepted definitions of industrial design, and I internally did not accept it as a principle. My attempts at find-ing deeper meaning in the profession were just not working out, and I was going down "the rabbit hole" in terms of design solutions, creating undue complexity where it was not needed. My mind was searching for something, but I wasn't able to understand what.

Thus, I can conclude that without a concrete path to what my soul knew was a purpose, I descended into a state of anxiety and fear wherein the only way to extricate me was the path to purpose. I have seen this in many young people around me as well. Gail Sheehy's Passages truly helped me gain a sense of perspective in my early twenties, helping me reason out some of what was happening, helping me to articulate for myself what I couldn't before. I am smiling as I write this since my articu-lation seems to be happening as I am typing these lines.

My Words of Advice in Navigating Toward Your Purpose

Today while having lived a life of purpose, I could say it's been a reason-ably balanced life. People around me are relatively well-balanced too. From those closest to me, only a rare person do I see with an internal conflict about who they should be and what they are doing to get there. I see them suffer a bit. These projections of the persona are also to do with time and space and usually naturalize in due course, as love for the inner voice grows and the ability to tune in and listen increases. Taking a path of purpose sounds glorious, but the most stressful times in my life were caused because I took too much upon myself and the organization in the quest to actualize its purpose. Physical leaps and steps are not mental. A mental promise made to oneself or a conceptual leap made in a second can take decades to actualize. Perseverance and patience require no boundaries. Well-meaning steps taken entrepreneurially sometimes take years to set within frameworks of the world of systems, processes, good governance, and the like, which is entirely essential to holistic growth.

Along the same lines, I have some thoughts for people exploring the quest of their lives and want to make a decent living. I can't say much about making a lot of money, but it should be enough to have a good life that does not make you stand out like a sore thumb in your family, community, or neighborhood. Resources should be enough to provide for your old age, lead a comfortable life, travel the world, but maybe not be in first-class or on your private jet. It is essential to try and do things alone first and then stabilize ourselves with a good life partner, parents, or offspring just in case. Doing it alone is the toughest, and good friends may not always be enough. It's the 4 a.m. blues one needs to counter— brought on by the dread of the workday that awaits. Life partners are support systems to split the years of togetherness to allow each other to explore life's quest while one of us serves as the chief breadwinner. A family, along with a purposeful life, is a balanced way to exist because a family helps you grow to tackle the challenges that your life brings as an entrepreneur or changemaker.

Also, my conclusive piece of advice to all about arriving at their purpose in today's environment where the opportunity to make a decent living in a life of purpose is boundless is—choose the path that your instinct propels you to take. It takes some effort to position yourself to avail opportunities strategically, and that's where you need to build a game plan. After that, the final plunge is instinct-driven. There are many inclusive businesses, the potential for part-time work, and the gig economy, but the idea is to always get the toe into the crack and lever yourself up. If you dream that you want to make a reality, a start, even a small one, like a part-time engagement, could lead to the dream. You can get into it with a bang, even after retirement. Though that's not the ideal option, many purpose-led people run organizations on their second wind. If I say that living a life of purpose is a fine art, it would be going too far. Trust the universe with the goodness of intention and go for it.

Neelam Chhiber, a well-known social entrepreneur, has been a voracious advocate of the "Creative Manufacturing Industry." She is an industrial design graduate from the prestigious National Institute of Design, who founded Industree to connect underserved rural artisans with urban and global consumers through strategic and sustainable market linkages. More than 90% of the craftspeople Industree engages with are women. Industree also engages with artisanal communities in capacity, infrastructure, and institution-building efforts, intending to organize them into productive ventures that could bring economic benefit to their families and communities. Neelam's organization Industree is working towards impacting 3 million artisans through sustainable livelihood over the next ten years. Industree and its network of entities serve as the ecosystem in the creative manufacturing space, boosting artisans' growth and economic viability and ventures. Eventually, Industree hopes to shrink its role as enabler and facilitator, while newly formed 100% and majority producer-owned enterprises continue to benefit artisans through business development and association. Find more information on Industree at https://industree.org.in/Follow Neelam at https://www. linkedin.com/in/neelamchhiber/

Concluding Remarks

By Dr. Alise Cortez,
Anthology Curator

How has reading these twenty-five stories affected you? We hope that sharing our paths to purpose and how we live it and express it through our work has inspired you. We hope it has helped you find the courage to pursue the path for yourself, discover and understand your own unique journey to purpose. You've learned that purpose is your directional compass, which can help you orient your life, choose appropriate goals, and opt into relationships that suit your path. It can undoubtedly inform your occupational expression, and we want that for you.

Stay true to your journey. You will undoubtedly need help along the way. Continue studying, surrounding yourself with people who pull you up and cheer you along. Avoid or sever ties entirely with people who desperately try to tell you a life of purpose will not work or is not practical. Frequently, the urgency of their dissuading is a measure of the dissatisfaction they feel in their own life. A typical human phenomenon shared across the world that those who feel an invested connection in us are highly motivated to ensure we don't ascend. Doing so represents a threat to their chosen way of life and makes them uncomfortable as they question their path.

By reading these twenty-five stories, you've entered the lives of us contributing authors. You have learned there are at least four paths to purpose, and your own life could involve more than one to get there. You know your long-held passions or central values can illuminate your path to purpose. What do you love that you can't possibly let go of? You have consistently battled that *thing* in life that you obsessively try to handle or deal with can be your path to purpose. Have you struggled your whole life with weight or a lack of self-confidence? It just might be that the unique way you have navigated those challenges toward healing and wholeness is just the ticket to help others who have also struggled with them. That overwhelming event or experience in your life that you've been trying desperately to make sense of and put yourself together again afterward? That adversity, that crucible moment could be enticing you, urging you to pull you to grow into a higher version of yourself and become someone you always wanted to be or never imagined was possible. And finally, that huge injustice, pressing need, or vexing problem in the world that is so enormous it just needs doing— well, *that* could be your purpose beckoning.

Whatever insights you've gotten about yourself by reading our stories are heartening. We offered our stories to both celebrate them for ourselves and help you find critical fuel and direction for your own purpose, discovery, and expression. We would like to know if our words matter, so reach out to any of us who gave you beneficial advice or examples through her story. We've included our bios and contact information for this very reason. We are officially passing the baton to *you*. It's your turn, your moment, your *life.* It is worth every bit of effort and pain to discover your purpose and then find a way to live and serve through it. The world desperately needs your gifts. By accepting the path to purpose and serving from it, you are helping to raise the world's collective consciousness to make it a better place. A place where we can all thrive, give our best gifts and do our part to steward the next generation onward continuously. Now, *that's* a useful and fulfilling way to spend *your* precious life.